Job Satisfaction

Job Satisfaction

A study of computer specialists

Enid Mumford
Manchester Business School

Longman

LONGMAN GROUP LIMITED
London
Associated companies, branches and representatives throughout the world

First published 1972

ISBN 0 582 45008 X

Set in Monotype Joanna
and printed in Great Britain
by Cox & Wyman Ltd,
London, Fakenham and Reading

Contents

Members of the Computer Research Unit Manchester Business School

Past members

Roderick Atkin
Susan Gates
Andrew Pettigrew
Malcolm Rigby
Krystina Weinstein

Present members

Valerie Kennedy-Browne
Dorothy Mercer
Stephen Mills
Enid Mumford
Mary Weir

Introduction and Acknowledgements

The research described in this book has formed part of a larger project into the processes by which organisations change themselves from one technological state to another, carried out by the Computer Research Unit at Manchester Business School under the direction of Enid Mumford. Studies have so far been confined to computer technology as the computer is seen as one of the major catalysts for change affecting contemporary society.

Associated with the computer is a group of new but influential technologists – the systems analysts who analyse business problems and redesign business systems using the computer as a data processing aide, and the programmers who translate the components of these new systems into a set of instructions which the computer can understand. These specialists are viewed by managers with some ambivalence. On the one hand there is a recognition that they have a valuable contribution to make to the increased efficiency of the company, on the other hand they are perceived as agents for a form of technical change which few managers yet fundamentally understand and many find threatening. Top management are anxious to use them effectively, to retain their services, and at the same time to control their activities; both top and line managers are anxious to understand them and their work.

This book is a small contribution to the understanding of computer specialists as an occupational group, particularly their needs in work and the factors which are likely to contribute to their job satisfaction. It also attempts to identify the origins of the demands which an organisation makes of its computer personnel and to establish how a good fit can be achieved between the needs of the organisation for an efficient computer service and the needs of the individual for a satisfactory and stimulating work environment.

The author would like to express her sincere thanks to the firms who co-operated in this survey and to all the programmers and systems analysts who so willingly talked about their work, many giving up several hours of a very full day in order to do this. She hopes that when they read this book they will feel that their interest has not been a waste of time. She would also like to thank

Susan Gates and Krystina Weinstein who did the greater part of the interviewing and Judy Butland, Greg Bowey and Roderick Atkin who helped with the statistical analysis. Also Dan Gowler whose original thinking greatly assisted the formulation of the job satisfaction model used in the text and Mary Weir, Dorothy Mercer and Geoffrey Dawe whose helpful suggestions throughout the writing period prevented a great deal of loose and misguided thinking on the part of the author. Lastly, she is very grateful to Mrs V. Gagan, Mrs M. Dickson, Mrs E. Stephenson and the Central Office Services of Manchester Business School for their excellent typing of the draft.

ENID MUMFORD

Manchester Business School
September 1971

1

Job satisfaction and computer specialists

This book is about computer personnel and their job satisfaction. The research findings discussed here form part of a larger study, carried out by the Computer Research Unit at Manchester Business School during the past five years, into the processes associated with changing an organisation from one technical state to another. Change cannot be understood without an appreciation of the attitudes and activities of those groups which have responsibility for its implementation. In the computer field these include the following.

- top management, who take the decision to use a computer to solve a particular set of business problems and who are responsible for formulating long-term computer policies, plans and strategies;
- personnel managers, who require a comprehensive understanding of the impact of computer technology on employees and their jobs;
- line management in those departments where computer-based solutions are to be introduced, who should take direct responsibility for the successful implementation and operation of new EDP systems;
- the computer personnel themselves who in practice appear to assume a range of responsibilities covering problem definition, systems design, planning for change, education and communication, systems implementation and in some cases, the eventual running of the new computer system in the user department.

In this book we are concerned with computer personnel and their attitudes to their work. Later publications in the series will cover the other three groups.

Industry is increasingly having to assimilate new breeds of specialists and of these computer men are some of the most interesting and influential. Yet they have been around for only a comparatively short period of time. Commercial data processing, the form of computer usage we shall be discussing here, was pioneered by J. Lyons and Co. in the early 1950s (31).[1] By 1957 the first Leo computer was producing a weekly payroll for 15,000 employees together with

[1] Bracketed numbers relate to the Reference section at the end of the book, pp. 227 ff.

a detailed analysis for costing and accounting purposes. But it was not until the late 'fifties and early 'sixties that computers in any numbers were in commercial use in this country. In 1968 it was estimated that there were around 3000 installed digital computers in use in the United Kingdom (32). Today, 1971, it is believed that there are 6000 machines in commercial use and it is forecast that by 1975, 3 per cent of the UK gross national product will be spent on computing, while by 1980 this will have increased to 8 per cent (14).

Computer men and women, despite the brief time since their first appearance, have managed to acquire considerable prestige and influence. As a rule specialist groups are in a position to influence the attitudes and behaviour of others only if they have a recognised status, and skills acquired as a result of several years of professional training. Doctors, lawyers and accountants all come into this category. Computer personnel, however, have managed to achieve credibility without up to now being required to demonstrate their professional competence through formal qualifications. The reasons for this unusual situation are interesting.

First, it is clear that computer technology has been associated with impeccable marketing strategies. IBM, for example, has the reputation of having the best marketing skills of any industry or firm in the world. This marketing has proved extremely effective and has convinced industry that here is a new technology with advantages which must be utilised as quickly as possible. Managements have been persuaded without difficulty that by using computers they will save money and become more efficient. Now, observers such as McKinsey are claiming that reality does not come up to expectations and there have been suggestions that up to 50 per cent of American computer installations have failed to reduce the operating costs of the organisations which use them (32). But despite this recent pessimism the industry continues to expand and the blame for inefficient computer use is, rightly or wrongly, laid firmly at the door of the internal management of user companies.

Second, computer technology is by its nature esoteric and difficult for the layman to understand. As a result management has tended to stand in awe of it and to subject it to less rigorous controls than would be the case with other forms of company investment. In particular financial controls have been weak with the result that doubts about the economic viability of the new technology are only now being voiced (4). It may be that there has been a tendency towards an 'Emperor's new clothes' effect, with firms suspecting that their own computer installations were not as effective as they might have been but refraining from speaking out because they believed that the majority of other firms were entirely satisfied.

Third, influential and prestigious scientists have spoken up for the computer, suggesting that on many counts its capabilities are superior to those of men. Two typical comments of this kind come from Stafford Beer (1), who says:

> Most of us will live to recognise the day when the only human prerogative left, the only entitlement to priority which will be left to us as men, will be the prerogative of error. The more helpful and clever things that man can do, can now be done better by machines.

and

> People just do not like to be told that the capabilities which make them distinctive are susceptible to automation. Not only can artificial systems reproduce such capabilities: they can vastly improve on them.

Professor David Hickson provides some interesting explanations of why organisations permit particular groups to have power (16). He suggests that a group is given power when it assists an organisation in coping with uncertainty – that is, when it gives the organisation a great degree of control over its external environment. This is certainly true of computer personnel whose activities normally provide a company with a more effective system of internal controls than has previously been possible and therefore enable it to respond better to the demands of customers and of the product market. A group is also given power if its activities are pervasive and infiltrate into many areas of the organisation's activities. Again, this is true of computer technology, which can impinge on most business activities and, for that matter, on most activities carried out by local and national government.

Another factor in the allocation of power is the appreciation that a particular group of specialists is unique and that its activities cannot be substituted elsewhere in the organisation. This too is true of computer personnel and is the source of both their successes and their problems. Other groups in the firm cannot at present carry out their functions and therefore have to give them responsibility for EDP innovation while at the same time often resenting the need for doing this.

Lastly a group is given power when it concerns itself with strategic activities – those activities which are central to the success of the organisation. This is certainly true of computer specialists, for our pundits again tell us that in the future most of industry will be run by means of computers and computer control. Herbert Simon (35), for example, states that 'technologically, machines will be capable, within twenty years, of doing any work that man can do'.

For all these reasons computer technologists are expensive, scarce, irreplaceable and powerful. It therefore seems important to secure some understanding of the kinds of things they are looking for in work and which a firm needs to provide if it is to keep these high talent personnel.

This book is an attempt to understand the attitudes, behaviour and motivation of computer personnel. It sets out to identify their needs in work, how these needs originate, and the nature of the constraints which may prevent these needs being met in full. It also examines how computer personnel define their own role, the influences which have led to the development of current definitions, and the reasons why firms see their computer personnel as having particular functions and responsibilities. These last are usually a result of pressures exerted by a firm's product market, of factors in its culture and ethos, of company technology and of the administrative structure. The way in which an individual defines his own role and has this defined for him by the organisation in which he works is, of course, inextricably bound up with his ability to achieve job satisfaction; it leads to certain sets of job expectations and to feelings of frustration if these expectations are not being met.

Job satisfaction as a concept

Job satisfaction is a nebulous concept. Many of us talk about it a great deal but, if pressed to explain exactly what we mean, are hard pushed to provide an acceptable definition. Vroom has defined it as 'the positive orientation of an individual towards the work role which he is presently occupying' (38). This can be freely paraphrased as 'an individual liking more aspects of his work than he dislikes'. This is a definition which most people would accept as substantially correct but again it is vague and tells us nothing about the components of job satisfaction.

The literature on job satisfaction is of equally small help in providing us with an understanding of the concept. There appear to be no all-embracing theories of job satisfaction and work on the subject has been focused on certain factors thought to be related to feelings of satisfaction or dissatisfaction in work. Few studies take a wide and simultaneous survey of a large number of related variables. Job dissatisfaction has been found easier to identify and measure than job satisfaction, and it has been customary to look at labour turnover figures as one indication of this. Here the hypothesis has been that the more satisfied a worker is, the stronger his inclination to remain in his job and the less the probability of his leaving it voluntarily. But for this hypothesis to be correct there has to be an assumption that the individual is prepared and able to change jobs to secure more satisfaction, and that the labour market is loose enough for him to do this.

Research on job satisfaction can be divided into a number of different schools of thought. There is what can be called the *psychological needs* school, exemplified by psychologists such as Maslow, Herzberg, Likert and others, who see the development of motivation as the central factor in job satisfaction and concentrate their attention on stimuli which are believed to lead to motivation – the needs of individuals for achievement, recognition, responsibility, status (25, 15, 21). A second school devotes its attention to *leadership* as a factor in job satisfaction. Psychologists like Blake and Mouton (3) and Fiedler (10) see the behaviour of supervisors as an important influence on employee attitudes and direct their observations at leadership style and the response of subordinates.

A third school, strongly represented at the Manchester Business School by Lupton, Gowler, and Legge, approach job satisfaction from a quite different angle and examine the effort-reward bargain as an important variable (22, 13). This leads to a consideration of how the wages and salaries of particular groups are constructed, and the influence of factors such as overtime pay and the state of the labour market on earnings and employees' attitudes to them. Some psychologists maintain that people have a subjective perception of what is a fair day's pay for a fair day's work and if they do not receive this their job satisfaction will not be high (19).

Yet another school of thought approaches job satisfaction from an entirely different angle and sees management ideology and values as an important influence. Writers such as Crozier and Gouldner distinguish different value systems in organisations (9, 12). For example, Gouldner categorises varieties of management behaviour as 'punishment centred', 'representative' and 'mock' bureaucracy. Punishment centred bureaucracy is the type of management behaviour which responds to deviations from rules and procedures with punishments. Representative bureaucracy is the kind of management practice which today would be called 'democratic'. Here rules and procedures are jointly developed by management and workers to meet a group of shared and mutually agreed objectives. Mock bureaucracy is when an organisation has rules and procedures but neither management nor workers identify with these or accept them as legitimate. In consequence they are generally ignored. Although a discussion of values as such does not appear often in the job satisfaction literature it is clear that the kind of legislation formulated by management, and employee perceptions of the legitimacy of this, must have an influence on job satisfaction.

Lastly, there are behavioural scientists who say that the factors described above are extrinsic to the tasks an employee is required to carry out and therefore a less important factor in job satisfaction than the work itself and the way it is structured. This group concentrates on the *content* of work and on job design factors. In Europe they are represented by Cooper at Liverpool Herbst, Thorsrud and Gulowsen in Norway and the Tavistock Institute in London (8, 17, 37, 11).

All the writers referred to above have made important contributions to the theory of job satisfaction although they may not have consciously set out to do so. For example, Lupton, Gowler and Legge would regard their work as a contribution to control theory, with earnings as a key factor, and not just as a contribution to job satisfaction. Similarly the school represented by Crozier and Gouldner are examining different manifestations of bureaucracy and only indirectly relate these to concepts of job satisfaction. Nevertheless a coherent theory of job satisfaction must embrace all these ideas.

Some contributors to thinking on the subject, including the Herzberg school, seem to suggest that it is only necessary to identify the needs of an employee. The organisation for which he works must then ensure that these needs are met if it wishes to secure the advantages of a labour force performing at a high level of job satisfaction. This approach appears to ignore the very real constraints under which most firms operate and which may severely limit the satisfactions which they can provide. We would see the most important of these constraints as arising from the pressure of a firm's product market, but others will be imposed by the factors we referred to earlier – the firm's culture, technology and administrative structure. A more realistic approach to job satisfaction may be to look at the individual's needs in work but to examine also the needs of the firm and the demands which it has to make of its employees because of pressure exerted by the environment in which it operates. This leads us to consider job satisfaction in terms of the degree of 'fit' between what an organisation requires of its employees and what the employees are seeking of the firm.

The fragmented nature of the thinking on job satisfaction made it apparent that computer specialists could not be studied in any meaningful way without first developing a viable theory of the subject. This had to be a theory capable of embracing not merely the needs of the individual but also the needs of the employing organisation. An idea on how to develop such a theory came from reading the works of Talcott Parsons, in particular his definition of pattern variables.

Parsons sees an individual's behaviour as influenced by a number of personal conceptions (30). These are first, what the individual wants from a particular situation in which he finds himself, second, how he sees the situation; and third, how he intends to use the situation in order to get what he wants from it. In other words how he develops his plan of action. Parsons suggests that we evaluate all situations under two heads; what we expect to happen, what we can influence in the situation so as to give ourselves a choice of outcome. He sees an individual as being confronted with a series of choices which must be resolved before a given situation becomes clear and specific action can be taken. These choices can be categorised into five dichotomies, which Parsons calls 'pattern variables', meaning a tendency to choose one thing rather than another in a particular type of situation. This choice will be made in terms of personal expectations, needs and objectives. The five pattern variables cover choices between:

1 seeking immediate gratification *or* deferring this until a future date (affectivity – affective neutrality);
2 seeking to further interests private to oneself *or* interests shared with others (self orientation – collective orientation);
3 deciding to accept generalised standards in the interests of conformity and control *or* to seek for an acceptance of individual differences and a unique approach which may be a response to emotion rather than intellect (universalism – particularism);
4 evaluating people and things because of what they are – their attributes, *or* because of what they do – their achievements (ascription – achievement);
5 choosing to react to a person or a situation in a widely different manner according to the perceived requirements of the situation, or reacting to a situation in a limited and specific way (diffuseness – specificity). For example, an individual may seek a variety of satisfactions from work or require satisfaction only on the earnings variable – a fair day's wage for a fair day's work.

These pattern variables are helpful when considering job satisfaction for two reasons. First, Parsons describes them at three levels: of personality, social system and cultural system. This means that they can be translated without too much difficulty into organisational demands and individual needs, and hence into the concept of 'fit'. Second, they are comprehensive categories which appear to cover all the factors that researchers have considered to be incorporated in job satisfaction. Unfortunately, as at present phrased and defined they are intellectually cumbersome and need some redefinition and simplification before they can be used operationally to study job satisfaction.

A first attempt at this simplification led to the following set of definitions (27). These were related to an organisation's role expectations – the behaviour which it expects from its staff in the roles to which they have been allotted. And to an individual's need dispositions – what he himself wants from his work situation.

1 *Company job requirements – personal job requirements.* What the company wants from the individual *and* what the individual wants from the company in terms of attitudes and behaviour. Some of these needs will be urgent and immediate, others will be deferred. That is the company and the individual will hope to achieve a number in the short term and others in the long term.
2 *Company interest – self interest.* The extent to which the firm expects its employees to identify with its interests and to forego their own. The extent to which an employee wishes to pursue his own interests in the work situation.
3 *Uniformity – individuality.* The extent to which the firm's objectives cause it to introduce uniform policies, methods and standards to which its employees must conform. The extent to which an individual wishes to behave in a unique and individual way (to express his own individuality, 'do his own thing') and seeks a work situation which allows him to do this.
4 *Performance – personal quality.* The degree of emphasis the firm places on performance as opposed to social and character qualities. The extent to which a man wishes to be recognised for what he *is*, as opposed to what he *does*.
5 *Work specificity – work flexibility.* The degree of work specificity which arises from the firm's technology and organisation. The degree of work flexibility which an individual requires to match his skills, knowledge and personality.

It can be seen that we are now starting to approach a coherent framework for examining job satisfaction, although even these new definitions are somewhat vague, especially the first, which appears to subsume all the rest. A more workable approach follows Parsons by viewing work relationships as a series of contracts between management and employees. These contracts are implicit rather than explicit and indicate that if the employer will meet the employee's needs then the employee will help further the employer's interests. Contractual areas are set out below and all except the first hold closely to the Parsonian model.

	The firm	*The employee*
The *knowledge* contract	Needs a certain level of skill and knowledge in its employees if it is to function efficiently.	Needs the skills and knowledge he brings with him to be used and developed.
The *psychological* contract	Needs motivated employees.	Needs factors which will motivate him e.g. achievement recognition responsibility status.

The *efficiency* contract	Needs to achieve set output and quality standards.	Needs an equitable effort-reward bargain; needs controls, including supervisory ones, which are seen as acceptable.
The *ethical* (social value) contract	Needs employees who will accept the firm's ethos and values.	Needs to work for an employer whose values do not contravene his own.
The *task structure* contract	Needs employees who will accept any technical constraints associated with their jobs.	Needs a set of tasks which meets his requirements for variety, interest, targets, feedback, task identity and autonomy.

If an employee's needs in these five areas are met then we can hypothesise that he has high job satisfaction. Similarly, if an employing organisation's needs in these five areas are met that firm should be satisfied with the performance and attitudes of its employees. A beneficial work environment for both sets of interested parties will have been achieved. The fit between company and employee needs may be good on all five variables or it may be good on some and poor on others. If the latter is the case then the question 'Why is this?' must be asked and answered. On the employee's side, he may see his needs as not being satisfactorily catered for because he has unrealistic expectations of what he may reasonably require of his employer. On the employer's side, the environment in which the firm is operating at a particular moment in time may prevent it meeting some of its employees' needs. For example, the economic climate may prevent it providing what its employees regard as an equitable effort-reward bargain; the technology it uses may make it impossible for it to meet employees' needs for a task structure which permits interesting and varied work, or increased competition in its product market may make it essential to tighten quality standards and controls and increase output. All these things can inhibit the ability of the firm to satisfy its employees and can result in a bad fit between what the company wants and what its employees want.

The five contractual relationships set out above will be dealt with in detail in each of the following chapters. As an introduction it may be useful here to describe each one briefly, starting with the knowledge 'fit'.

The knowledge fit

Once a firm has decided what its skills and knowledge requirements are, and many are not good at doing this, it has either to recruit at this level or to train to this level. If it cannot do either it is likely to have difficulty in surviving in its business environment for it will be operating with low quality personnel.

Whether it can recruit or train to meet its requirements will be a product first of the labour market and the availability of skills there, and secondly of its own training procedures and their capacity for developing staff to the required skill and knowledge level.

Looking at the individual employee there appear to be considerable differences in the extent to which people recognise their own skill and knowledge potential and, once recognised, wish this to be fully utilised. For example, research into the attitudes of clerks has shown that many older women clerks are looking for an easy life and do not want to be mentally stretched. In contrast, another clerical group, bank clerks, who entered employment with good educational qualifications, complained that their jobs were too easy and that they were not able to exercise fully the skills and knowledge which they possessed.[1]

Studies of highly qualified specialist groups such as engineers and scientists show that their group norms and expectations are such that they actively seek challenging work. They pride themselves on their problem solving and creative ability (36).

From a firm's point of view the desire of staff to have their skills and knowledge fully used can have both advantages and disadvantages. If the firm can do this successfully it has a group of effective problem solvers who feel that an important part of their job satisfaction needs are being met; if it cannot it is likely to have a group with a high labour turnover. Its employees will be lured away by the opportunities of more intellectually challenging jobs in other firms. As the number of specialists in industry increases it seems certain that firms will have to pay more attention than they do at present to ensuring that there is a good fit on the knowledge variable. All the manpower predictions suggest that in the foreseeable future there will be a worldwide shortage of high talent personnel. Specialists who are lost to a firm because they believe their skills are being wasted will be very difficult to replace.

The psychological fit

A great deal of attention is now being paid by behavioural scientists to those aspects of work which motivate individuals to identify with their employer's interests. The theory behind this research is that we all have powerful psychological needs, many of which we seek to gratify within the work situation. If the employing organisation can ascertain and meet these needs it will develop motivated employees. Psychological needs are influenced by a variety of personal factors including sex, family background, education and class. They tend to vary over an individual's life cycle so that the needs of a person starting his career are likely to be different from those of a person nearing retirement age. The studies of motivation undertaken by Herzberg suggest that certain psychological needs are common to a majority of people (15). Herzberg and his fellow

[1] This research is being carried out by the Computer Research Unit, Manchester Business School. The results will be published.

psychologist Maslow also believe that there is a hierarchy of needs, and that as certain basic needs become satisfied so they become less urgent and are replaced by others which assume greater urgency (15, 25). Most investigators of job satisfaction would agree that needs within a work situation must not be viewed as being the same for all people. As an individual succeeds in meeting his lower level needs for food, safety and social relationships, so he proceeds to higher level needs such as a desire for status, respect and self-realisation.

The theories of both Maslow and Herzberg stress achievement as a motivating factor – Maslow calls this the need for esteem and self-actualisation. This need appears to be very much a quality of western culture, particularly middle-class western culture. Evidence suggests that scientists and professional men are above average in their desire for achievement and that as an individual progresses up an organisation so this need becomes greater rather than less.

The efficiency fit

Here we have a contractual relationship based on the organisation's needs for quality and output standards and the individual's willingness to meet these, provided:

- the effort-reward bargain is seen as fair and his economic needs are met;
- work controls are seen as reasonable – neither too rigid nor too loose;
- supervisory controls are acceptable.

The effort-reward bargain is the amount that a firm is prepared to pay to get the skill and competence it requires, set against the evaluation of individuals on how much their skills are worth, and their expectations of what they are likely to receive. This contractual area has traditionally been seen by management as the most important, and the one with greatest influence on employer–employee relationships. Yet studies of many white-collar and some blue-collar groups have shown that in certain circumstances employees will place financial rewards low down on their list of needs. This is not because they are uninterested in money but because they perceive their financial rewards as adequate and therefore give higher priority to needs which they believe are less well catered for and therefore more important. A critical factor in this evaluation of fairness of pay is the earnings of those groups with which an individual compares himself. These may be internal or external to his own work situation. For example, a university lecturer may compare his pay with that of other lecturers or he may compare it with that of senior civil servants, architects or doctors.

Work controls constitute our second factor and here we find that firms vary greatly. Some favour tightly structured rules and procedures which they believe reduce the margin of misunderstanding and error. Others leave their staff wide limits within which to set their own targets and monitor their own performance. McGregor, in his analysis of Theory X and Theory Y management styles, suggests that Theory Y, with its emphasis on autonomy and self control is more effective than Theory X, but other evidence suggests that people adjust to the kind of controls which are in operation, and it is possible that this is not an important element in job satisfaction (23). The critical factor may be the relevance of selected controls to the needs of a particular situation.

Supervision as a form of control also appears to evoke different reactions in different kinds of groups. For example, girl clerks working for a large mail order company stressed their need for close but helpful supervision. Specialist groups, in contrast, are usually seen as responding best to a form of supervision in which the supervisor becomes a facilitator and a resource rather than a mechanism for tight control.

The ethical or social value fit

In work most people wish to be evaluated not only for their performance but also for their qualities as people: for example, their success in making friends, winning respect and inspiring confidence. Some organisations place a great deal of importance on what might be called civilised behaviour in work. Others are more interested in efficiency as an end in itself and want efficiency orientated men. Clearly an individual who believes strongly in the importance of personal relationships will not be happy in a firm which cares only for its output figures and views its employees solely as the means to this end. If he works for such a company his job satisfaction is likely to be low. Similarly a tough, efficient man may become irritated in a situation where he is expected to pay great attention to the feelings and interests of his colleagues and subordinates.

The contractual relationship between an employer and employee on this ethical/social value variable is an interesting one about which a considerable amount has been written but little relating to the subject of job satisfaction. It is likely to be an increasingly important factor in job satisfaction as employees demand better communication and consultation and more involvement in decision-taking.

Many of us have strong personal values which have developed throughout our lives and exert a powerful influence over the way we behave. We believe that there is a 'right' and 'wrong' way of relating with others. Organisations are also seen as having values, and firms are perceived by the communities in which they operate as 'welfare minded', 'paternalistic', 'ruthless', etc. Values are not easy to change, and men and women who have a strong sense of 'right' and 'wrong' may find it difficult to achieve job satisfaction if they have an employer whose values do not coincide with their own on matters which they regard as important.

The task structure fit

The task structure contract is the agreement by the individual that he will perform the work activities required of him if, in return, the employer does not require him to undertake anything that he regards as too onerous, too demanding or too simple. The fit on this variable will be a good one if the level and kind of work provided by the employer meet the employee's needs for stimulus and variety.

This contractual area is strongly influenced by technology for many of the jobs a firm requires its employees to perform will be directly related to the processes it uses to make its product. Technology has received a great deal of attention in the literature on job satisfaction and organisational structure (33, 35, 39, 41). It appears to exert a powerful effect on behaviour at shop floor level but its influence on the jobs of specialists and managers may be less potent. Many of these are located at some distance from production processes and their work may be more affected by the constraints and opportunities arising from pressures in the product market and from the administrative structure of the firm. Nevertheless when a person is allocated a particular work role he is instructed by his supervisor that certain tasks and responsibilities go with it. Some of these are prescribed – that is, they must be done; others are discretionary and the individual has a degree of choice over whether and how he carries them out (6). The nature of these tasks and responsibilities is clearly an important element in job satisfaction although one that until recently has only received limited attention. Social psychologists who have studied job content and design suggest that work can be analysed in terms of

- the number of skills that need to be used;
- the number and nature of targets that have to be met and the feedback mechanisms that tell the individual when these targets have been achieved;
- the identity of the task as shown by its separation from other tasks by some form of work boundary, and its visibility as an important and meaningful piece of work;
- the degree of autonomy and control that an individual has in the performance of work activities.

Jobs differ greatly in their blend of these four characteristics, and if a particular job mix does not meet employee expectations of what is desirable there will be a bad fit between company and individual needs on this task structure variable and job satisfaction will be reduced.

These five variables – knowledge, psychological needs, efficiency and its associated components of rewards and controls, values and task structure will be used for our analysis of the job satisfaction level of computer specialists. An attempt will also be made to identify those factors which influence both the demands firms make of their employees and their ability to cater for employee needs.

Most studies of attitudes to work focus on job dissatisfaction rather than satisfaction and attempt to identify the reasons for the former. First impressions of the motivation and morale of computer specialists suggest that on the whole it is a group with a considerable amount of job satisfaction. If our research data supports this then the emphasis of our study will be on identifying those factors which contribute to this job satisfaction.

Product market, technology, administrative functions and structure and organisational culture as determinants of personnel requirements

Product market

Sociologists believe that four factors exert a great deal of influence on what an organisation requires of its staff. These are product market environment, technology, administrative functions and structure, and organisational culture. Of these the first will generally exert the strongest influence. The product market in which a firm operates is made up of those external groups which seek its goods or services. The pressures of this market influence all its activities; the product it makes and how often this changes; its marketing and production activities, and the social climate it creates for its employees. Non-commercial organisations also have a product market. With hospitals this is the community they have been set up to serve and the sick people who form part of this community. In the case of a national or local government body the product market is the section of the community for which it is providing facilities and services.

Factors in a product market which exert most influence on an organisation are:

1 Demand. How much of the product does the firm have to produce in order to meet its customers' needs?
2 Stability of the demand. Do customers require the same product all the time or does the nature of demand vary so that the product has to be altered at intervals to meet new requirements?
3 Stability of the market. Does demand fluctuate so that the organisation has to vary the amount of goods and services which it produces?
4 Competitor behaviour. Does the firm have to be continually reviewing its production and marketing policies so as to maintain its profits and share of the market and prevent encroachments from competitors?

The pressures the product market exerts on particular groups of staff in an organisation will depend on their closeness to it. Marketing and production departments will always require a capacity for fast response, but this may be less important in other areas such as personnel or sections of R and D. In the firms which use computers the influence of the product market on data processing staff will be less immediate than on groups located in other parts of the firm. The introduction of computers is more often a response to perceived long-term needs such as a future inability to recruit clerks, a desire for greater internal control and efficiency, a wish to provide a faster customer service, than it is to the day to day pressures of the market. Nevertheless the nature of the product market is likely to have considerable influence on the kind and amount of data-processing services which the firm decides to invest in. If the firm is a computer manufacturer or a computer consultant then it is in business to provide these services to the outside world. Its staff will be constantly in touch with customers and the nature of the service it provides will be geared to the needs of those customers which make up its actual or potential product market.

Technology

Technology is the second major influence on personnel requirements and the demands an organisation makes of its staff. It is, of course, related to the product market and what will sell there, for the nature of the product must affect the technology that is used to produce it. Technology can be defined as 'any tool or technique, any product or process, any physical equipment or method of doing or making, by which human capability is extended' (34). Using this definition technology is seen to stretch from rudimentary aides such as simple filing systems to complex automated processes for operating and controlling production plants. An organisation's technology will affect its data processing specialists in a number of ways. For example, the overall nature of company technology will influence the use that is made of computers. If a bank has a clerical technology of typewriters and accountancy machines its first use of data processing technology is likely to be related to this accountancy area. If, in contrast, a steel plant has a complex production plant which requires exact monitoring, then a process control use of computers would logically follow. Computers, as they are at present used, appear to enhance existing systems technically, rather than to change them drastically – a cautious approach that is much criticised by the more innovative computer professionals.

Administrative functions and structure

The way an organisation defines its product market assists it in answering the critical question, 'What business am I in?' The manner in which it organises its technology helps it to answer the question, 'How shall this business be carried out?' The answers to both questions lead to the organisation recognising that it has certain functions which relate both to its external environment and to the conduct of its internal affairs. In turn, the way these functions are defined and arranged produces an administrative structure which affects the demands it makes on its staff. In organisations which make a product, the role and function of data processing departments will be influenced by how the firm interacts with its product market and how it arranges its internal affairs so as to supply this market most satisfactorily. Similarly, in service organisations the role and functions of data processing departments will be related to the needs of the external groups the organisation has been set up to serve and to internal administrative decisions on how best to meet client needs.

Organisational culture

Organisational culture is the fourth factor seen as influencing employer–

employee relationships, though this influence is likely to be much less direct than that of product market and technology. An organisation's culture emerges as a result of a variety of historical factors. It stems from the origins of the firm and from its early business interests. It is greatly affected by powerful men at senior level who inculcate their personal values into the rest of the company. It is shaped by the perceptions of employees at every level of what the firm's business is and how it shall be carried out, and these perceptions exert a particularly strong influence on skill and knowledge demands. A firm which defines its objectives purely in economic terms and maintains 'we are in business only to make a profit' will be interested in acquiring staff whose knowledge will assist in the maximisation of profits. A company which sees itself in a professional service and problem-solving role, and which has clearly defined codes of conduct, will look for staff with an appreciation of professional ethics and a good all-round problem-solving ability.

The research situations

The computer personnel whose level of job satisfaction is examined in this book were employed by eight different organisations. Three of these were computer users who were participating in a larger study of the processes of technical change carried out by the Manchester Business School Computer Research Unit between 1968 and 1972. The first, a mail order company, had used computers since 1956, initially for stock control and supplier payment purposes, later for order processing and customer payment procedures. The second firm, Industrial Products, had a large management services department which had been in existence for six years and had introduced many different computer systems into the company. The third organisation was not a firm but a large Civil Service department. This had a new management services department whose data processing activities were not dissimilar to those found in our commercial firms but would eventually be on a much larger scale. The remaining five firms were two computer manufacturers and three computer consultants. Two of these consultants were providing a general problem-solving service in the computer area; one had a major innovation and research role.

Product market environments

There is not space here to go into detail on the nature of the different product markets in which each of our eight firms operated and some broad generalisations will have to be made. The two computer manufacturers were competing in what was virtually the same product market and this was also true of the three computer consultants. The computer users were operating in very different product markets though those of the mail order company and Industrial Products had similar characteristics. The government department was in a different environment for it was offering a service to its clients and was not faced with competition from organisations which also wished to supply this particular service. Despite this absence of competition the government department was anxious that the service it provided – that of paying the wages and salaries of a very large and mobile external group – should be of the highest quality.

The product market situation of the mail order company was a healthy one. Mail order house sales reached almost £500 million in 1968, a figure which was 8 per cent above the 1967 level. By the standards of retailing as a whole this was a satisfactory increase for retail sales overall rose only by 6 per cent. But by the standards of the mail order houses themselves and their past performance it was a disappointing outcome. The journal, *Retail Business*, tells us that the high-flying days of the mail order houses are over and that their progress is likely to be in line with the more dynamic sectors of the traditional retail trade. Yet mail order houses still continue to increase their share of the retail market and in 1968 their proportion of all retail sales reached 4 per cent for the first time. However, this rate of increase is now slowing down. Competition between the leading mail order houses is considerable and they are all fighting to improve their share of the mail order market while containing rising prices and rising costs. Increased postal charges are a major factor in these rising prices. In addition many mail order houses, and this was particularly true of the one we describe here, are having difficulty in recruiting clerical labour. This has been a major factor in stimulating computerisation. The economics of mail order depend on the ability to generate sales from a large force of part-time agents who work on commission. Mail order companies have to find these agents and encourage them to sell, while at the same time providing high quality goods and an efficient administration service so that these agents can please their customers.

Industrial Products was in a not dissimilar market situation. It had always been in the forefront of its own manufacturing and market field but at the time of this survey was experiencing heavy and increasing competition. Throughout its history it had invested considerably in research and development and because of this had maintained the competitive cost of its products.

The two computer manufacturers had an excellent and growing demand for their products but they operated in an extremely competitive environment and were highly motivated to reduce costs and provide a better customer service, thus securing a larger share of the market. The computer consultants were in an easier market situation. Demand for their product was excellent, and there were, when this research was carried out, only a small number of top-class consultants in the EDP business, although competition was rapidly increasing. They too were interested in improving their services and increasing their share of the consultancy market. Consultant A at the time of the survey was in a more difficult situation than the others. It had only recently been created and still had to establish its reputation with industry and commerce. It did, however, have government backing and this greatly assisted its market opportunities.

A summary of the product market environment of the three groups is set out opposite.

USERS	*Mail order company and Industrial Products.* Good demand for product. Serious pressures from competitors. The two firms had to reduce costs and improve efficiency if they were to retain their share of their product markets.
	Government department. Stable demand for product. This was an efficient wage and salary service. No competition, but external pressures for increased efficiency and reduced costs.
MANUFACTURERS	Good demand for product which was computer hardware. Serious pressures from competitors. They must reduce costs and provide improved customer service if they were to increase their share of the product market. These two firms competed with each other and with a third major manufacturer.
CONSULTANTS	Good demand for product. This was problem-solving ability in the EDP area. Pressures from competitors were not great, but likely to increase. They wished to provide an excellent service in an area where there was rapid technical innovation. They wanted also to increase growth and income.

Before going further with this discussion of our eight firms and the programmers and systems analysts who participated in the survey, it may be useful to provide a brief description of those activities which normally come within the sphere of responsibility of programmers and systems analysts.

Programmers and systems analysts – job definitions

There are many different types of programmer and hence many definitions of a programmer's functions. Some of these are both complex and confusing. Perhaps the clearest are provided by Papetti in an Anbar Monograph (29). He defines a programmer as a person who 'is responsible for the writing of computer programs on the basis of block diagrams and charts prepared by the analysts, under the general supervision of a senior programmer'. The programmer carries out the following activities:

1 prepares block diagrams and translates them into a program of instruction for the computer;
2 tests his own program on the computer;
3 brings up to date, modifies and carries out the necessary maintenance on individual programs already in operation, in order to reduce the processing time or to improve results;

4 assists in the training of other programmers and collaborates in the analysis of particularly complex processing operations and in planning integrated program systems.

A senior programmer also:

5 analyses the documentation provided by the systems analysts.
6 defines the principal breakdown for the programming;
7 plans programs for the solution of commercial, scientific and technical problems;
8 establishes the arrangements for the use of the storage, input and output units available and the organisation of relevant data for processing.

A systems analyst is defined by Papetti as a person who:

1 looks at departmental procedures and, in consultation with user staff, analyses information needs and assesses the possibilities of better meeting these using electronic data processing;
2 studies and suggests new procedures using electronic data processing;
3 defines these in detail looking at forms, document flow, the codification and verification of primary data and the conversion of this to magnetic records;
4 collaborates with the programming staff in drawing up a schedule of programs to be written;
5 Prepares a complete documentation of procedures in such a way as to give a clear indication of programming steps;
6 collaborates with the programming staff in planning and writing programs for the computer;
7 follows through the procedures with which he is concerned into the operational stage so as to introduce necessary modifications and improvements.

A senior analyst also:

8 plans the arrangements for revising a department's procedure, defining the specific activities to be subjected to analysis.

There are many other definitions of the work of programmers and systems analysts including a comprehensive but rather obscure set produced by the United States Department of Labour. These distinguish 'business' programmers and systems analysts from others working in more purely scientific areas, but essentially they cover the same activities as those set out by Papetti.

Our hypothesis is that, although the work of the programmers and systems analysts in our survey will broadly conform to the job definitions set out above, there will be a variation in work activities and these will relate to the demands of the product markets in which our firms operate and to the skills of the staff which they are able to recruit.

The characteristics of data processing departments

In the two computer manufacturers and three computer consultants data processing was a primary goal in the sense that the profitable existence of these companies depended on their ability to make others believe that their data processing products or skills were worth purchasing. In the three user EDP departments this was not the case. Here data processing was not an end in itself but a means to assist the more efficient attainment of organisational goals (26). Data processing staff provided a service to other parts of the organisation by designing computerised systems for tasks which might otherwise require large numbers of employees for their completion. Unfortunately these activities were often seen as a threat rather than a service because people simply did not understand what the computer specialists were trying to do and in some instances, once they did understand, did not like what they were receiving.

Data processing departments do not all operate in the same way and a number of writers have pointed out that the objectives which they set themselves or have set for them, together with the manner in which they are organised, have an important effect on their activities. The internal division of tasks may differ. The nature of the problems selected for data processing solutions will vary and will be influenced by first, the perceived needs of the company, in turn related to pressures exerted by the firm's product market; second, the firm's technology; third, the kinds of skills and knowledge residing in the data processing department; fourth, its stage of development; and fifth, the interests of data processing management and the computer policies laid down by the board of directors. Most data processing departments have three main functional areas: operations, programming and systems design. In addition they will look after miscellaneous control functions and some management services groups also have responsibility for management science activities such as operational research and economic model building. Some departments will prefer to transfer responsibility for computer operations – the production function of the computer – to the line management of those departments which use the computers' output, and retain only development work. Others will take responsibility for computer operations and will have specialists who liaise with those departments which are dependent upon computer output.

Computer departments, like research and development groups, have tended to assume an organisational form and structure which differs considerably from that found in the normal line department. Organisational theorists Lawrence and Lorsch suggest that research departments have broader spans of control, fewer hierarchical levels, longer time spans of review for performance, less specificity in the review of performance and fewer and less comprehensive rules (20). In other words they operate in a more organic way than the traditional line department which tends to be bureaucratic and mechanistic (7). Data processing departments appear similar to research departments in structure with the exception of one characteristic – that of hierarchy, where they appear to have more grades and levels than many line departments. The reason for this may be an attempt by data processing managers to seek to provide their staff with promotion opportunities within their own departments. This can persuade individuals not to leave but may lead to situations where there appear to be more supervisors than subordinates. Meyer points out that this often means that data processing supervisors have narrower supervisory responsibilities than supervisors located elsewhere in the firm (26).

As yet, few data processing departments suffer from major organisational constraints because of the technology they use. Whereas the miner, the steel worker and the chemical process operative exist in a work environment which is largely a byproduct of the technology used by their industries, this is less true of the computer man. The programmer requires only a pencil and paper in order to do his work. Thus, although computer personnel can impose technological constraints on user departments as a result of the new systems they introduce, they are rarely the victims of their own technology. The factors which constrain their work are more likely to be administrative than technological. Our user EDP departments may differ in the extent to which they restrict their activities to development work or assume an operational role and produce computer data for line departments. In the computer manufacturer group the organisation of departments will be a product of their function in the total organisation of the company. They may be concerned directly with customers in a sales or service relationship or they may provide a service to staff who have this direct customer contact.

In the consultant firms, departments may be organised in terms of specialised knowledge so that there are groups of experts in, for example, process control systems, or accountancy systems or stock control systems. Thus departmental structure in all three groups will be influenced by the nature of the work programmers and systems analysts are called upon to do. In the user EDP departments this will be a product both of line managers requesting assistance and of the computer group itself devising projects in an effort to increase company efficiency. In the manufacturer group work will be related to the nature of the systems which are being sold to customers, and these are likely to vary in size, function and complexity. Similarly, in the consultant group work will be determined by the form and content of client problems.

In the user EDP departments the stage of development reached in data processing will exert a major influence on task structure. The work and size of departments which are developing major new computer projects will differ from those which are merely ensuring the continued running of existing computer systems. The abilities of data processing staff will also be a factor influencing the nature of the work undertaken. Highly creative and novel problem solving activities are unlikely to take place in departments where staff have only limited experience and training. Lastly, the precision with which long-term plans have been formulated will also have an influence on work activities. Those firms with well-developed computer plans and policies are likely to have development groups working in areas related to the perceived organisational needs of five or ten years ahead.

Our three user EDP departments differed considerably in size. In 1969 Industrial Products had the largest department with a staff of 177, the government department came next in size with a staff of 78 and the mail order company was the smallest with a staff of 59. Of these 314 employees, 116 were women, but only three were programmers and none systems analysts. Women were almost entirely located in ancillary computer functions such as punched card machine operators and clerical jobs. One reason for the differing size of the three data processing departments was the nature of their functions and responsibilities. The smaller size of the mail order company's department was partly due to the fact that it did not count data preparation personnel in its staff complement. Also, at the time our survey was carried out it concentrated entirely on research and development activities – analysing existing methods in the company and recommending to the management new and improved methods. It had taken a decision to hand over responsibility for the operation of computers and the production of data to those divisions of the company which used the computer output. Each of these had its own computer manager and data preparation staff. This restriction of activity to research and development was a deliberate policy on the part of the head of the department. He believed that operating responsibility would hinder the ability of his staff to survey the company from a broad and objective perspective. This is not to suggest that the department concerned itself only with long-term planning. It was also responsible for document design, training schedules, implementation and the selection of hardware and software.

The mail order EDP department originated as a computer department but later amalgamated with an organisation and methods department formed in 1959. These two functions combined with an operational research unit and became a group management services department in 1963. Although most of its activities were concerned with computer applications, a large number of its recommendations concerned the improvement of existing manual systems. This department has expanded greatly since this survey was carried out and now approaches one hundred staff. It has shifted somewhat from its development role and now assumes responsibility for some EDP production activities.

The Industrial Products management services department originated in 1962, though before that date there had been both an organisation and methods group and a punched card installation. Its activities covered research, development and the provision of a service to those departments which used computer systems to assist their operations. This service required a large number of management services staff to concern themselves with the preparation of input data and the production of computer output. Another group of staff were concerned with applying mathematical and operational research techniques to the marketing, production and planning activities of the company. A third group had responsibility for office methods. The function of the whole department was described by its manager as a contribution to the profitability of the company by providing specialist knowledge and the work of specialist staff as consultants or as project teams. These could be essentially management services department teams or joint teams with 'client' departments.

The government department data processing group had been set up in 1964 but because it controlled a very large and complex project its work was still in the development stage at the time of our survey. This department was also responsible for the production of data as well as for development work and so it was acquiring a large staff of ancillary computer personnel.

It was impossible with the time and resources available to the research team to interview all the staff of the two computer manufacturers. A department in each firm was therefore selected, the basis for choice being amount of customer contact. We wanted groups whose work was not greatly dissimilar from that of the staff in the user EDP departments. In the event we found that the staff of Manufacturer A had more of a direct selling role than that of Manufacturer B. The function of Manufacturer B's department was 'to provide the Company's customers with a contract systems design and programming service to assist them in using the computers purchased from the firm'.

The three consultants had a wide range of activities, including the provision of a computer consulting service to clients, the development of new computing techniques and the provision of an education and training service. They described their business as 'innovation' and told us that they were always seeking to develop new computer application areas and new techniques. Their staff had a good knowledge of all types of computer hardware and became involved with new makes and models as soon as they appeared on the market. At the time of our survey they had been in existence for between two and five years with consultant A the most recent entry to the business.

Interviewing sample

In the mail order company all the programmers and systems analysts working in the management services department were interviewed. The firm also had a number of maintenance programmers in line departments but these were not included in the sample.

Industrial Products, as we have seen, had an extensive management services department and employed a number of computer specialists who were working in very advanced areas of data processing. In order to make valid comparisons with the staff of the mail order company, only those people working in the commercial data processing areas were interviewed. In the government department all programmers and systems analysts were interviewed but as the installation was so new these were few in number.

The work of the two computer manufacturers was organised in a somewhat different manner with the result that in Manufacturer A we interviewed programmers and systems analysts who had a large sales responsibility in their work. In the three consultants we interviewed all staff who were available at the time the survey was carried out.

Departmental functions

In the user group there was some variation in the number and kind of projects for which the EDP departments were responsible. The mail order company had already successfully introduced an inventory control system which included mechanisms for the automatic payment of suppliers. It was about to introduce a comprehensive order processing and customer payments system to cover the whole company. Industrial products had a much wider range of activities than this and had already introduced sixteen computer projects of at least medium size, including payroll, stock control, costing, order processing and sales statistics. The government department was still developing its first major computer project and this covered payroll, manpower planning and personnel records. The nature of the projects undertaken by the computer manufacturers and the consultants was related to the demands of their product markets and their own long-term development plans. Although all companies had some difficulties in recruiting staff there was no evidence that their activities were restricted in any way through an inability to attract staff of the necessary calibre. Their recruitment policies will be discussed in chapter 2.

All three user EDP departments had long-term computer policies and these included the development of comprehensive management information systems. A brief description of the functions of the department in each establishment where interviewing was carried out is set out below.

MAIL ORDER COMPANY

Staff numbers	Managers 4, plus 55 staff in total (a number of these were OR staff).
Staff interviewed	Systems analysts 17, programmers 17.
Functions	Responsibility for analysing existing methods in the company and recommending new and improved methods generally involving the use of computers. The management services department in this firm was interested in the whole range of business systems. It had no executive responsibilities at the time of this study, but occupied itself entirely with research and development. Computer operation in the sense of producing control data was the responsibility of the individual mail order divisions.

INDUSTRIAL PRODUCTS

Staff numbers	Managers 7, plus 177 staff in total.
Staff interviewed	Systems analysts 17, programmers 17. (These were application programmers and systems analysts working on commercial projects.)

Functions	To provide specialised knowledge and staff to the Company. This knowledge covered office methods and operational research as well as computer technology.
GOVERNMENT DEPARTMENT	
Staff numbers	Managers 4, plus 78 staff in total (many not concerned with computers at the time the interviews were carried out).
Staff interviewed	Systems analysts 7, programmers 20.
Functions	This was a new department set up to design and implement a centralised personnel record and wage payment system.
COMPUTER MANUFACTURER A	
Staff interviewed	Systems analysts 16, programmers 34.
Functions of departments where interviews were carried out	The sale of the firm's EDP products in a defined geographical area.
COMPUTER MANUFACTURER B	
Staff interviewed	Systems analysts 29, programmers 20.
Functions of department where interviews were carried out	Providing the firm's customers with a systems design and programming service to assist them in using the firm's computers.
CONSULTANT A	
Staff interviewed	Systems analysts 14, programmers 11.
Functions	Very comprehensive, can be summarised as to further the wider and more effective use of computers.
CONSULTANT B	
Staff interviewed	Systems analysts 7, programmers 12.
Functions	The provision of management and computer consulting services to industry, commerce and the public sector.
CONSULTANT C	
Staff interviewed	Systems analysts 13, programmers 15.
Functions	As for Consultant B.

It is important to note here that although the staff of the three consultants has been divided into programmers and systems analysts this division was much less clear than in the user firms and the manufacturers. The majority of these specialists were general problem solvers in the computer area although their previous experience and interests inclined them towards problems with a programming or systems analysis bias.

The enigma of computer specialists

Computers and the specialists associated with them are proliferating in industry, government, the health service and education. A considerable number of organisations are now moving from the early stages of computerisation in which mainly routine jobs were affected and anticipated savings were in time and labour. Today the future of computer systems is seen in their capacity to assist decision-taking and organisational control by providing detailed and sophisticated management information.

Yet industry and commerce are as perplexed and ambivalent about computer systems as they have ever been. Confusion stems from a number of things. First, managers are bombarded with conflicting information. On the one hand the computer manufacturers and the data processing press continue to put out the message that the way to efficiency and cost saving is via computers. On the other hand influential observers of the computer scene, in particular major consultants such as Brandon and McKinsey, describe the picture in many firms as one of costs and problems rather than savings and successes (5, 24). There is everywhere a lack of clarity about the profit and loss account aspect of computers. The computer manufacturers tell industry 'you will save money through computers', yet industry has few satisfactory methods of establishing that this saving has in fact been made. The economic evaluation of computer-based systems is an area which is still very short on techniques and knowledge.

The realities of many computer-based systems are that computer specialists talk of efficiency and savings while causing their firms long periods of expensive chaos before anything like an efficient system appears. A McKinsey study (24) tells us:

> In terms of technical achievements the computer revolution in US business is outrunning expectations. . . . The basic current problems for EDP management stem from the successes of the past. In thirty of the thirty-six companies [examined by McKinsey] the conversions of routine administrative procedures to computer systems are complete or nearly complete. The EDP staff who completed these conversions are under pressure to show results in the form of new computer systems. In terms of technical competence they are well equipped to do so. But they are seldom strategically placed or managerially trained to assess the economics of operations fully or to judge operational feasibility. These limitations are raising even more obstacles to the success of new corporate computer efforts. . . . Over the past five years most computer staff have doubled. Typically the department that had 40 people in 1962 has 80 or 85 now. Yet no overhaul of the management practices of earlier years has taken place.

These doubts alone provide a good argument for taking a hard look at computer specialists as a group and identifying the satisfactions they seek from their work; the factors which influence their attitudes and hence their behaviour, and the nature of their responsibilities in those situations where they exercise their talents and skills.

Secondly, the predictions of computer experts are showing us a highly uncertain future. For example, Bjerrum writing in *Futures* (2), makes the following forecasts:

> A 50 per cent reduction of the labour force in present industry is expected in the late 1980s. The reduction will be partially compensated for by shorter working hours, together with new industries to absorb the labourers; but the problem of unemployment is expected to be more serious in the future than it is today.
>
> In the year 2000 all major industries will be controlled by computers. Small industries will not be automated to the same extent; but it is estimated that not many of these will exist by then.

Sceptics may laugh at these predictions yet experience has shown that technological forecasting is frequently too conservative. For example, predictions made in 1953 took no account of the space age even though it was only four years away and sputnik 1 was launched in 1957. Maxwell Hunter points out that at the moment the majority of forecasts about computers are a product of a crude projection of the consequences of foreseeable technological developments (18). Yet it is very likely that computer technology will advance in association with the knowledge of other disciplines such as sociology, psychology, ergonomics and cybernetics. This makes forecasting particularly difficult.

We shall not know whether these predictions are correct for some time. But it is clear that the computer and computer-based systems will cause great changes in society and this means that the more we know about the group of specialists associated with this technology the better. Above all we must reassure ourselves that they are socially responsible and capable of setting themselves human as well as technical objectives. Computers can bring with them immense advantages but they can also bring disastrous disadvantages if they are controlled by those Lewis Mumford calls the 'priests of power' – people who have little respect for man's autonomy, his unpredictability and his moral responsibility (28).

This chapter can usefully be ended with a warning note from Norbert Wiener (40), quoted by Lewis Mumford in *The Pentagon of Power* (28).

> If we use, to achieve our purpose, a mechanical agency with whose operation we cannot efficiently interfere once we have started it, because the action is so fast and irrevocable that we have not the data to intervene before the action is complete, then we had better be quite sure that the purpose put into the machine is the purpose which we really desire and not merely a colourful imitation of it.

Above all we must check that the specialists who design computer systems are civilised men with imagination and breadth of vision. Lewis Mumford tells us that 'technicians who themselves lack other purposes and values, memories and feelings, see no human deficiency in their seemingly superhuman machine, or in the kinds of demands they themselves make of it'.

2

The knowledge contract

This chapter considers in detail what we have called the knowledge contract. In exchange for an individual's skill and knowledge, or skill and knowledge potential, an organisation offers, or should offer, him the opportunity to use and develop his skill and knowledge. For this knowledge bargain to work successfully there must be a good match between what the organisation requires from its staff, what they can supply, and how they wish their skills and knowledge to be used. If a firm requires a level of data processing skill which it cannot obtain, it will be unable to operate efficiently. If, on the other hand, its data processing employees have a level of skill which the firm cannot fully utilise they will become frustrated and look elsewhere for more satisfying employment. It is therefore essential for a firm to work out with some precision what its data processing skill requirements are, both in the short and long term, before recruiting staff.

Product market pressures

In the last chapter we discussed the influence of product market, technology, administrative structure and function, and company culture on the demands an organisation makes of its employees. In terms of the knowledge contract, the product market environment is likely to affect skill and knowledge requirements, and hence recruitment policies in the following way. If a firm is operating in a highly competitive market with a product demand which changes rapidly both in quantity and kind, then it will require staff who can respond quickly to these new demands and who are efficient, good decision-takers and innovative. If, in addition, the firm makes a product which is complex – for example, advanced electronic equipment – then it will require staff who are sufficiently intellectually versatile to enable them to acquire new knowledge rapidly.

The EDP departments of user firms are not, as a rule, in close contact with their product markets and therefore may be protected from direct pressures of this kind. However, they will not be entirely unaffected. In all three of our user organisations computer systems were introduced in an attempt to reduce costs and improve customer service and the nature of computer usage was closely related to these objectives. In so far as the computer applications chosen for implementation reflected product market influences, so they also had an impact on the level of skill and knowledge required by the EDP department.

Product market pressures had a much stronger impact on the skill and knowledge needs of the computer manufacturers and computer consultants, for both had to meet two sets of knowledge requirements: their own and those of their customers. This meant that they required a wide diversity of talent and experience and might be expected to seek staff with a high level of education and considerable EDP experience.

Technology and administrative structure

We have seen that the manner in which these are organised depends on the answers which firms give to the two questions 'What business are we in now and in the future?', and 'How shall we best conduct this business now and in the future?' In the context of our user EDP departments, the firm's production technology – that is the technology used to make the principal product – is important only in so far as it has influenced data processing developments and hence the demand for a particular kind and level of data processing expertise. The nature of the data processing technology chosen to solve a particular business problem will have a more direct influence on EDP skill and knowledge demands. For example, a firm which is introducing a real time data processing system will require a different level of skill in its programmers and systems analysts from one which is introducing its first batch processing system. Data processing specialists working for computer manufacturers and consultants will again be affected both by the EDP technologies of their own companies and by the technologies of their client firms. This is another factor causing their employers to demand a wide range of knowledge and skill from their staff.

Before the advent of computers the mail order company had a traditional clerical technology which made use of large numbers of women clerks using conventional technical aides such as filing systems and mechanical accounting machines. Early computer developments in this company were directed at computerising clerical operations related to stock control, thus reducing the number of stocks which needed to be held at any one time and greatly enhancing the efficiency of the stock forecasting and ordering service. Later developments have been directed at computerising office activities associated with the processing of orders sent in by agents. Because five mail order companies would eventually be involved in the general office computer system, the company had chosen an on line EDP system with graphic display units for input purposes.

Industrial Products had a considerable number of data processing projects in hand at the time of our survey. These included an invoicing system; a stock control system for a supply department, introduced to reduce buying costs, and an engineering works project intended to optimise and monitor the flow of fabrication work in the site workshops. All these projects had a labour-saving effect in that they involved the computerisation of operations previously carried out by clerks, but they also brought new and more sophisticated techniques to bear on organisational activities. The government department was responsible for the control of wage and salary payments for a very large number of personnel and this involved the computerisation of work previously handled by large numbers of clerks.

All three user organisations were therefore upgrading manual work previously associated with simple technical aides such as typewriters, accounting machines and traditional files. The philosophy of the problem-solving processes behind these clerical activities remained largely unchanged although the technology was now computer based. The three user organisations therefore required competent and efficient personnel who were interested in solving the problems of their employers. In the applications area with which programmers and systems analysts were concerned at the time of our survey, knowledge of the objectives and administration of their own companies, together with a high level of data processing skill and an ability to relate easily with user departments, were the most important requirements.

The situation in the computer manufacturers and computer consultants was somewhat different. Here the greatest influence on the work of programmers and systems analysts was not the computerisation of their firm's own work procedures but the computer requirements of their clients. These were likely to range from first attempts to apply computers to clerical processes such as payroll, to advanced management information systems.

The computer manufacturers, with their emphasis on development and on selling more machines through excellent marketing strategies and an efficient customer service, needed staff who could meet their work standards and work to tight job specifications and targets. They had the advantage, as did Industrial Products, of being able to offer some employees the possibility of working in areas located at the forefront of computer technology. Most functions in the firms were, however, influenced by the primacy of selling computer hardware. Gillis, referring to American practice, says that any examination of a computer manufacturer's marketing organisation will reveal an unprecedented growth rate and recruitment objectives that are skewed towards the hiring of graduates with engineering or technical qualifications. He suggests that this indicates a recruitment shift from *any* graduates to those who can make a technical contribution and says that the reason for this is not difficult to ascertain. Computer manufacturers today must have a source of talent which is capable of sustaining the evolutionary growth of the computer as a management and control tool (8). This demand by computer manufacturers for more and better technical staff is also true of Britain, though there has not been the same stress here on recruiting university graduates – perhaps because there are fewer on the labour market.[1]

[1] See footnote on p. 9.

The functions of the computer consultant firms were influenced by the demand for their problem-solving services, by their ability to get high calibre staff capable of assuming this problem-solving role and by the way in which they and their clients perceived the nature of their problem-solving role. The three computer consultants in our survey all defined their roles in broad terms and were prepared to tackle a wide diversity of problems in the EDP area. Computer Consultant A was more research orientated than the other two and also had a particular interest in computer education.

A summary of those environmental and technological factors likely to influence EDP skill and knowledge requirements in our firms is set out below.

COMPUTER USERS

There has been a traditional clerical technology in most work areas affected by computers. Computers have been introduced with the objectives of making clerical procedures more efficient and less expensive. All three organisations hoped to make savings in the number of clerical staff employed, although this was nowhere the principal reason for investment in computers. A high level of programming and systems analysis expertise was required for application areas and EDP staff must be able to establish good relationships with the rest of their organisations on a long-term basis. All three users regarded software development as one of their functions and Industrial Products also had groups of programmers and systems analysts with mathematical and scientific skills who were working in very advanced areas of operational research. These were seen as outside the scope of our survey.

The role of all three user EDP departments has been defined as service to the rest of the organisation. In the mail order company and Industrial Products until recently there has been a stable or increasing demand for company products – in other words the two users operating in a commercial environment have been doing well (16). This has been reflected in a willingness to invest in computer hardware and in an expanding demand for the services of data processing staff.

COMPUTER MANUFACTURERS

They were in the business to sell computer hardware. They therefore required a high level of technical and marketing expertise in many of their staff. Their business functions were market orientated – that is based on selling, backed up by service.

There was an expanding demand for company products.

They had an important EDP research and development role. Therefore a group of staff were needed of a calibre to perform this activity.

COMPUTER CONSULTANTS

They were in business to sell problem-solving ability. They therefore required staff who were expert problem solvers in the data processing area.

Their business role was defined by how each consultant firm saw its functions and by how clients structured the problems for which they requested consultant assistance.

At the time of this survey there was an expanding demand for their expertise.

They saw themselves as having an increasingly educational role and this was especially true of Consultant A.

ORGANISATIONAL CULTURE

Although any culture directly associated with EDP will be recent in origin data processing departments will be influenced by the cultures of those organisations which contain them. Our three users had cultures which were not dissimilar. All were established institutions with reputations for treating their staff benevolently and with a tradition of keeping their employees for the duration of their working lives. But there were differences in the manner in which they recruited staff for their data processing departments. Whereas Industrial Products and the government department recruited internally, the mail order company brought in the majority of its EDP staff from outside. This policy affected the age structure of the departments and we found that in the mail order company the computer staff were young, 70 per cent of them having less than four years' service. This was only true of 11 per cent of Industrial Products staff and of 7 per cent of the staff of the government department. Both Industrial Products and the government department had some EDP staff who had worked for their companies for twenty years, while 70 per cent of programmers in these two organisations were over thirty years of age.

These long-service employees were strongly identified with the culture, philosophy and values of their employers and had friends and ex-colleagues in many other departments. This was less true of the mail order company where new data processing staff had not had time to form these close relationships throughout the business and were less enmeshed in the firm's culture and tradition.

The computer manufacturers had a quasiscientific culture in which the development of EDP technology was a major interest. Their culture was strongly influenced by their marketing orientations and there were pressures on staff to gain new customers and to retain old ones. Staff who were in contact with customers were likely to experience some conflict between a desire to look after the interests of their own company while at the same time looking after those of the computer purchaser.

The culture of the computer consultants was based on the need to create a work environment in which high level problem solving could be carried out. Great emphasis was placed on providing clients with an effective problem-solving service. This was achieved not merely through solving clients' problems but through assisting clients to develop their own problem-solving skills. The firms all regarded themselves as communities of professionals.

To summarise. EDP staffs' skill and knowledge requirements will be influenced by the following aspects of organisational culture:

COMPUTER USERS

Mail order company. This was a paternalistic company culture but the EDP group defined its role as that of a 'ginger' group, bringing new ideas to a somewhat conservative company. These two conflicting ideologies could cause some internal conflict and EDP staff needed to have the social skills to resolve this. EDP staff who were new recruits to the company also required an ability to learn quickly about the ethos of company and to appreciate areas where tradition might place constraints on their work.

Industrial Products and government department. The policy of recruiting the majority of EDP staff internally meant that there was a high acceptance of institutional norms and values. Although this has advantages, too strong an association with past procedures can sometimes lead to conservatism in innovation. This was not a problem in this instance and the fact that EDP staff had experience in other parts of the organisation contributed to the design of acceptable computer systems.

COMPUTER MANUFACTURERS

Culture here was quasiscientific with strong technical objectives and a selling orientation. There were likely to be cultural differences between those parts of the firm which had marketing responsibilities and those which were engaged on research and development. Field staff had to have the skills and experience necessary to resolve difficulties when the interests of their own companies came into conflict with those of their customers.

COMPUTER CONSULTANTS

Employees here saw themselves as a group of professionals dedicated to solving the problems of their clients. There were strong imperatives to provide an excellent client service and considerable identification with client problems. Staff were required to subscribe to this approach and to work with ethical and service considerations continually in mind.

This analysis of the product market, technology and culture of our three groups shows that external influences, internal processes and procedures and company traditions all influence recruitment policies. Our firms required data processing staff whose knowledge, skill and personal ideologies conformed with company policies and needs. These needs were affected by pressures exerted by the markets in which the firm operated; by their pattern of internal organisation and the technology they used to assist them in their production or service functions, and by the intra-organisational culture which had developed as a result of events and relationships in their histories. Our eight concerns would no doubt have liked to have been in a position to recruit staff who met their requirements exactly. They were not always able to do this because of the tight labour market for EDP personnel. However, they had all developed mechanisms for moulding new staff into the required employee image. This was done formally through procedures and informally through an indoctrination process which communicated to the newcomer the norms and attitudes of the group he had joined.

Skill and knowledge requirements

Let us now examine the mix of skill, knowledge and personality factors that programmers and systems analysts in our firms were required to have, recognising that because of the factors discussed in the last section users, manufacturers and consultants did not have identical requirements. The range of skills and attributes is set out below. This consists of:

Technical skills
Problem-solving skills
Administrative skills
Marketing skills
Personality factors
Creative ability
Human relations skills

Technical skills

By technical skill is meant a knowledge of the techniques and equipment available to the programmer and systems analyst to assist him in doing his work. The staff of user EDP departments will require skill in the use of techniques associated with their specialism, together with a sound knowledge of the computer hardware used by their own organisation. Computer manufacturers' staff will not only have to have a knowledge of those techniques available to help them carry out their own work, they will also have to know a great deal about the range of hardware which their own firms are selling if they are to persuade customers that this is the equipment to buy. They must be able to advise on the computers in their company's range which are best suited to solve a particular data processing problem, and they should know enough about all makes of data processing equipment to be able to advise their clients on the most suitable configuration for their needs. In addition both manufacturers and consultants are likely to have a major software development function; the design of software systems to cater for new problems or to improve on the methods for handling old ones. Whereas the three computer users will in most, though not all, computer areas require staff with only an average technical knowledge, the manufacturers and consultants are likely to require considerably more staff with advanced technical qualifications.

Technical skill and knowledge is not inherent but has to be acquired through learning. Therefore a good measure of the extent to which people have this can be obtained by looking at the number and kind of technical courses which they have taken either before joining their present employers or while working for them. In the last paragraph we suggested that the technical knowledge requirements of manufacturers and consultants would generally be greater than those of users. We can now establish whether the staff of these firms had taken more courses than the DP staff of the users and whether they took these at a different point in their data processing careers. We will begin by looking at the number of courses related to data processing taken by staff before joining their present firms.

DATA PROCESSING COURSES TAKEN BEFORE JOINING PRESENT EMPLOYER

Users. Virtually no one had taken a data processing course of any kind.

Computer manufactuers. 31 per cent of programmers and 39 per cent of systems analysts had taken courses. Most of these courses were in programming and we found that computer Manufacturer A was recruiting more trained staff than computer Manufacturer B.

Consultants: 72 per cent of programmers and 79 per cent of systems analysts had taken courses. These courses covered a wider variety of data processing subjects than those taken by the staff of the manufacturers.

In summary, the consultants were recruiting individuals who were already knowledgeable in data processing subjects, the manufacturers were doing this to a lesser extent, and the users were recruiting staff who had little previous formal training in either programming or systems analysis.

DATA PROCESSING COURSES TAKEN WHILE WITH PRESENT EMPLOYER

Users: 100 per cent of programmers had taken programming courses. 76 per cent of systems analysts had taken programming and various other courses related to EDP. The average number of courses taken was three, but the range varied from one course to ten.

Computer manufacturers: 91 per cent of both programmers and systems analysts had taken a variety of EDP courses. The average number of courses taken was three: the range, one course to ten.

Computer consultants: 61 per cent of programmers had taken programming or systems analysis courses. 47 per cent of systems analysts had taken various courses. The average number of courses taken was one: the range, one course to three.

All three groups were therefore undertaking a considerable amount of internal training once new staff had been recruited. The users had the problem of training new staff from scratch. The manufacturers, despite the fact that a third of new entrants already had some formal training, had to ensure that their staff kept up with the latest technical developments. The consultants provided rather less training, particularly at systems analyst level, but made sure that their recruits had already received a considerable amount of formal training before accepting them as members of staff.

The amount of technical knowledge which staff are *expected* to show in work can be identified by looking at individual job descriptions. Programmers and systems analysts were asked to describe the technical, administrative and human relations aspects of their jobs and in all three groups we found that programmers were much more likely to define their jobs in purely technical terms than systems analysts.

In the user EDP departments the task of programming was defined by most people as writing instructions for the computer. Programmers told us, for example:

> I write programs, test them, put them into operation and then maintain them. I also make input and output alterations when necessary.
>
> I take specifications from the systems analysts and say how they are to be applied to the machine.

The majority of answers were of this kind, and few programmers had much contact with line departments. They knew a great deal about their own machines and the software associated with these but little about the data processing problems of business.

The programmers of the manufacturers made many more references to interaction with other groups such as customers. They also had a more comprehensive knowledge of hardware and software.

> I have to be able to appreciate systems and customer requirements.
>
> I must modify software to suit customer requirements and develop the operating system.
>
> I have to have a thorough knowledge of the applications of my Company's software packages from the programming and operating angle.
>
> I have to have an absolute and detailed knowledge of the machine and of the software available.

The consultant programmers gave a very different set of answers demonstrating the very wide variety of problems with which they were associated.

> I am investigating programming techniques for information retrieval in general and designing software packages for use in this.
>
> I visit clients and see how their problems can be put on to a computer. I then help break systems down into programming modules.

Here the programmers of Consultant C appeared to be on more conventional work than those of Consultants A and B. Consultant A in particular was breaking a lot of new ground in programming techniques.

Systems analysts in the user group spoke of devising solutions for line management's problems and of examining existing methods and improving these using computer techniques.

> I need an overall appreciation of hardware and software available and of techniques needed to deal with routine problems and not so routine problems.

Manufacturer's systems analysts were mainly in an advisory role to customers.

> I need a fairly high level of understanding of my firm's equipment and its limitations. I also need a knowledge of applications which are relevant to industries requirements. I need to appreciate the capabilities of hardware and software and to advise customers in this area.

The systems analysts working for consultants stressed the variety of their work.

> The technical content varies from one project to another. I determine a client's requirements, design systems to meet these requirements and get specifications from Computer Manufacturers.
> I need to know management science techniques, operational research model building, investment analysis and business principles.

All three groups therefore had mechanisms for ensuring that their staff had the requisite level of technical knowledge to meet their requirements. Users secured this through internal training, manufacturers and consultants through the recruitment of trained staff and by the further development of skills and knowledge through internal training.

Problem-solving skills

Problem-solving ability implies the use of logical processes to solve ill-defined problems. Problem-solving in data processing covers many activities. These range from defining the information needs for large areas of a business and providing computer-based systems to meet these, to the simpler tasks of transferring payroll or invoicing procedures to a computer. Problem-solving ability is difficult to define. It has been suggested that it covers *predictive* effectiveness – the ability to predict future results on the basis of known regularities; it covers *formal* effectiveness – the ability to look at the structure of a problem in a new way; and it covers *metaphoric* effectiveness – the ability to see relationships between things which have not previously been thought to have any kinship (3). The computer man is most concerned with the second of these. He has to be able to look at business problems from an entirely fresh angle and to answer fundamental questions such as: What is this section of the organisation set up to do? What problems does it have to solve in performing its function? How can the solution of these problems best be achieved using (if required) the technical assistance of a computer?

A working party set up by the education committee of the British Computer Society has set out three levels of problem-solving ability in relation to systems analysis (2). The greatest amount of skill is required in what they call 'information analysis'. This they define as the use of logical structure within complex and ill-defined areas of administrative work; creative ability to conceive new possibilities, and ability to make objective judgments while taking account of a large number of factors. Below this in skill comes 'systems design': this is similar to information analysis but deals with problems of reduced scope and depth.

Last comes 'procedure design'. Here procedures are subordinate to the understanding and experience of using recognised techniques.

Gillis suggests that computer users are primarily interested in securing a payoff from their data processing investments (8). To do this they require EDP personnel who can establish and implement the pay-off objectives. Broadly these personnel will be of three kinds:

1 those who can establish the information processing needs and plans for the enterprise;

2 those who can translate the statements of needs and plans into computer applications;

3 those who can operate the data processing installations.

Computer manufacturers and consultants also require staff who can perform these activities, although objectives 1 and 2 will figure more strongly than 3. But, as they are in close association with many client firms, programmer and systems analyst versatility in problem solving will be particularly important. Because consultants are small in comparison with users and manufacturers, they must recruit at a uniformly high level if they are to acquire this versatility.

Although some people are better natural problem solvers than others, the educational process is usually seen as one method for improving an individual's problem-solving abilities – particularly the higher educational process. Therefore it can be argued that organisations with a need for high level problem-solving skills will tend to recruit university graduates. Figure 2.1 shows the percentages of graduates in our user, manufacturer and consultant groups.

Fig. 2.1 Percentages of data processing staff with university or technical college qualifications

Users	Programmers 38	Systems analysts 44
Computer Manufacturers	Programmers 31	Systems analysts 38
Computer consultants	Programmers 42	Systems analysts 68

It can be seen that whereas there was little difference in the percentage of programmers with high qualifications, the systems analysts of the consultant group were more likely to have degrees than those of the other two groups. This may reflect the complexity of the problem-solving processes in which senior staff of consultants are involved for the job descriptions of the systems analysts indicated that they dealt with problem areas of considerable magnitude.

I am assisting a local government authority to reorganise itself using computers. I am looking at the information needs of education and health services.

I have to be able to advise in all areas of data processing on the methods and standards relevant to a client's business activities. I must always be able to improve on their ideas and to implement my solutions.

Administrative skills

Administration covers the way work is organised, controlled and documented. It was an important function in all our firms but again desired standards of competence in this area differed. In the user group administration was chiefly an internal matter related to the efficient running of the data processing department. In the manufacturers those programmers and systems analysts who were in contact with customers had to show considerable administrative skill as ineptness in this area could result in the loss of a contract. For similar reasons, efficiency was very important to the consultants. They would not be able to persuade clients of their ability to produce results in the client's business if they were seen to be inefficient in their own. Because of the smaller size of the consultants, a higher percentage of staff would have client associations and therefore the majority were likely to need administrative skills.

Administrative responsibility is frequently a consequence of holding a supervisory position and we found that whereas only a third of all programmers and a third of the systems analysts working for users and manufacturers spoke of a supervisory role, two-thirds of the consultants' systems analysts had supervisory commitments. Few programmers who were not team leaders had any administration duties with the exception of a number of the manufacturers' programmers who were responsible for customer contracts. For user and manufacturer systems analysts, administration was associated with running projects, documentation and scheduling. In contrast consultant systems analysts spoke of project 'management' and one consultant placed a great deal of emphasis on developing the managerial expertise of his staff. The administrative role of systems analysts working for consultants appeared to vary between acting as an adviser to a client and taking up a temporary line management position with a client. Few of the programmers and systems analysts we interviewed were enthusiastic about administration and hardly anyone had a job which he described as purely administrative.

Marketing skills

Marketing skill is defined here as the ability to sell successfully in one's product market. This does not apply to our user firms whose success in persuading line departments to use computer systems will be covered in the section on human relations. Both the manufacturers and the consultants had something to sell. In the case of the manufacturer this was a tangible product – a computer – and selling it successfully required giving the customer confidence in the performance of the product through before sales information and after sales service. The consultant was selling something much more intangible – the skills of his staff. His reputation would grow as a result of his problem-solving performance in client firms. Therefore marketing in the traditional sense would be less important for him than for the manufacturer. He would be indulging much more in the 'soft' sell. The computer manufacturer required staff who could sell his computer hardware, the consultant required staff who could sell themselves.

Selling relationships almost always involve a degree of conflict for the salesman, particularly between his desire to serve his customer and his need to look after the interests of his employer. One would therefore expect that the staff of the computer manufacturers, who were selling hardware, would experience more conflict in this respect than the staff of the consultants who were selling a service.

We asked all programmers and systems analysts in these two groups the question, 'Does your loyalty to your firm ever conflict with your responsibility to your clients?' Somewhat surprisingly there was little difference in the percentages of systems analysts in each group who said 'yes' – 40 per cent of those attached to computer manufacturers and 47 per cent of those working for consultants. A larger variation was found between the programming groups, with consultant programmers experiencing more of this kind of conflict. Only a quarter of computer manufacturer programmers in our sample had any direct contact with customers, whereas 47 per cent of consultant programmers spoke of some kind of client contact.

Staff in both of these groups were well aware of their marketing responsibilities and of the personal dilemma in which a conflict of interest between a client's needs and their employer's interests might place them. The staff of the computer manufacturers resolved this conflict by either putting the client's interests first or by trying to act as an arbitrator between the two sets of interests.

> I believe that what is good for the customer is good for our company too. If customers are happy, this is good for the firm's reputation.

However, many staff attached to computer manufacturers recognised that there was a point at which they could no longer side with the customer against their own firm and this moment could cause them problems.

> My company promised to meet a delivery date for equipment and then broke this promise. I felt I should tell the customer but I didn't. It wasn't the right moment in terms of the Company's interests.
>
> We are a profit-making organisation. Customer service is the prime object but it must have a return; I wouldn't give anything to a customer unless the company gained from it. You must know where to draw the line.

Consultant staff also experienced conflict but it was less severe and they were usually able to resolve this by supporting the interests of their clients, thus maintaining their 'helper' role.

> I am pro-client when I am on a project. Our professional image is important and I hope my firm will support this point of view.

It seemed that the needs of the computer manufacturers for staff who recognised that they had a 'selling' role were being well catered for. Computer manufacturer systems analysts made many references to their marketing responsibilities and appeared to enjoy these. Their skill lay in being able to persuade customers that their firm's equipment and knowhow fitted customer needs. In contrast the staff of the consultants were selling themselves and this made them extremely conscious of the human relations aspects of their work. One told us:

> This problem is continually with one. I must be able to sell myself positively and also my firm. One has to get the confidence of the client.

Personality factors

The kinds of personality characteristics that a firm looks for in its staff will relate to the nature of the problem-solving skills that the organisation seeks. Here the greatest differences may not be between firms but between programmers and systems analysts. In all our firms programmers needed a capacity for concentration, perseverance and attention to detail. The computer manufacturer required a wider range of programming skills than the users, and the consultants required a higher multiskill level than the other two groups. Programmers who interacted with customers also needed to be good communicators and excellent representatives of their companies.

The greatest differences in personality requirements were perceived as being in the systems analyst group. Here the users required competent systems analysts who were experts on the business procedures of their own companies, sympathetic to the problems of line departments and aware of the culture constraints of the environment in which they were operating. In contrast the systems analysts of the manufacturers needed to reflect the marketing interests of their employers and to show marketing flair and drive in their relationships with clients. The most important personality characteristic of the consultant systems analyst was the willingness to develop a helper relationship with clients. To identify with their problems and direct all his attention to solving these in a sympathetic and intelligent manner. This meant that users required good systems analysts whose personalities fitted in with the cultures of their employing organisations; the manufacturers required staff who were motivated to serve marketing interests and who saw providing a good customer service as one of the best ways of doing this. The consultant required systems analysts who had a strong service orientation and who were sympathetic and personally involved in the problems of their clients.

Thus all three groups had a need for individuals who were highly motivated to perform well in demanding roles and who had the kind of temperament necessary to sustain these roles successfully. We asked our programmers and systems analysts if they believed that temperament was an important factor in job success and received an overwhelming 'yes' in reply. Temperament requirements did not vary between the three groups but between the jobs of programmers and systems analysts. Whereas programmers said that having the right temperament was important so that the programming task could be performed – programmers required the ability to concentrate, to persevere etc – systems analysts spoke as much of the human relations aspects of work – the ability to get on with people, to be tolerant etc – as of task needs. Figure 2.2 sets out these answers.

Fig. 2.2 Reasons why temperament is important (percentages)

	Task reasons		Human relations		Other reasons	
	Progs	*SAs*	*Progs*	*SAs*	*Progs*	*SAs*
Users	71	48	18	39	11	13
Computer manufacturers	71	39	17	50	12	11
Computer consultants	73	36	16	44	11	20

Creativity

Computer work because it is innovative requires a degree of creativity in the people associated with it. Knight has attempted to define the characteristics of creative individuals (11). He sees creative problems as a high risk activity, often erratic and unpredictable. He suggests that creative people have a detached devotion to their work; they have a deep commitment to the problem they are trying to solve, yet they are not so deeply immersed that they are unable to see the problem in a broader perspective. Creative people are receptive to all sorts of new ideas. They will consider them and judge them on their merits. They rely on free exploration in that they actively go out and search for new ideas and opinions from a wide variety of sources. They appear to commit themselves to a specific solution to a particular problem at a later stage than their less creative fellows. They spend a long time considering alternative approaches before arriving at a conclusion. They tend to be unconformist and continually to question existing solutions.

In so far as data processing specialists are continually surveying business procedures in order to find improved ways of handling them, using the computer as a data processing aid, they require a considerable amount of creativity. But here again the need for radical and innovative solutions from programmers and systems analysts will vary with the nature of the firm and its environment and culture. Many firms will prefer a minor improvement which does not drastically change existing work procedures, to an innovative solution which leads to greater efficiency but also to a major change in methods and structure. Looking at our users, manufacturers and consultants we find that although users did need some creative individuals they were not usually looking for many radically innovative computer solutions. In contrast the manufacturers required a great deal of creativity in some groups, for example hardware designers and software development staff, but the majority of programmers and systems analysts were working on conventional business problems and did not need exceptional abilities in this direction. The consultants, who were frequently asked to bring a new approach to a wide variety of client problems, were likely to have the greatest need for creative staff. Here again their smaller personnel resources meant a majority of their staff must have creative talent.

Surprisingly, when programmers and systems analysts were asked to describe the skills required in their work there were very few direct references to creativity. Programmers were asked to say what kinds of people were most successful at programming and their answers were again in terms of individuals with logical ability, who were tenacious and would pursue problems until they were solved. There were also many references to a requirement for average or above average intelligence. Systems analysts seemed uncertain about the kinds of people who made the best systems analysts. One said: 'I don't know. In my department some of the best systems analysts are quite different kinds of people. One can't generalise.'

Answers varied from, 'They must be patient, persevering types who aren't deterred by problems', to such curious answers as: 'Sportsmen are good analysts. It is part of their nature to get on well with people and to get a wide knowledge of different subjects.'

Many of the consultant systems analysts spoke of systems design as a major part of their responsibility and it would seem that this requires a considerable degree of creativity if an imaginative solution is to result. There was an intuitive recognition of this as shown by the Consultant systems analyst who told us that the best systems analysts were 'those capable of standing back and seeing the system in its entirety and in the whole context of business'.

Consultant systems analysts were certainly working in pioneering areas of data processing and this kind of responsibility must require creative resources. But it is difficult to specify these in detail without a recognition by those concerned that creativity plays a part in their work. Certainly the definition of creativity provided by Torrance would seem to fit many of the activities carried out by programmers and systems analysts (18). The first part of this is:

> Creativity is the process of becoming sensitive to problems, deficiencies, gaps in knowledge, missing elements, disharmonies and so on; identifying the difficulty, searching for solutions, making guesses or formulating hypotheses about the deficiencies.

Perhaps programmers and systems analysts are less concerned with the second part of his definition:

> Once hypotheses are formulated they are tested and retested and the results are finally communicated.

It may be that our manner of solving business problems would be improved if systems analysts did incorporate a more experimental approach into their work.

Computer technologists do not yet have the characteristics of an established professional group, for entry to the work is not entirely controlled by professional examinations, although these are securing increasing recognition. But they do appear to be showing some of the group norms which are thought to be characteristic of professional scientists. One is the desire to be working at the frontiers of their discipline. Lee suggests that the professional norms of scientists demand the creation of new knowledge and its practical application (13). Hence scientist's work goals are generally centred round working on novel aspects of scientific phenomena in order to establish themselves in the forefront of their profession. The answers of the programmers and systems analysts working for the manufacturers and consultants suggested that their norms were not dissimilar. The ability of these two groups to provide interesting, innovating work was therefore a powerful mechanism for maintaining and increasing job satisfaction in their staff.

Human relations and 'change' skills

By human relations skills we mean the ability to develop in others trust, enthusiasm and friendship. We also mean the ability to communicate effectively and in such a way that interest is aroused and cooperation secured. Data processing specialists are essentially agents for change. They are not merely interested in designing new methods but in getting these introduced and used. This is one of the most important aspects of their work yet, as we have seen, also the one that is least recognised in job definitions, in computer literature and in training courses. Knight has pointed out that the process of organisational innovation consists of two major phases (11). First, the creation of the idea and its development, second, the introduction and adoption of the idea. Most of the thought that has been directed at the use of computer systems has looked at the first and neglected the second. Yet all new data processing systems will require the production of change in people. There will be a need to alter behaviour and attitudes through motivation, education and training while at the same time maintaining high morale and job satisfaction. Technical change is unlikely to secure improvement unless people are in favour of it, and its introduction and operation can mean that individuals and groups are required to accept new and demanding work standards and controls. Computer specialists must therefore have the knowledge and means to bring about change. Their human relations skill will be crucial here – the extent to which systems analysts can design and introduce computer systems in such a way that these assist rather than frustrate the needs of staff in line departments.

Users, manufacturers and consultants all expected a considerable amount of human relations skill in their staff. The greatest requirement, this time, was by users and consultants. Computer personnel working for users had to establish and maintain good relationships with other parts of their firms on a long-term basis. Unlike the staff of manufacturers and consultants they were not transients who came and went but a permanent group whose reputation was a product of relationships built up slowly over many years. Again, unlike manufacturers and consultants, they had to live closely with their mistakes. If defects showed up in a system twelve months after it had been introduced they would still be around to receive the complaints and would have the responsibility for putting these right. Human relations expertise was therefore of vital importance to them and this had to be of a genuine 'helping' as opposed to a 'selling' kind.

The manufacturers also had to have a staff who were efficient in establishing good relationships, but here again marketing interests would dominate and if staff experienced a conflict between the interests of the customer and the interests of their employer, then they would be expected to put the interest of their employer first.

The consultants were in a position similar to that of the users but for a different reason. Human relations expertise was essential for them, not because they were establishing permanent long-term relationships with clients, but because the ability to convince clients of a desire and competence to help would influence the extent to which clients would entrust them with their problems.

Thus both the users and consultants required staff who were good at developing sincere helping relationships. The manufacturers would be in an advantageous position if they too could get this kind of staff but we have seen that their staff could experience a conflict of loyalties because their principal interest lay in selling computers. Marketing would be assisted if they had staff who could make an excellent impression on clients, but too many staff who put the maintenance of good human relationships with customers first could hinder an effective marketing approach.

At present human relations and the ability to manage the human part of change are skill areas which are dealt with intuitively and unsystematically and this is in striking contrast to the technical side of computer systems where programmers and systems analysts continually stress the need for a logical approach. Sociologists would argue that this logical approach can be applied as well to the human as to the technical aspects of computers. None of our firms would be able to get their systems accepted and efficiently operated without securing a commitment to the new approach from their clients. We would argue that the human relations and change agent area of computer work is far too loosely defined at present. It needs thinking through much more clearly and this we shall attempt to do in chapter 5.

Generalisations are always open to criticism because they oversimplify complex situations. The needs of our eight firms cannot readily be placed in categories without a considerable amount of distortion. Nevertheless there were differences in the skill, knowledge and personality requirements of users, manufacturers and consultants and these were reflected in the qualifications and experience of their programmers and systems analysts.

These broad differences are set out in Figure 2.3.

In summary, the manufacturers and consultants required high technical qualifications in their staff, the users less so. The manufacturers and consultants also required excellent problem-solving skills, because of the variety of clients with which they interacted. This was particularly true of the consultant group which was in business to sell these skills. All three groups required administrative skills in their staff but this was especially true of the consultants whose ability to make their clients more efficient depended on their own efficiency. Marketing skill in the sense of selling a product to an external group was important to both the manufacturers and the consultants although the two were selling somewhat different things; the manufacturers hardware and service, the

Fig. 2.3 Variance in qualifications required by users, manufacturers and consultants

Qualification requirement	*Users*	*Manufacturers*	*Consultants*
Technical knowledge	Average (in commercial application areas)	High	High
Problem-solving skills	High	Very high	Very high
Administrative skills	Average	Average	High
Marketing skills	Not required	High (selling hardware)	High (selling skill)
Personality factors (the ability to inspire trust and confidence)	High	High (if in contact with customer)	High
Creativity	Average (unless in R & D)	Average (unless in R & D)	High
Human relations skills	High (service orientation)	High (marketing orientation)	High (service orientation)

consultants problem-solving ability. Rather different kinds of motivation would be required in the three groups for the users and consultants must be strongly motivated to provide a service to their line departments and clients; the manufacturers to market their firm's product. We found that there was little expressed recognition of the need for creativity in the job, but consultant staff in particular were likely to find this a necessary attribute in task success. All three groups needed human relations and change agent skills, but especially users and consultants who often assumed responsibility for the entire change process when new computer systems were being introduced.

Skill and knowledge content of EDP work

In an attempt to obtain more specific information on the skill and knowledge content of EDP work we asked all the computer personnel we interviewed to define programming and systems analysis. We also asked them to say what, in their opinion, distinguished a good programmer and analyst from a bad one. Programmers' answers to the first question could be placed in the following activity categories;

Innovation: activities related to designing something new.

Planning: the organisation of sets of activities.

Information transfer: receiving briefs and work specifications from systems analysts.

Logic activity: solving defined problems and thinking in an ordered way.

Translation: putting instructions into a form which could be understood by the computer.

Instruction: the process of giving the computer a set of orders.

Figure 2.4 sets out the number of references that *programmers* in each of the three groups made to these different activities.

Fig. 2.4 Programmers' views of programming and systems analysis activities. (percentages)

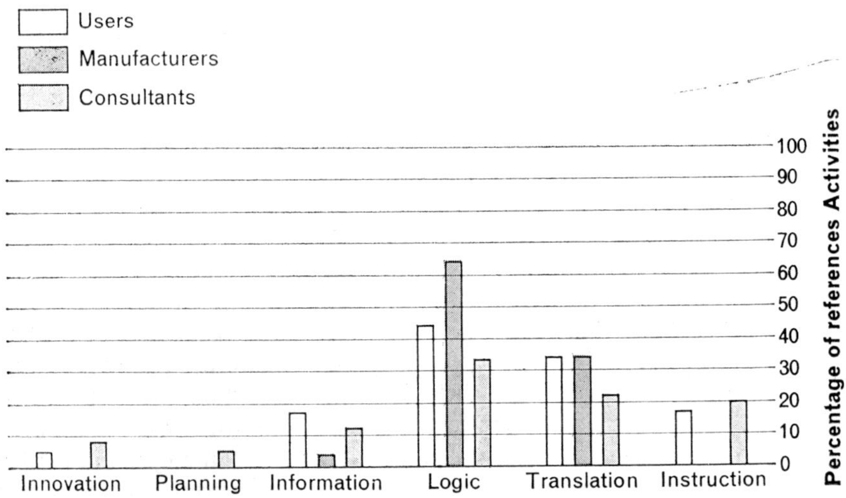

This analysis is interesting in that it shows up differences in programmers' perceptions of the scope of programming work. Computer Manufacturer programmers gave the narrowest definition – speaking almost exclusively of logic and translation activities. User programmers were more conscious of interacting with systems analysts and with the computer itself and consultant programmers defined programming in terms of a wide and varied set of functions.

Answers to the question 'What makes a good programmer?' are analysed in Figure 2.5.

It can be seen that in all three groups the favoured skill characteristics were for efficiency, particularly in regard to use of machine time, and for good logical ability. These two categories are not far removed from each other for it takes a logical person to write a really efficient program. Almost all the other references were to personality characteristics such as adaptability, intelligence and patience. The consultant programmers were the only group to see creative ability as a factor which distinguishes a good from an average performer. All the references in the 'other' category were to a programmer's willingness to document his activities.

Fig. 2.5 Assessment of programmer qualities (percentages)

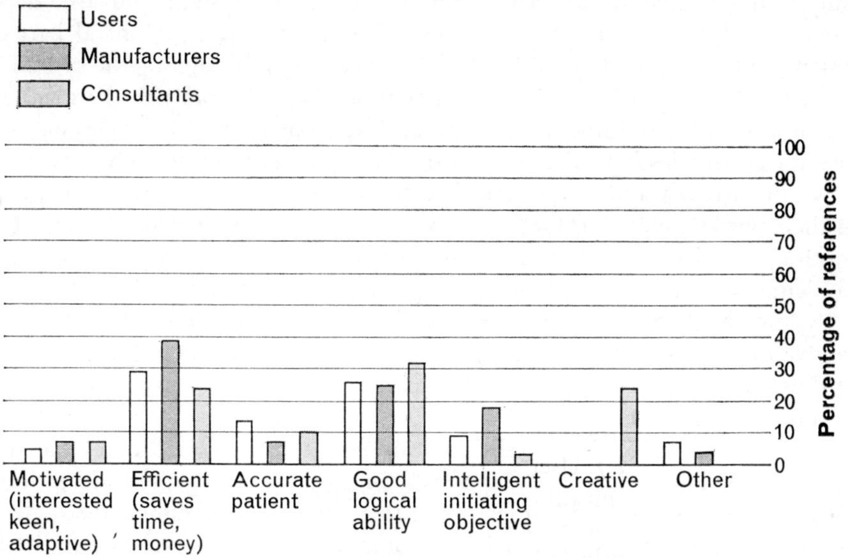

The *systems analysts'* definition of their work focused primarily on problem definition, problem analysis, and problem solution leading to systems design. Their answers could be divided up into the following activity categories:

Fig. 2.6 Systems analysts' definition of their work (percentages)

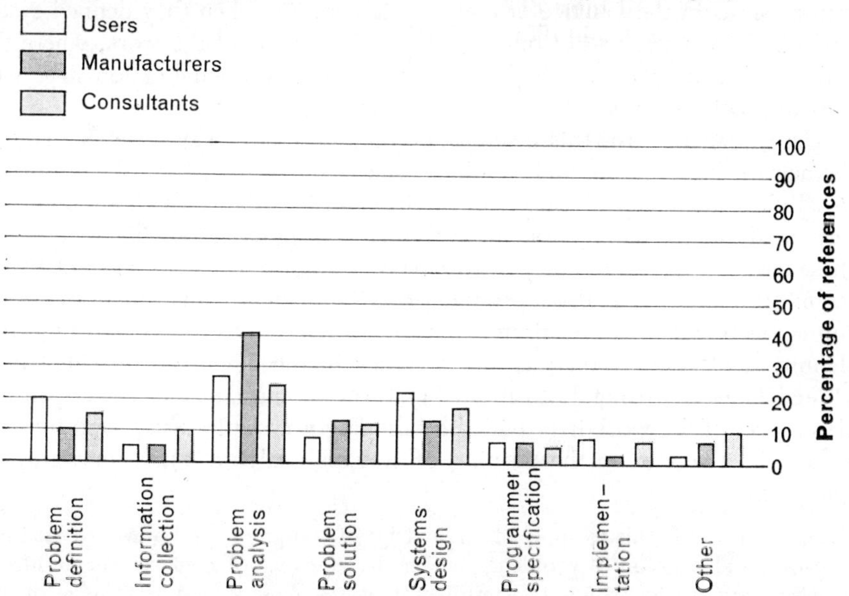

There were few references to implementation as part of systems analysis. In the User group only systems analysts working for Industrial Products included this in their definitions, even though systems analysts in the Mail Order Company were responsible for introducing new computer systems into line departments. Implementation again appeared to be viewed as a peripheral part of a systems analyst's job; an addition to his key activity of designing the system. Yet it is clear from our observations of systems analysts at work that the manner in which systems are implemented is an important factor in their successful operation. This leads to the conclusion that systems analysts are defining their jobs too narrowly and too technically. They need to recognise that a major part of their work is ensuring that systems are introduced with a minimum of disruption, and that this requires a great deal of attention to the human aspects of implementation.

Systems analysts working for users, manufacturers and consultants appeared to give more or less the same weight to the same things, except for the tendency of those working for computer manufacturers to refer more frequently to analytical processes.

Systems analysts' answers to the question 'What makes a good systems analyst?' are set out in Figure 2.7. User and consultant systems analysts considered human relations and communication factors as items which most clearly distinguished good from average systems analysts. Computer manufacturer systems analysts referred more frequently to logical ability and were also more inclined to speak of personality characteristics such as motivation and flexibility. Few saw excellence in terms of ability to meet the needs of the client and fewer still in terms of creativity. There appear to be some interesting contradictions here. Systems analysts were clearly aware of the importance of human relations and communications skills in the practice of their specialism. Yet when they defined systems analysis they referred most often to the analytic parts of the work, where these skills are less needed, and they did not refer to the implementation stage where human relations skills loom large in importance.

The explanation for this discrepancy may lie in the way systems analysis is defined in the literature and in educational programmes. Here the emphasis is usually on the technical aspects of the job and it is these which are commonly written about and taught. Systems analysts therefore learn to define their work in these terms, even though they instinctively recognise that success is not a purely technical matter but is also a product of the competent management of complex human factors. Human relations skills are not referred to by Pappetti (15) in his definition of systems analysis, nor are they in the definition provided by the United States Department of Labour (4). More recently, however, recognition of this aspect of the work is provided by the Engineering Industry Training Board which, in a report on the training of systems analysts (7), defines a systems analyst as

> a person who is able to apply his knowledge of computer applications to the investigation and solution of problems. Under the guidance of management he identifies what needs to be achieved, determines how the required results can be obtained, selects appropriate methods and *plans the implementation of the system* designed to meet the objectives.

Fig. 2.7 Systems analysts assessment of required personal qualities (percentages)

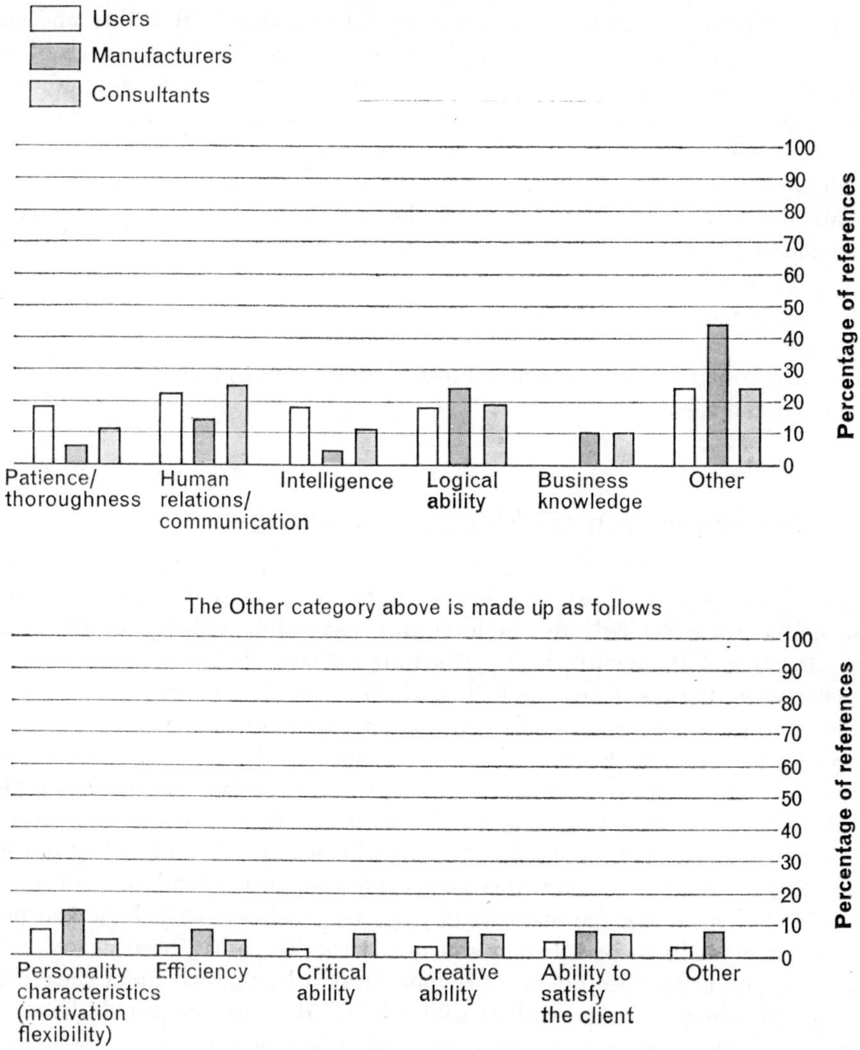

The descriptions of personal qualities set out in Figure 2.7 show that programmers and systems analysts have clear, if narrow perceptions of their activities and believe that they can identify those skills and characteristics which distinguish a good performer from a bad performer. Computer manufacturer's programming staff placed more emphasis than other groups on the logical aspect of programming and on efficient performance, in the sense of saving time and money. These attitudes reflect the needs of marketing organisations which require highly qualified and specialised data processing 'solvers'. Consultant programmers are the only group referring to a need for creativity; a reflection of the complex problem-solving activities which their firms undertake. Systems analysts attached to computer manufacturers also stress logical and analytical ability and refer less to human relations skill as an aid to job success. They also speak of personality factors such as drive and motivation. Users and consultants are more similar to each other in their responses than they are to the manufacturer group.

An interesting question is: 'Why do programmers and systems analysts define their work in this narrow way?' Perhaps the answer is that most people in occupational roles accept without too much thought the definitions of their activities provided by tradition or popular opinion. They do not sit down and produce an analytical model of their functions and responsibilities in terms of the needs of their employing organisations. A result of this can be that activities which logically fit into a group's sphere of responsibility, and which could improve their performance, are overlooked because they are not perceived as part of the occupational role.

The acquisition of skills and knowledge

Vroom suggests that if a task measures a highly valued ability then performance tends to be increased (19). In other words, if an individual believes himself to possess a particular skill and believes that successful performance of his task requires that skill, he will prefer performing the task effectively to performing it ineffectively. On the other hand, if he thinks that effective performance is unrelated to this or to other skills which he possesses then he will be indifferent whether he performs the task effectively or ineffectively. We have little information on whether this hypothesis is correct, though the first part appears logical. But we have been able to ascertain those skills and abilities which programmers and systems analysts thought were required in their work; and to find out how they had acquired these and which they had found most difficult to acquire.

We discovered that the majority of *programmers* believed their logic and problem-solving skills to be inherent and not learnt. These had been developed by training and experience but our programmers had possessed them since childhood. In contrast, *systems analysts* told us that they had acquired their skills through experience in doing the work and in the user and consultant groups these skills were seen as primarily in the management and human relations area. We asked both programmers and systems analysts which particular skill they had found the most difficult to learn. Answers are set out in Figure 2.8.

In the manufacturer and consultant groups those programmers saying that temperamental attributes of patience, thoroughness etc, had not proved easy to develop were young (under twenty-six years of age). Analysts in all three groups said that human relations and management skills had been particularly difficult to learn and, as might be expected, the group stressing this fact were mature and

Fig. 2.8 Which skill did you find the most difficult to acquire? (percentage replies)

	Technical	*Mental*	*Temperament*	*Human relations & management*	*None*	*No answer*
Programmers	4	14	21	13	24	24
Systems analysts	7	11	13	35	22	12

in their late twenties or thirties. With both programmers and systems analysts, the reason most frequently given for an inability to develop certain skills was a lack of the necessary temperament. Thus, although programmers believed that they had the right amount of logical ability to do their work successfully, many said that they had not yet learnt the patience and thoroughness essential to maintain the meticulous accuracy which programming required. Others said that it had taken a number of years to acquire this. In contrast, systems analysts, many of whom had begun their data processing careers as programmers, had had to develop the human relations skills and management expertise necessary for supervising their own colleagues and for successful interaction with user departments.

Vroom's comment that if a task requires a valued ability and an individual possesses that ability, then his performance should be high, while if he does not possess the necessary ability he will be less motivated towards high performance, was supported to some extent in the programming group. EDP managers in two user firms and one manufacturer were asked to rate their data processing staff on creativity and efficiency. We found that there was a strong correlation between being a young programmer (under twenty-six years of age) and being rated low on efficiency. This may have been because of the difficulties the young programmers had in developing the temperament necessary for painstaking and accurate work.

Programmers and systems analysts were unanimous that it was important to have the right temperament to succeed in data processing, though their reasons for this opinion were very different. Programmers said that if they did not have this – again referring to patience, thoroughness etc – either they could not do the job or they would find the job hard to tolerate; it would become irritating and frustrating. Systems analysts emphasised that their chief temperamental requirement was social skill and tact; the ability to explain what they were doing, to avoid conflict and to maintain good relationships.

The same emphasis on temperament appeared in answer to the question: 'What kinds of people make the best programmers and systems analysts?' It was stressed that anyone who was impatient or bad-tempered could not function successfully as a programmer or systems analyst; temperamental defects were seen as more disabling in terms of job success than an absence of problem-solving ability.

This stressing of temperamental qualities as the key to job success is interesting and has implications for data processing selection procedures. At present most selection tests concentrate on identifying logical ability and general intelligence. Yet tests to ascertain whether candidates have the right personality qualities may be equally important. Many firms have had experience of programmers who have suffered mental stress of sufficient severity to cause them to leave. One of the firms in our sample attempted to evaluate programmer selection tests by giving all available tests to their applicants for programming posts. This firm found that the only man to succeed in passing all the tests left with a nervous breakdown after six months with the company. But despite these difficulties it is clear that most people do not find the necessary qualities of temperament difficult to acquire or we would not find such unqualified enthusiasm for data processing work.

Manpower problems which affect the skill and knowledge contract

An organisation may have given a great deal of thought to its skill and knowledge requirements and successfully obtained a nucleus of staff who meet these and who are satisfied because they believe the work fits their talents, yet if it cannot continue to recruit at this level it will experience manpower problems and its efficiency may suffer. Here the state of the labour market is a critical factor.

A source of anxiety in all data processing departments is whether they will be able to get staff in the numbers and quality they require. All the forecasts on this subject have been dismal. The *Computer Weekly* of 24 April 1969 points out that systems analysts, in particular, form the major bottleneck in the speedy development of successful computer applications. Estimates produced by the Ministry of Technology some years ago predicted that by 1970 there would be a shortage of 11,000 systems analysts. This shortage appears to have been somewhat offset by the increased development of formal courses in data processing, in particular those designed by the NCC.[1] Nevertheless many firms complain bitterly that they cannot get systems analysts of sufficient experience. In 1967 a report produced by the Department of Education and Science also stated that the most critical shortage of skilled staff in EDP was in the systems analysis area (6). This conclusion was endorsed in the same year by the report of the Engineering Industry Training Board referred to earlier (7). There are fewer comments about the shortage of programmers and it may be that both computer manufacturers and the newly formed software houses are helping to meet the need for programming skill. Despite this apparent lack of competent personnel young people have difficulty in finding firms which will train them from scratch in programming or systems

[1] Evidence submitted to the 1969/70 Parliamentary Select Committee on computing suggests that current training turns out 1500 systems analysts each year, compared with a need for 3600 in 1970 and 11,000 by 1975.

analysis. The *Computer Weekly*, 25 July 1968, points out that about the only people prepared to employ raw recruits are the computer manufacturers and they provide work which is not always to a young person's liking (5).

Although the 1971 recession led to some companies reducing the numbers of their data processing staff there are no signs that these shortages will not persist and it seems that the only way that an organisation can ensure a supply of really competent EDP personnel is by training its own. This means that a firm must be clear about the nature of its data processing needs and have methods for identifying people with the potential to meet these. For example, it is generally accepted that a programmer needs aptitude and motivation. There are numerous tests which claim to identify the former, though programming aptitude does not necessarily mean eventual success. Motivation is less easy to identify and is, in any case, more often a product of the environment in which the programmer finds himself than of his own personality. People with a potential to become good systems analysts are even more difficult to find. Firms would be well advised to spend time working out with some precision the role they wish their systems analysts to play and the activities for which these specialists are to accept responsibility.

Two of our three user EDP departments were not in serious difficulty over the recruitment of data processing staff. Industrial Products and the government department were able to find staff with the right potential inside their own organisations, and they had excellent training facilities. The mail order company did have problems and found it very difficult to attract experienced staff from outside. This firm preferred to recruit externally, except for some systems analysts, but they were prepared to train inexperienced applicants and they kept their staff because they had incorporated a cumulative bonus scheme into their salary structure. Under this scheme staff who stayed a certain length of time received a generous bonus and this bonus increased with length of service.

The problems of user firms in obtaining staff may increase in the future but it looks as if their internal training facilities will prevent serious difficulties arising. More intractable staff problems are forecast for the computer manufacturers. An article in the *Sunday Times*, 'Computers: the cuckoo in the economic nest', suggests that the industry is expanding at such a rate that it will need to hire two new people in the next two years for every one it has hired up to now (10). The article points out that large parts of the industry are at present located in areas where there is a serious shortage of labour: north London, central Scotland and Manchester. It suggests that the computer industry will either have to rob other industries or open plants near different major conurbations if it is to satisfy its appetite for labour.[1] The computer manufacturers are members of a new industry. They have not been around for sufficient time to have long-service staff and there is no tradition of providing a lifetime of work for individual employees.

Consultants are likely to be in a happier situation than users or manufacturers. The work they provide is varied and interesting. A certain prestige attaches to

[1] The 1971 recession has, of course, greatly slowed down this expansion.

working for a consultant and industry is greatly attracted to young men who have had consultant experience. They should have fewer recruitment problems.

Although the staff situation is not easy and may become more difficult none of our firms appear to be in the situation of some United States companies described by John Hoskyns, the computer consultant, in the *Sunday Times* article. He sees these as afflicted with poor quality labour: 'They have to hire more people because those they have got are no good – and the people they hire are even worse than the ones they have got, so they have to hire still more people.'

In a tight labour market the attraction of a company for its potential employees is a powerful factor in helping it to recruit at the right skill and knowledge level. We have seen that Industrial Products and the government department recruited the majority of their data processing staff internally and then gave them the necessary EDP training. Many of these individuals had taken jobs with their employers because they were attracted by their public image and reputation or because friends and relatives had recommended them to do so. At that time they had not envisaged ever moving into computer work. In contrast, programmers in the mail order company, 94 per cent of whom were under thirty, tended to have joined this firm because they actively wanted to work in EDP. This was less true of the systems analyst group, some of whom had worked in other jobs in the firm before moving into EDP.

In the two computer manufacturers, 65 per cent of programmers said they had joined their firms because they were attracted by their images, because they had a friend who already worked there, or simply because they wanted to work in EDP. The majority of systems analysts gave the same reasons. These employees were already committed to the idea of computer work and their choice of employer was based on who would provide them with the best self-development opportunities.

They described their firms to us:

> There is a good atmosphere and enthusiasm. It is a go-ahead company.

> I fancied programming and thought it better to go to a manufacturer as there would be more opportunities.

In all the consultant firms the majority reason for staff joining their employers was company image and this image was generally related to perceived opportunities for self development. They said '... I wanted an atmosphere where I could be creative and use ideas'. In this group were many references to professionalism.

> This firm has a good reputation. This is important in career terms. Also there was the attraction of a professional environment.

> The variety of work and applications attracted me, and the more professional background.

This desire for self-development appears to be a major motivating factor with computer specialists and we shall examine it further in the next chapter. It is clearly an important factor in whether an individual believes that his skill and knowledge needs are being met by his employer, and it is strongly related to the existence of formal training mechanisms which permit this self-development to take place. Computer people seek, first, the opportunity to acquire and develop the knowledge to be accepted as data processing specialists; second, as data processing becomes professional the opportunity to go further than merely achieving acceptability with employers, and to acquire qualifications and work standards which will ensure entry into the professional body.

Training provisions

These two skill and knowledge requirements lead us to a consideration of the training provisions now available to those people who wish to make data processing their career. We have seen that our user EDP group were almost entirely trained by their own employers through the media of internal courses, though the mail order company sent its systems analysts on outside courses. A third of the computer manufacturers' staffs, more in Manufacturer A than B, had already received training before joining their present employers and this tended to be through short, internal courses organised by previous employers. Of consultant programmers, 71 per cent, and of systems analysts, 59 per cent, had been on courses organised by previous employers, but again these were short internal courses, usually in programming and systems analysis. A number had been on computer manufacturers' courses.

Generally internal training courses were short and intensive and people had to acquire a great deal of their expertise while actually doing the job. At the time our survey was carried out, formal training was still relatively undeveloped. Today the situation is very different and there are many excellent courses for imparting the technical skills which a programmer and systems analyst requires to become competent in his work.

Few of our programmers and systems analysts had a university degree in computational science, though courses in this subject are becoming common and it is probable that in future young men and women interested in making data processing their career will enrol for these. The *Computer Bulletin*, June 1967, tells us that these courses have a long history, dating from the 'twenties and 'thirties. The war years gave impetus to the development of numerical techniques and after the war these became the subject of post-graduate diploma courses (17). Between 1950 and 1959 the emphasis was on numerical analysis; then, when computers arrived in universities, programming was included in the subject content. Since 1964 the number of these courses has increased and the majority now provide an MSc. degree rather than a diploma. There has been a shift away from numerical analysis to topics such as the theory of computation, logic design of computers, symbol manipulation, information processing and so on.

Many degree courses are academic in content and perhaps more suited to the backroom men of computing than to the programmer and systems analyst who is going to be concerned entirely with business applications. The Engineering

Industry Training Board has now completed an excellent analysis of what a systems analyst operating in a commercial environment ought to know (7). The Board divides skill and knowledge requirements into three areas:

- business training;
- computing training;
- systems analysis training.

It suggests that training for each of these topics can best be accomplished through an off-the-job course and a period of planned on-the-job experience. The purpose of business training is to give the systems analyst an understanding of the main functions of business and the problems of introducing computer-based systems into industrial concerns. A course of at least two weeks is recommended for this purpose. Training in computing is directed at providing an understanding of computer hardware and software; data collection and data preparation, and the organisation of data processing departments. Here again a course of not less than two weeks is recommended. Systems analyst training covers a working knowledge of the practice of systems analysis together with the acquisition of skills and knowledge which a systems analyst requires to perform satisfactorily in his first post of responsibility. Here a four weeks' course is recommended. This Engineering Industry training plan is one of the few to recommend some coverage of the human relations aspects of computer introduction.[1] It suggests that the systems analyst needs to know something about individual and group attitudes to change; how to overcome resistance and the importance of user participation in decision-taking in doing this; and the role of training and education in securing cooperation. He also needs to know about his firm's trade unions, salary procedures and manpower planning activities. The Engineering Training Board report also provides one of the better job specifications for the work of a systems analyst. Nevertheless it still focuses on the technical aspects of the job and ranges very rapidly over his responsibilities in the human relations area.

As we have seen earlier in this chapter, there is a measure of agreement on the technical nature of a systems analyst's job but very little agreement on his responsibilities once he moves outside this narrow area. An article in the *Computer Weekly* points out that the development of training programmes has been handicapped by almost total lack of agreement on the functions of a systems analyst (14). It suggests that at times it has seemed that the only common ground was that he appeared somewhere between the user of a system and the computer. Within that area the boundaries of his responsibilities were almost infinitely variable. This problem has been compounded by the variety of backgrounds from which the potential systems analyst has been recruited.

Another article in the *Computer Weekly* describes the courses which exist to provide the would-be data processing expert with the knowledge he requires (12). It states that four broad types of course are offered:

[1] The BCS working party on Education and Training also emphasise the need for human relations skills.

1 course run by manufacturers;
2 courses run by consultants or bureau;
3 courses run by independent colleges;
4 courses run by computer users who have opened their own internal courses to outsiders (for instance the National Coal Board).

Computer manufacturers were the first to enter the training field, for the simple reason that they could not sell computers if people did not know how to use them. Their courses are usually short and hardware based so that they give the new analyst very little understanding of the business problems he is likely to encounter in his work. Consultants were the next to offer systems courses. These tend to be very varied in content, and also expensive. As a rule they take a much wider view than the manufacturer and, if not considering all human relations problems, at least provide some information on communication needs.

Technical colleges now provide a considerable number of systems analyst courses. The stimulus here has been the National Computer Centre together with the Department of Education and Science. A working party set up by the NCC devised a course package designed to take six weeks of full-time study. This course was to be offered initially by twenty-two technical colleges and, in the long term by thirty-five. Candidates are drawn from among programmers, work study and O & M groups, and the intention was that by 1970 up to 5000 students would be receiving training in this way. The problem here has been one of providing good teachers. The course was originally conceived to be given by practising analysts. But it has been found that few technical colleges have systems analysts with the breadth or up-to-date experience to expand and interpret the basic course framework in the way that the NCC authors intended. In an attempt to overcome this problem attention has recently been given to the provision of industry-based courses. The Engineering Training Board report referred to above has been a product of effort in this direction.

A useful method of creating resources is now being provided by organisations which, over a long period of time, have developed courses to train their own data processing staff and have now opened these up to industry in general. Rolls-Royce was a well-known example here and the National Coal Board still is. This is an excellent contribution to the training problem, though only a very few firms are in a position to provide an educational service of this kind.

So far we have been looking at the training provisions for systems analysts. Programmers are better catered for in terms of the numbers of available courses as their work is less varied than that of the systems analyst and it is therefore easier to set up special educational establishments to provide this kind of training. Here the vexed question is one of standards. Programmers receive their training from technical colleges, from computer manufacturers, from private programming schools and from correspondence courses, and there has been a great deal of criticism of the two last methods in the data processing press. Programming schools are rebuked for providing inadequate training and for accepting applicants for their courses whose attributes would normally bar them from finding a job afterwards. For example, they may lack academic qualifications, be older than the acceptable age or be foreigners. The same criticisms are levelled at correspondence courses. Yet for many people courses of this kind can provide an entry to a profession which, though short of personnel, is still reluctant to accept the completely untrained applicant from outside. It has been suggested that programmer training should cover three stages (9):

1 producing a high level language applications programmer;
2 extending his knowledge to assembly language programming;
3 progressing to systems programming or the computer side of systems design.

Some companies are now looking into programmed learning as a method for training their programmers. But it seems likely that this will only be economically worthwhile in firms which constantly train large numbers of programmers – for example, computer manufacturers.

Opportunities to meet the first needs of a would-be data processing specialist, that of acquiring the necessary technical knowledge to ensure acceptance by industry, are therefore good at the present time. Increasingly employers will look for data processing staff who have formal qualifications of some kind and qualified personnel will possess a high value on the labour market. The programmers and systems analysts in our survey got into data processing by a variety of routes, and many got there through chance rather than intention. This is much less likely to happen in the future.

The individual who wishes to develop his talents and to progress in the data processing world of tomorrow will increasingly have to meet standards of work and behaviour set by and for data processing specialists through their professional body, the British Computer Society. Eventually, as in many other occupations – for example, accountancy and engineering – it may be difficult to obtain a senior post without professional qualifications. Members of new occupations which require a high level of skill and knowledge are usually anxious for the prestige which comes from belonging to a recognised profession and they will frequently attempt to restrict entry to those who have passed approved examinations. Data processing is now in this stage. In June 1967 details of the plan for professional qualifications in computing were announced by the British Computer Society, and it was stated that the first examination would be held in the summer of 1969. In July 1968 an article in *Computer Weekly* by Donald Yeates stated:

> We must equip potential systems analysts with the skills of their profession. I use the word 'profession' quite deliberately. It is high time that all data processing staff introduced into their work the working practices of true professionals. We can no longer offer to have people becoming 'systems analysts' and picking up the skills, techniques and working practice as they go along. Systems analysts must now be recognised as a profession in its own right (20).

Yeates then goes on to point out that the framework for professionalism has now been set through the introduction of the British Computer Examination scheme and through the setting up of a UK coordinating committee for examinations in computer studies. The latter would concern itself with courses other than at degree or final professional qualification level and would 'ensure that a clear structure of educational opportunities related to courses with national currency shall be provided for the various categories of computer staff required by industry and commerce'.

In the *Computer Weekly* for 8 October 1970 Maurice Ashill, Secretary General of the British Computer Society defines a profession as he sees it:

> The prime factor is that members of a profession accept special responsibility and voluntarily work to a code of practice which goes beyond the minimum legal obligations. They accept these higher standards to ensure the confidences of those for whom they work as well as the general public. This confidence is essential to any profession. From its members a profession expects a high standard of skill and knowledge and a high standard of business ethics (1).

And so we find data processing specialists now adding ethics to technical competence as a necessary qualification for being a member of the data processing profession. The data processing career man can now call himself a professional once he has passed the British Computer Society examinations and accepted their code of ethics. This again adds attraction to the work for those who wish to be esteemed by society as well as by their own colleagues.

At the time of our survey the British Computer Society was still struggling for members. Membership figures for our users, manufacturers and consultants are

Fig. 2.9 Percentage membership of the British Computer Society

	Programmers		Systems analysts	
	Member of BCS	Non-member	Member of BCS	Non-member
Users	9	91	7	93
Manufacturers	33	67	60	40
Consultants	40	60	65	35

set out in Figure 2.9. It is clear that the staff of manufacturers and consultants were more interested in membership than the staff of users and that in these groups systems analysts were more likely to be members than programmers.

Once having recruited and trained data processing staff the next problem is to keep them. It has been suggested that, from the point of view of management, continuity of employment in data processing departments is a key factor in the successful use of computers (8). Formalised career paths with built-in training opportunities are essential if expensive computer staff are to be retained. Increasingly firms will have to abandon attempts to recruit experienced staff and shift to a policy of taking on graduates with the expectation that by the time they have completed their training programme there will be jobs waiting for them. Many observers believe that the need for internal company training for data processing will be acute in the next decade.

Summary and conclusions

The principal hypothesis on which this chapter is based is that important elements in job satisfaction are:

- the fit between the skill and knowledge requirement of an employing organisation and the skill and knowledge attributes of its employees;
- the fit between how an individual's skills are being used by an organisation and how he wants these skills to be used.

We have concentrated here on the first more than the second because we propose to examine in detail the attitudes of programmers and systems analysts to their work in chapter 6. We have related skill and knowledge requirements to the environment in which organisations operate – in particular the product market environment – and have noted that because the EDP staff of computer manufacturers and consultants were in direct contact with their product market and subject to its pressures, they tended to have a different pattern of recruitment and training to that of EDP departments located in user organisations.

The diagram opposite sets out in a simplified form the variables which influence a Company's EDP skill and knowledge requirements.

The next diagram shows those variables within an individual's personal environment which influence the level at which he wishes his skills and knowledge to be used.

An individual's perception of the state of the labour market is an important influence on his attitudes and behaviour. If he believes that his skills are being underemployed he will normally look for another job. In an easy labour market he will have little difficulty in finding one and he is therefore likely to have a low tolerance of a poor use of talents. If, in contrast, the labour market is tight and he knows and will have difficulty in obtaining another job then he may lower his expectations of how his skills and knowledge should be used.

Level of EDP training is an obvious influence on an individual's idea of how he should be employed. Job expectations are normally related to an individual's perceptions of his own competence, and competence is a product of both training and experience. Professionalisation, in so far as it involves the acquisition of professional qualifications, is also tied in with level of training. Membership of a professional society which restricts entrance to people who have passed its exams implies a certain level of competence. Membership of the British Computer Society is not yet restricted in this way but there are signs that the Society is under pressure to move in this direction.

Somewhat surprisingly, degree of institutionalisation has been found to exert an influence on employment expectations. Men and women who have worked for one firm for many years become very bound up with the company and

Fig. 2.10 Factors influencing an organisation's skill and knowledge requirements

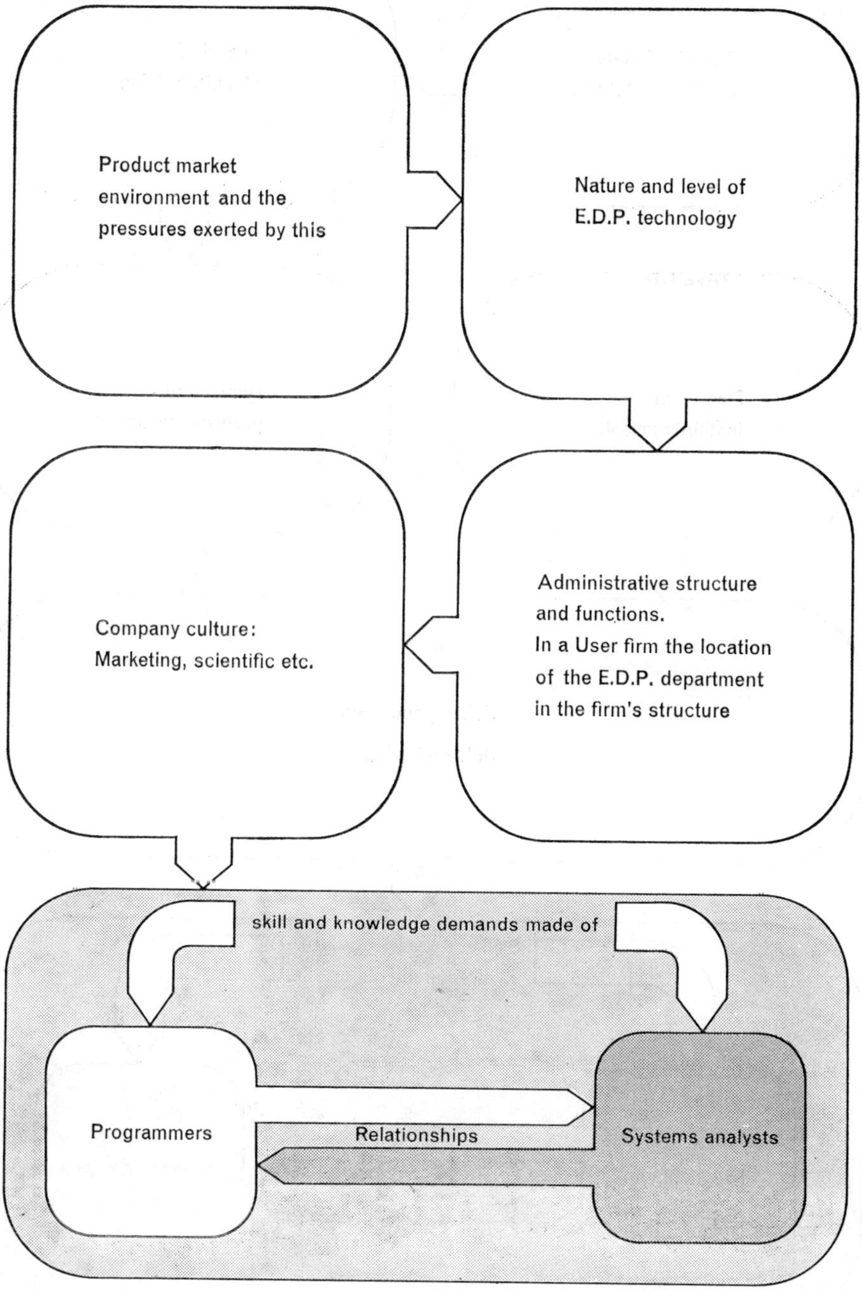

Fig. 2.11 Factors influencing the skill and knowledge requirements of an individual (the level at which he wishes to use these)

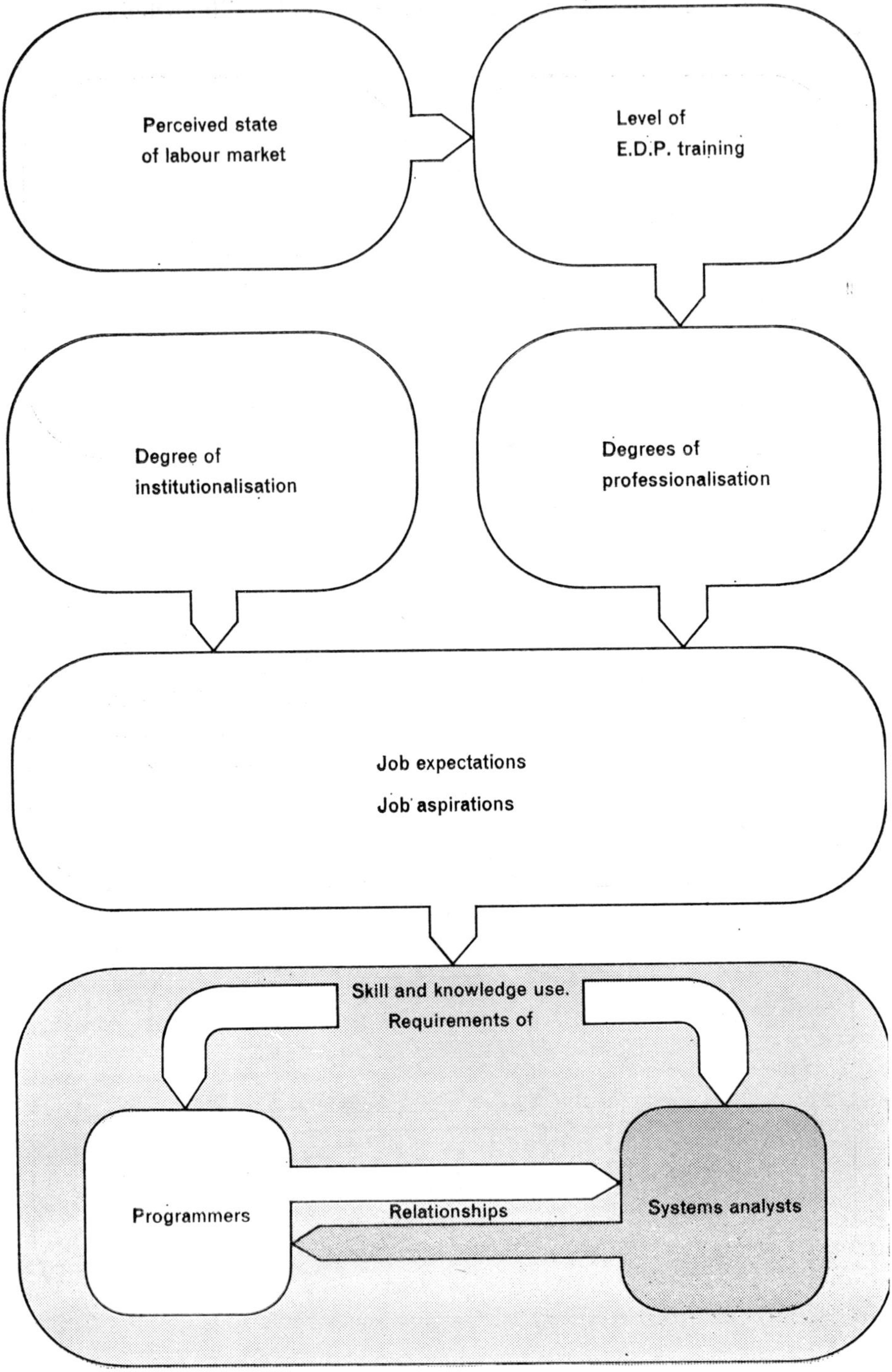

reluctant to leave. They are then often prepared to tolerate what they regard as a misuse of their abilities rather than dig up their roots. This was not an important factor in our computer manufacturers and consultants, where staff length of service was universally short, but it did affect attitudes to work in our user EDP departments where, as we have seen, a length of service of up to twenty years was not uncommon.

An individual's satisfaction with the use of his skill and knowledge will be high when his expectations of how his talents *will* be used by his employer, his experience of how they *are* being used and his aspirations of how they *should* be used all overlap. In our eight firms there was little dissatisfaction in this respect. Programmers and systems analysts spoke enthusiastically about their work and there was a general belief that the nature of this led to their being intellectually stretched. There was, however, some criticism of training provisions and this we shall discuss in the next chapter.

3

The psychological contract

This chapter considers the psychological contract between a firm and its employees. By psychological contract is meant the willingness of the employer to provide a situation which caters for the individual's psychological needs in exchange for a commitment by the employee to his work and to the firm's interests – a condition that is usually referred to as 'motivation'. Employers and employees will vary in what they expect or will accept from each other in this exchange relationship. In Parsons' terms both organisations and individuals can be either self or collectively orientated (17). An organisation is self orientated if it allows its employees to give priority to their personal interests regardless of the effect on the interests of the organisation. Few organisations approach this but some, for example professional associations, come close to it. The organisation is collectively orientated if it expects its employees or members to give priority to the interests of the organisation. Most employing establishments come into this category although they vary in the extent to which they demand conformity to their interests.

An individual is 'self' orientated if he takes account of his own interests regardless of the interests of others in his firm. He is collectively orientated if he is strongly influenced by his perceived obligations to others and will subordinate his private interests to these.

Schein has pointed out that although the psychological contract implies that the firm has expectations of the employee and the employee has expectations of the firm, these expectations are not written into any formal agreements (21). Despite this they act as powerful determinants of behaviour. In most employing organisations conformity to company interests will cover a willingness on the part of the employee to stay with the firm so long as his services are required and adequately rewarded, a high level of performance and a personal identification with the culture and objectives of the organisation. The psychological contract is implemented by the organisation through the concept of authority. A decision by an individual to join an organisation is seen as an acceptance of the authority system of that organisation. Authority can rarely be imposed on an individual or group unwilling to receive it, thus the individual has to give his tacit consent to this authority and agree to submit to it. He will only do this if he believes that a fair exchange is taking place and that he is getting something worth while in return for his commitment to the interests of his employer.

Theories of needs and motivation

At present there is still some confusion regarding psychological needs in work. What compensation will the individual accept in exchange for subordinating some of his personal interests to the interests of the organisation? Schein suggests that broadly the individual requires freedom and influence. The knowledge that he can influence the organisation or his own immediate work situation in such a way that he can achieve his most important personal needs. In other words so that he can persuade his employer to look after his interests. This poses the very large question of what people's needs in work are. Psychologists have now completed a great deal of research on the motives and needs of employees and have related these to the incentives and rewards provided by the organisation. But, before setting out the main strands of thought on this subject it is important to define what we mean by needs.

Leggatt has defined the concept of need as a system requirement which must be met if the system is to survive in a satisfactory state (12). From the point of view of the individual in work this relates to those of his requirements which must be met if his job is to be done with effectiveness and satisfaction and his career to be advanced. From the point of view of the organisation it is those requirements which must be met if its current goals are first to be realised and then modified so as to ensure continuing survival in response to changing environmental conditions. It can be seen from this definition that needs in a work situation are usually considered within the context of motivation.

Chung has described the different approaches of psychologists and managerial practitioners to the problem of motivation (2, 3). Whereas psychologists tend to approach it from the angle of human needs and motives, management theorists have looked at the development of motivation through incentives and inducements. Another group of experts, led by Gestalt psychologists, have developed perceptual theories of motivation. These stress that an individual's perception of a situation – the way he sizes it up – is the only basic determinant of behaviour because it conditions the way people respond to incentives. In contrast, other groups of experts, especially personnel managers, appear to assume that performance is a product of an individual's ability. They seek to acquire motivated employees through sound selection and training practices. All these play a part in the development of motivation but in this chapter we shall restrict ourselves to the psychological needs of employees and the organisation's ability to meet these.

Psychological needs will vary from person to person according to sex, family background, education, career aspirations, as well as many other factors and these influences will lead to different patterns of behaviour. Needs will also vary over different stages of an individual's life cycle. A young unmarried man will have a different set of needs from an older man with a family to support. Most theorists also accept that as some needs are satisfied so they become less important and are displaced by others of greater urgency.

The 'hierarchy of needs' theory was first developed by Maslow as an alternative to theories which viewed motivation in terms of a number of separate and distinct drives (14). Essentially Maslow's approach is to see an individual's needs as being on a series of levels ranging from low level physiological needs to the ultimate goal of self actualisation. His theory is a dynamic one in that man is seen as a wanting being who constantly strives for the fulfilment of needs in an ever-expanding need system.

Maslow's approach is often oversimplified by students who do not appreciate its sophistication. It is in fact much broader than a simple listing of a need hierarchy. Maslow believes that an individual's system of needs must be studied as a whole if his behaviour is to be understood. Needs are found in clusters rather than in isolation and this means that most behaviour is a result of a number of motivations. Maslow thus looks at groups of needs within a larger need system (3). These clusters form subsystems which can be categorised in different ways. They can, for example, be classified into the needs which are common to different age or occupational groups. Or they can be classified, as Maslow prefers, into a hierarchy of needs covering physiological needs, safety needs, social needs, self-respect needs and self-actualisation needs. This human need system is seen by Maslow as an expanding one with higher needs emerging as a result of the satisfaction of lower order needs. However, lower level needs are never completely displaced; they will recur whenever an individual is unable to satisfy them. They will become powerful motivators if, for example, a man has to work in a situation where there is physical danger or a shortage of food.

Maslow's hierarchy of needs is in no sense a rigid theory. He accepts that the order will vary from one individual to another and from one culture to another. He also recognises that the movement of needs from one level in the hierarchy to another is only a tendency and not a certainty. Again as an individual's goals and objectives alter so a different structure may appear. Maslow therefore accepts that needs within work must not be viewed as the same for all individuals, or as static over time. As an individual succeeds in meeting his lower level needs for food, safety and social relationships, so he will proceed on to Maslow's highest order needs and seek self respect and self actualisation.

Another important contribution towards a theory of human needs has been developed by Herzberg (7, 8). His research was designed to test the theory that man has two sets of needs. First, his need as an animal to avoid physiological pain and deprivation – corresponding to Maslow's lower level needs. Second, his need as an individual to grow intellectually – corresponding to Maslow's higher level needs. This hypothesis was first tested out on 200 Pittsburgh engineers and accountants but has since been applied to many different groups including housewives, unskilled catering staff, professional women, scientists and nurses. It has also been tested in a number of different countries.

At the time Herzberg began his research the conventional explanation of job satisfaction was that satisfaction and dissatisfaction were two ends of a continuum with a neutral condition midway in which the individual was neither satisfied nor dissatisfied. This approach assumes that individuals shift along this continuum in response to changes in their jobs or in the situation in which they work. Dissatisfaction is seen as an absence of factors which cause satisfaction, for example, adequate pay, good supervision, interesting work. If there are an equal number of factors causing dissatisfaction with work and an equal number causing satisfaction then the individual is perceived as being neutral towards his job.

Herzberg's approach differs from this in that he assumes that certain aspects of work act as satisfiers and other, different, aspects act as dissatisfiers. If there is an absence of factors which produce job satisfaction then the individual will not feel actively dissatisfied; he will revert to a state of 'no satisfaction'. Similarly if an individual is not subject to influences liable to cause him job dissatisfaction then he will not necessarily feel actively satisfied and motivated by his job, he will merely move to a state of 'no dissatisfaction'.

Using Herzberg's approach five factors stand out as strong determinants of job satisfaction. These are recognition, achievement, responsibility, advancement and the nature of the work itself. A different set of factors is associated with job dissatisfaction. These are supervision, salary, working conditions, interpersonal relations, and company policy and administration. It has been noted that these two groups of factors can be distinguished in terms of 'what a person does' and 'the situation in which he does it' (11). Critics of Herzberg's approach suggest that this split into clusters of motivating and hygiene factors came about as a result of the methods used by Herzberg to collect his data. This was a semi-structured interviewing approach in which respondents were asked to identify 'critical incidents' which led to feelings of job satisfaction or dissatisfaction.

Other research methods still support the traditional uniscalor approach in which there is a continuum with feelings of satisfaction and dissatisfaction at either end (1). Vroom has suggested that Herzberg's research methodology tends to overemphasise the importance of actions within the individual's personal control as sources of satisfaction and matters beyond the control of the individual as sources of dissatisfaction. The individual can take credit for his successes and blame others for his failures (23).

Despite these methodological doubts, Herzberg's work has led to a great deal of serious thought on the nature of job satisfaction and to practical attempts to provide work situations which are conducive to its development. Two points emerge clearly from the work that has been done up to date. One is the elusiveness of the concept of job satisfaction. What does it mean? Does it mean quite different things to different age, sex, and occupational groups? The second is the complexity of the whole subject. There is little evidence that individuals have simple feelings of satisfaction or dissatisfaction towards their jobs (1). On the contrary any researcher tackling this subject must consider a large number of factors contained both in an individual's job, in the situation in which he works, and in his personal environment outside work, and relate these to his attitudes towards his job. Most of us have mixed feelings towards work. We like some aspects and dislike others. Our feelings are related to what we are called on to do, to the situation in which we are asked to do it, to the attitudes and beliefs of those we work with, and to the demands and pressures of our domestic and social environments.

Despite these difficulties, managements are well aware that if people are generally dissatisfied with their jobs there are likely to be some manifestations of this discontent and these will take the form of employees looking for more congenial work elsewhere, taking time off if permanent removal from an unpleasant situation is not possible, or becoming disinterested in work activities with a consequent reduction in efficiency and productivity.

The theories of both Maslow and Herzberg stress the importance of achievement as a motivating factor, although Maslow prefers to call this the need for esteem and self-actualisation. This need for achievement seems very much a quality of western culture, particularly middle-class culture. A number of studies have been made of the need for achievement of different occupational groups. McClelland has found that businessmen have relatively more achievement motivation than other groups in society (15). Scientists and professional men are also above average in this although there is a considerable variation within their ranks, and they tend to be striving for long-term rather than short-term goals. Porter has related this need for achievement and self-actualisation to organisational properties such as job level, company size, sub-unit size, and the amount of diversity in the groups with which the individual has to interact at work (19, 20). He found a strong relationship between perceived possibilities for self-actualisation and job level. Higher level managers generally felt they had more opportunities for autonomy and personal development than lower level managers. The same relationship was not found with the security and social esteem variables.

For some time now management has recognised the necessity to meet what it has perceived as the most important personal needs within work. At shop floor level it has, rightly or wrongly, seen the most fundamental need as an economic one, and has directed considerable attention to wage payment systems, incentive schemes and productivity deals. Generally it has viewed its clerical, technical and managerial employees as rather different, more complex, kinds of animals with higher level needs than those of blue-collar workers and more responsive to motivating factors other than financial incentives. Essentially these have taken the form of personnel practices such as career development schemes, management by objectives and different varieties of McGregor's Theory Y approach. These are now well documented in management literature and there is only space here for a brief description of the philosophy which lies behind their use.

McGregor has set out two alternative views of man which broadly coincide with the more extreme assumptions of the traditional management theorists and the human relations school (16). The first of these is Theory X which sees man as a competitive, lazy and irresponsible animal who has few of Maslow's higher level needs and who has to be pushed, directed and controlled if he is to be made to produce anything at all. This approach has been common in industry until recent years and has been found to produce results. It has led to a great deal of thought about incentive schemes of the monetary kind, to measurements of performance and to job specialisation leading to easier work control. It is now being seriously questioned for it is not seen as meeting Maslow's higher level needs or Herzberg's motivators and, because of these defects, it is likely to produce a waste of human potential.

McGregor's Theory Y perceives man as cooperative, industrious and responsible, with an urge to maximise his own talents, to grow and mature. If this view is accepted it then becomes important for management to make it possible for people to develop these characteristics for themselves by providing work situations where there are opportunities for self-development and self-control. The acceptance of a Theory Y approach by an increasing number of managements has led to policies of job enlargement and enrichment, to the provision of opportunities for participation in decision-taking and for self-discipline rather than supervisory monitoring and control of performance.

Likert has also done considerable research on this subject and has concluded that managerial systems which parallel Theory Y make significantly better use of human resources and increase both the efficiency and effectiveness of human performance in industry (13). He categorises management systems in levels of one to four. System 1 equates with McGregor's Theory X type organisation and secures performance through punishment and reward. In Likert's experience these kinds of systems lead to low productivity. System 2 is more benevolent but still authoritarian. System 3 is consultative and System 4 is participative and similar to McGregor's Theory Y. In this last kind of management system there is considerable group involvement in the setting of objectives, the design of policies and procedures to achieve these and in the allocation of responsibility. Likert believes that high producers are to be found in firms with management systems close to his System 4 model and he suggests that a shift towards System 4 can be a method for reducing costs and improving earnings. For Likert, meeting employee needs is not just a method for increasing job satisfaction but also a method for improving profitability.

The thinking and research described here show that industry is becoming very much aware of the importance of the psychological contract between an employer and his employees and is making efforts to identify needs in work and to ensure that work situations provide opportunities for individuals to meet their personal needs. Only in this way can a firm ensure that it has effective and motivated staff. Efficiency and motivation are clearly very important with specialist staff such as computer personnel. They are scarce and expensive and yet play a critical role in ensuring the technical development of a company.

EDP specialists and their psychological needs

Let us now look at our EDP specialists and try to answer the question 'What are the personal interests which they wish to be able to pursue in their work situations?' When considering these we will pay particular attention to Herzberg's motivating factors – the need for achievement, recognition, responsibility and advancement. Some consideration will be given to attitudes to work content but a detailed analysis of the task activities of the computer programmer and systems analyst will be set out in chapter 6.

Current mythology provides a very clear picture of the computer man although it remains to be seen if it is an accurate one. Yearsley describes him as a complex prima donna, a person who carries great responsibility and who has the power to change other people's working lives, yet who may have had little formal education in his specialism and who is without the wisdom of age (25). He also sees him as working in a particularly favourable personal environment, one in which he does not have to conform to conventional office mores and is allowed a freedom of intellect and behaviour which would not be tolerated in the older established sections of industry.

Let us begin by ascertaining which of the Herzberg factors were of greatest and least importance to the majority of our programmers and systems analysts. This information was obtained by giving them eleven pairs of statements based on the Herzberg variables.[1] For example, on self-development the statements were:

> It is essential to have a job which allows for personal 'growth'. Otherwise one becomes frustrated.
>
> Self-development is never possible, one has to accept that one's potential will not be realised.

On recognition:

> I know when I am doing a good job and I want other people to recognise this too.
>
> So long as I know I am doing good work, it doesn't matter to me if others are not aware of this.

And on responsibility:

> I'd rather get on quietly with my own work than have responsibility for the work of others.
>
> Responsibility is a challenge. I enjoy it.

The individual being interviewed was asked to indicate which statement in each of these pairs came closest to his own point of view. Statements of a similar

[1] These pairs of statements are set out in full in Appendix A.

kind were set out for a majority of the Herzberg variables. Those not included were two of the hygiene factors – supervision and working conditions; the first because it was covered in detail elsewhere in the interview, the second because it was not seen as very relevant to computer personnel. Questions on the importance of company policy and administration were replaced by questions on the importance of company image. Achievement was not retained as a separate variable as it was thought to be covered by questions on self-development, advancement and status. Answers were totalled and ranked in terms of the numbers of programmers and systems analysts saying that particular factors were important to them. They therefore represent a consensus view.

Most and least important needs – those needs seen as important by more than two-thirds and less than one-third of programmers in each group – are set out in Tables 3.1–3. These figures are based on majority opinions and do not necessarily reflect the way in which individuals would rank the Herzberg factors. In the user firms the factor which the greatest number of programmers (91 per cent) saw as important was opportunity for self-development, although there were some variations in opinion after this.

The mail order company programmers were less likely to want recognition than the programmers of the other two user organisations. These programmers were a high status group who saw themselves as on an equal level with the firm's systems analysts. They were also less likely to be interested in the image which their firm presented to the outside world.

This might be expected for they were a young group with few emotional ties with the firm. Many had joined the company because of the excellent reputation of its data processing department. In the user group it is apparent that many of the factors viewed traditionally as motivators – salary, status, advancement – were not seen as important needs by programmers.

The programmers of the computer manufacturers showed similar need patterns to the programmers of the user firms.

It can be seen that the two computer manufacturers had different need patterns from each other. Programmers in both Manufacturer A and Manufacturer B had a strong need for self development, but the programmers of Manufacturer B were more likely to want recognition. Manufacturer B was the only firm in our sample which employed a considerable number of women and 50 per cent of the programming group were in fact women. Many women in industry believe with some justification that their abilities are not given the recognition which they deserve and this could have accounted for the different results. If this is really the case in a new industry like computing then it is a disappointing state of affairs. New industries bring new skill opportunities and equity suggests that these should be equally distributed between the sexes.

The needs of the programmers of the three consultant firms are set out in Figure 3.3.

With consultant staff self development was the need referred to by the largest number of programmers (84 per cent) while salary was only seen as important

Fig. 3.1 Needs of user programmers

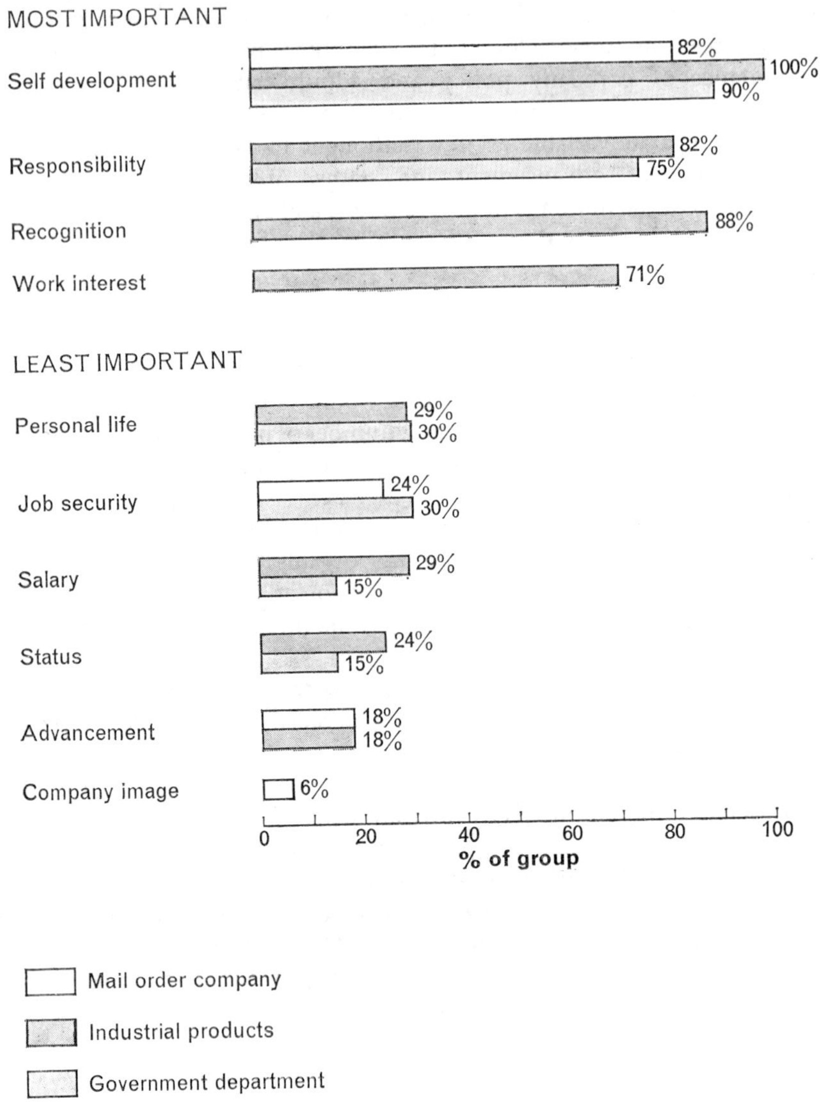

[1] Personal life refers to the importance of family and social life to the individual.

Fig. 3.2 Needs of computer manufacturer programmers

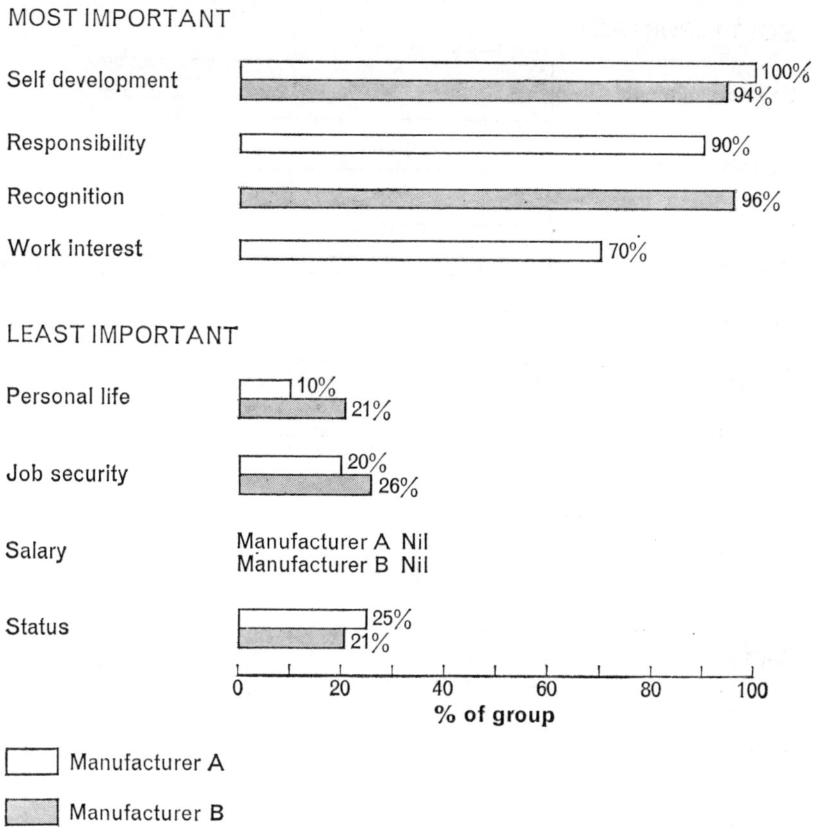

by 10 per cent.[1] This is not to suggest that these individuals were working for the intrinsic pleasure of programming without thought of financial reward. Almost certainly they were reacting in accordance with Maslow's hierarchy of needs theory and, because they saw their salaries as adequate, giving other needs higher priority.

Looking at the three programming groups of users, manufacturers and consultants together it can be seen that in all except one, Manufacturer B, the need for self-development was referred to most frequently. Salary was given a low priority by all programmers except those in the mail order company and Industrial Products. In the mail order company it was seen as important by more than

[1] We would regard salary as an economic rather than a psychological need and it is discussed in detail in chapter 4. Where salary is equated with status, as it may be by some individuals, then it will legitimately fall in the psychological need category.

Fig. 3.3 Needs of consultant programmers

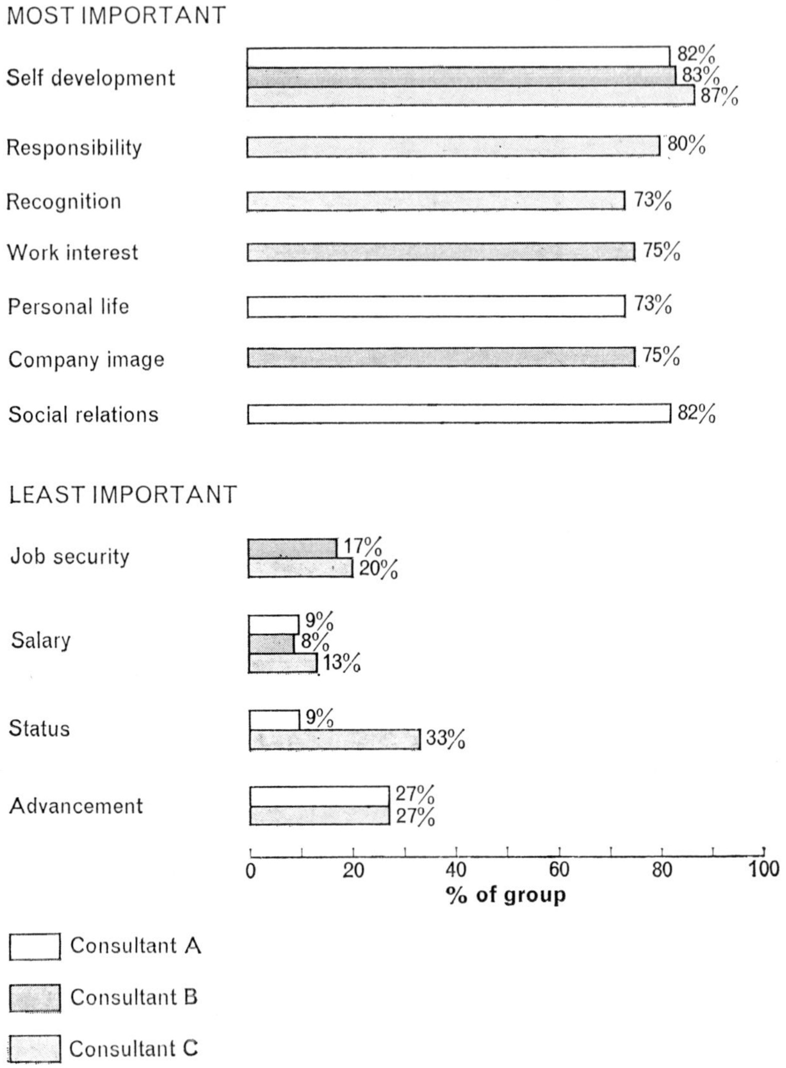

one-third of programming staff, although not by as many as two-thirds. The importance of salary in this firm may have been because part of the interviewing was carried out during the labour government's wage and salary freeze. An interesting feature of the overall results is that those needs seen as important by a majority do not all come into Herzberg's motivator category. Pleasant social relationships were sought by Consultant A programmers and they were also keen to have jobs which did not conflict with their family and social lives. The programmers of Consultant B were particularly interested in working for a firm with a good external image.

With the exception of two of the consultant firms the results fit the Herzberg model, with motivating factors being seen as important needs by the majority and hygiene factors by only a minority. However, two motivating factors do figure in the less important needs. These are status and advancement. The lack of emphasis on the first of these may be related to the quasiprofessional nature of the programming group. Many scientists look for status in their professional group rather than in their firms and data processing staff may be moving in this direction. Advancement for many was a deferred rather than an immediate need. Because of the youth of the programming groups many wished to acquire experience before seeking promotion.

Let us now consider the needs of the systems analysts (Figures 3.4, 3.5, 3.6).

Once again self development, recognition and responsibility head the list of majority needs. The systems analysts of Industrial Products were also anxious for pleasant social relationships in work and for their firm to have a good reputation in the community. Company image had the same low priority from mail order company analysts as it had had for programmers there. We have seen that this computer department had a technical and innovative ideology which separated it off from the rest of the firm. Salary and status again figure in the list of least important needs and all analysts were uninterested in job security.

With analysts, as with programmers, self development came top of the list except in the government department where it ranked second to responsibility. Company image was seen as important by more than two-thirds of systems analysts in each organisation except the mail order company, the government department and computer Consultant C. Social relationships were a majority need in all the consultant firms, in one of the manufacturers and in Industrial Products.

If the needs of more than two-thirds of staff in all the organisations are looked at together it can be seen that for programmers these were for self development, responsibility, recognition and work interest. Programmers in two of the consultant firms were similar to systems analysts in seeking an employer with a good company image and a work situation which provided pleasant social relationships. But for systems analysts the pattern was somewhat different. Their majority needs were again for self development, responsibility and recognition but a larger number looked for a firm with a good image and for pleasant social relationships within the work situation.

Fig. 3.4 Needs of user systems analysts

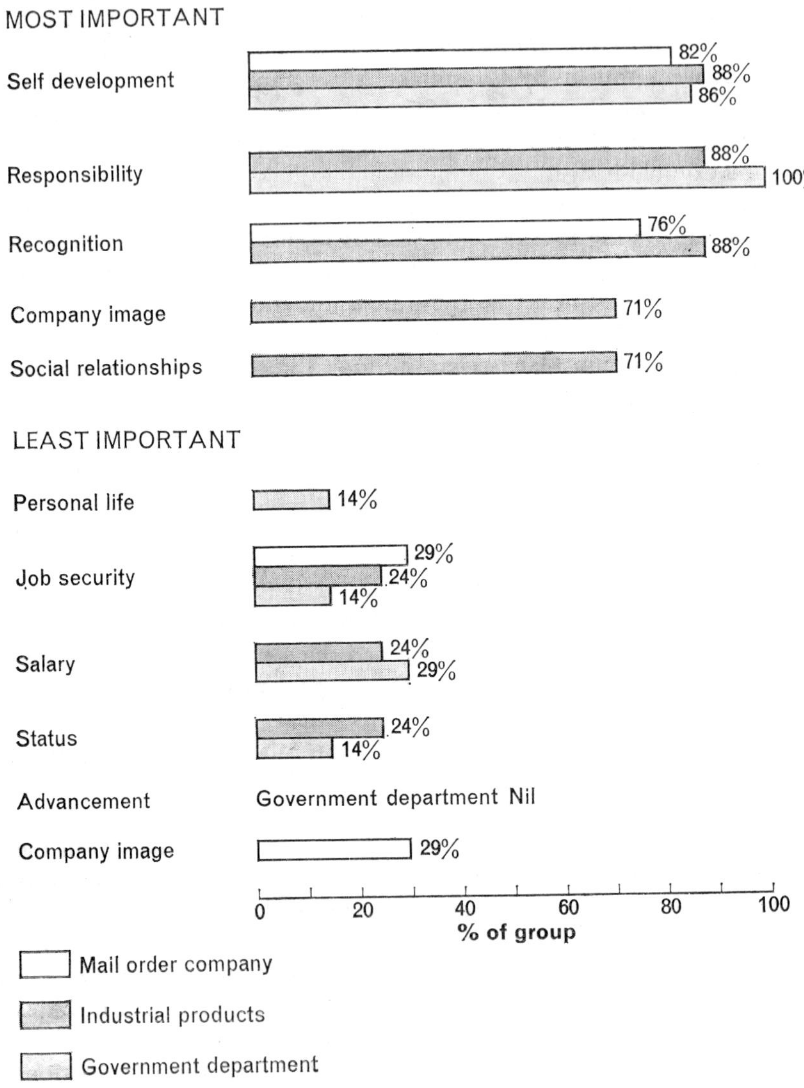

Fig. 3.5 Needs of computer manufacturer systems analysts

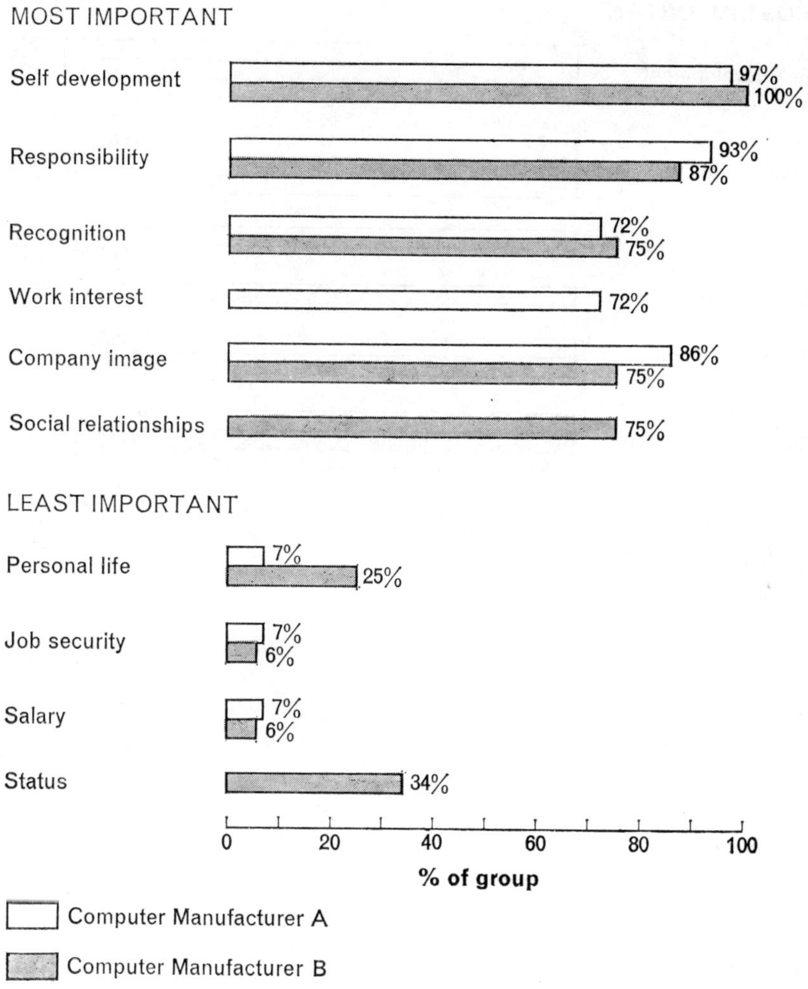

Fig. 3.6 Needs of consultant systems analysts

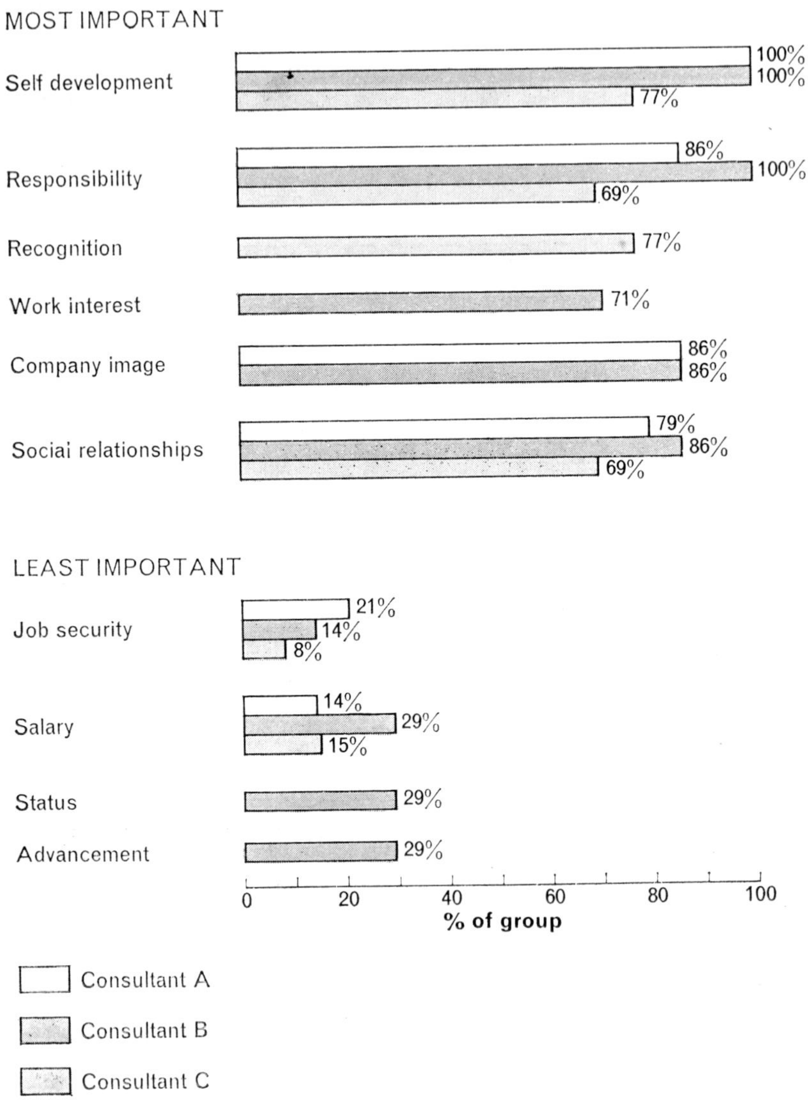

Fig. 3.7 Most important needs: programmers and systems analysts

Programmers	
Self development	given a high priority in all 8 firms
Responsibility	given a high priority in 4 firms
Recognition	given a high priority in 3 firms
Work interest	given a high priority in 3 firms
Systems analysts	
Self-development	given a high priority in all 8 firms
Responsibility	given a high priority in 7 firms
Recognition	given a high priority in 5 firms
Company image	given a high priority in 5 firms
Social relationships	given a high priority in 5 firms

Fig. 3.8 Least important needs: programmers and systems analysts

Programmers	
Salary	given a low priority in 7 firms
Job security	given a low priority in 6 firms
Status	given a low priority in 6 firms
Personal life	given a low priority in 4 firms
Advancement	given a low priority in 4 firms
Systems analysts	
Job security	given a low priority in all 8 firms
Salary	given a low priority in 7 firms
Status	given a low priority in 4 firms
Personal life	given a low priority in 3 firms

The importance of particular job factors to individuals might be thought to be related to their age and educational background but there were few statistical correlations. In the user group, programmers and systems analysts seeking self development were likely to be over twenty-six years of age and married. This was also true of those wanting responsibility. In contrast those seeking recognition were young and unmarried, as were those looking for interesting work. In the computer manufacturers those who were anxious to work for a firm with a good image and reputation were likely to be over twenty-six years and this relationship between age and company reputation was a strong one. Those who thought company image was not important were young and unmarried. We had asked the heads of departments in three of our eight firms to rate their staff in terms of creativity and efficiency and we found that manufacturer's programmers and systems analysts who said that advancement was not important to them were rated by their supervisors as low on both of these. However, individuals who swung away from popular opinion by saying that job security was important to them were also rated low on efficiency and creativity. It seemed that those of the computer manufacturers' staff who placed little importance on company image, were not keen on advancement and sought job security were not perceived by their supervisors as effective, motivated individuals. An alternative but less plausible explanation is that these individuals had come to terms with their own level of competence and did not seek advancement because they knew that they would be unlikely to get it.

An interesting question is whether the pattern of needs of our programmers and systems analysts resembles that of other groups of middle class young men. In order to check on this the same alternative choice questions were given to a group of forty post-graduate students at Manchester Business School, the majority in their twenties. They too wanted self-development, recognition and responsibility but, whereas advancement had been low on the list of programmers' and systems analysts' needs, it came third in the priorities of the business school graduates. These young men appeared to be more upwardly striving than our computer personnel, with greater motivation to get on and get to the top. It would be interesting to get more information on patterns of needs in various occupational groups and to establish the reasons for any differences. For example, one criteria for admission to a business school is motivation to succeed: therefore it is not surprising that our business graduates were high on this factor.

Western culture normally assumes that most people aspire to upward mobility in society. That they wish to move as high as possible up the job hierarchy in which they find themselves. Sociologists are now questioning whether career advancement is striven for in the same way by everyone. Most of us acquire our values from the work and social groups with which we associate and we judge our position from these rather than from society at large.

There are now increasing opportunities for upward mobility due to the changes which are taking place in the occupational structure of industry. But it seems that many groups, particularly those located in the working classes, are not interested in getting on above a certain level (18).

Our programmers and systems analysts were interested in obtaining promotion within their own departments although, as we shall see in a later section, the aspirations of many were restricted to data processing management and they did not wish to move into other managerial jobs higher up the organisation. There were two reasons for this attitude. First, many obtained great satisfaction from EDP work and promotion outside this offered little attraction. Second, many wisely related their aspirations to their competence and had little confidence in their ability to handle senior management jobs. There is some evidence that young people are today weighing up the costs and benefits of advancement in a way that was unknown ten years ago. Doing an interesting job may be regarded as more important than promotion into high-status, but routine, administrative work. Similarly, the possibility of coronaries and ulcers may cause a reluctance to seek advancement as an end in itself (24).

The extent to which psychological needs were being met

We have now established that our computer staff had needs which they perceived as opportunities for self-development, for responsibility, for recognition, and for work interest – the Herzberg motivators. Some also wanted the satisfaction of knowing that they were working for a firm with a good image in the outside world, and the opportunity for agreeable social relationships in the work situation. Let us now try to ascertain if there was satisfaction with the way psychological needs were being met.

Self-development as an important need

Self-development has been described by Jung as follows: 'The supreme goal of man is to fulfil himself as a creative, unique individual according to his own innate potentialities and within the limits of reality.' Schein (21) tells us that, 'Man seeks to be mature on the job and is capable of being so. This means the exercise of a certain amount of autonomy and independence, the adoption of a long-range time perspective, the development of special capacities and skills, and greater flexibility in adapting to circumstances'.

For most people the image presented by computer work is one of growth, challenge and excitement. We are told that the firm of the future will be increasingly dependent on efficient management information systems and that it must look to the computer man to provide it with these. One of the most effective methods of self development today is through improving one's skill in a particular knowledge area or increasing one's range of skills. Jobs which provide opportunities for further formal training would therefore seem highly desirable to groups motivated in this way.

In chapter 2 we saw that all our employers offered training to their data processing staff. In the mail order company and Industrial Products every programmer and almost every systems analyst had been on courses of some kind. In the government department all programmers and systems analysts had taken courses. Industrial Products and the government department offered a very large number of courses and some of their staff had taken seven or more. Most of these courses were internal to the organisation although the mail order company sent its systems analysts away to college for training. With the exception of the government department, programmers tended to have taken programming courses only, whereas systems analysts had taken a varied selection of subjects related to their specialism. In the computer manufacturers there was plenty of opportunity for staff to educate themselves. Here too some individuals had taken as many as eight different courses. The consultant firms were also keen to provide internal training although Consultant A was newly formed at the time of the survey and had not had time to organise a training programme. In Consultants B and C between 70 and 80 per cent of the programmers had taken courses, usually in programming, while between 60 and 70 per cent of the systems analysts had completed studies in a number of different EDP topic areas.

Despite this proliferation of opportunities for gaining new knowledge, around 50 per cent of computer staff in each user organisation were intending to take further courses. Programmers spoke of taking systems analysis training, seeing this as the way to progress up the data processing career ladder. Systems analysts referred to advanced systems courses and a small number in the mail order company and in Industrial Products said that they wished to obtain some management education. In the computer manufacturers nearly everyone was proposing to take further courses: 90 per cent of programmers and analysts in Manufacturer A and 50 per cent of programmers and 81 per cent of analysts in Manufacturer B. Programmers were interested in computer languages while systems analysts wanted to learn about real time applications, communications, operational research and business administration. In the consultants there was less interest in further training but on average 50 per cent were intending to take this. Once again the majority wanted courses in subjects related to EDP and there were a few references to business courses.

Most programmers and systems analysts saw these courses as a means for developing their own talents, adding to their market value and keeping up with a rapidly advancing technology. We were told: 'One must keep on taking courses in this job to keep up-to-date. . . . Yes, further training is inevitable because the technology of computers is developing so rapidly and it is desirable for me to extend my own knowledge.'

In terms of training provisions the opportunities for self-development clearly existed in all our firms and the speed of technical development in EDP was an added incentive to study. Most people saw their self-development interests as relating to data processing and few were interested in acquiring skills in other areas, for example, management.

There were very few references to management education and only 7 per cent of the entire group said that they were thinking of taking management courses of any kind. Although more than 50 per cent of programmers and systems analysts had told us that they hoped to end up in a management job they did not perceive the need to increase their formal knowledge in this area. This seems to be a shortsighted approach and there is some recognition of this within the data processing profession. An article on career building in *Computers and Automation*, September 1967, tells computer specialists:

> If you have a thirst for management responsibility here are a few things you can do to broaden yourself out.
>
> 1 Go to classes in business administration.
>
> 2 Join discussion groups where you can talk about aspects of management. In other words try to make yourself as broad and flexible a problem solver as possible.
>
> 3 Try to persuade your firm to let you go out occasionally with the sales representatives.
>
> 4 Try to persuade your firm to give you plant experience.

5 Develop an understanding of finance by working around your finance department as much as possible.

6 Work also with the personnel department.

All very sound advice but none of the programmers and systems analysts in our group were taking it.

Although training in terms of course provision was very good, not everyone was satisfied with the standard of training. Between a quarter and a half of the computer manufacturers' staff criticised the courses they had attended and there was also criticism in Consultants B and C. Consultant A was so new at the time of the survey that few courses were in operation there. Programmers working for either user EDP departments or consultants were generally more critical of their training than their systems analyst colleagues. The reverse was true in the manufacturers and here systems analysts had more complaints. In the user group, programmers criticised the mechanistic teaching approach, the fact that they were merely taught to write programs without being given an overall picture of company operations and of EDP systems. They also criticised the standard of teaching and the poor planning of courses. In the manufacturer and consultant groups the complaints of programmers were similar. They spoke of too much reliance on textbook material – often out of date, and a too theoretical approach.

Systems analysts in the user group deplored the fact that there were few formal courses available for them and said that their on-the-job training lacked guidance and good project selection.[1] They pointed out that when training was left at an informal level its success depended very much on the skills and teaching quality of the man the systems analyst was working with. Systems analysts attached to computer manufacturers were especially critical of their instructors and of the level of teaching. The staff of computer Manufacturer A said that the training which they received was inferior to that provided by their firm for programmers. Computer Manufacturer B's staff thought that their training had improved although it was recognised that the high labour turnover in EDP jobs made it difficult to keep lecturers. Systems analysts in the consultant group were less critical than those elsewhere but they too spoke of the need for experienced lecturers and for more participative learning processes.

Training for EDP was therefore an area where the fit between what programmers and systems analysts sought in order to meet their need for self-development and what the firms were able to provide was good, but perhaps not as good as it might have been. Looking at individual firms, the mail order company was not providing as many formal courses as its staff would have liked and the computer manufacturers and two of the consultants were not providing courses at a high enough standard for their staff. All three users and both computer manufacturers had excellent training departments and so had the physical facilities for providing good training. The problem was a shortage of competent teachers. Here data processing is experiencing a difficulty common to all new

[1] This was true at the time this survey was carried out.

occupations; the fact that the best people would rather practise it than teach it to others.

The solution to this is not easy to find. People may be persuaded to take EDP training posts if the rewards are seen as good enough, but in teaching others to become competent, they run the risk of falling behind themselves through lack of opportunity to practise what they are preaching. This is particularly true in such a rapidly evolving technological occupation as data processing. If firms are willing to second their best programmers and systems analysts to training posts for limited periods and reward them well for making this change then this may help the situation. But 'best' here means best in teaching as well as in doing and this may require the setting up of courses to develop and improve teaching skills. Only a very few people are natural teachers. Most professional teachers develop their skills slowly over time. Teaching methods can, however, be much improved if attention is paid to instructing the instructors in the skills of communicating and to providing them with the teaching aids to enable this communication to be effective.

Responsibility as an important need

Responsibility in work, the second need most actively sought after by programmers and systems analysts is difficult to separate from self-development, for self-development requires more than the acquisition of new skills and knowledge, it also requires the opportunity to use these. This is generally achieved through moving up the job hierarchy into larger and more responsible jobs.

Responsibility means different things to different people, but it is not unrealistic to assume that it frequently implies overseeing the work of others and that responsible jobs are as a rule broad rather than narrow, and demanding rather than easy. These are the somewhat crude indicators of responsibility which will be used here. Clearly all our firms saw supervisory duties of some kind as providing staff with opportunities for showing responsibility. Among the user programmers almost a third in each firm had charge of the work of others. The proportions were similar in the manufacturers and somewhat higher in the consultants. Systems analysts had even more responsibility; 53 per cent of Industrial Products systems analysts said that they supervised the work of others and in computer Consultant B the proportion was 86 per cent – a case of all chiefs and no indians. As a rule the number of subordinates under any one person was small; very few had as many as six. There seemed to be few problems of wanting responsibility and not getting it in data processing. If anything the opposite was true, programmers, in particular, said that they were given responsibility for the work of others when they would have preferred not to have had this.

Responsible work was defined as work which contained technical, administrative and human relations elements. All programmers and systems analysts were asked to describe their jobs and it became apparent that some contained only a rather narrow technical content. These jobs were seen as less responsible than others. This is a somewhat arbitrary definition as some tight, narrow jobs can be very responsible, but the job descriptions which we received made it clear that it was junior not senior staff who had their jobs defined in purely technical terms. Firms in which more than 25 per cent of programmers saw their work as entirely technical – that is solely concerned with the mechanics of programming – were the mail order company, the government department, Manufacturer B and Consultant A. This did not indicate a poor fit between a need for responsibility and the amount of responsibility which the firm was able to provide, for only in the government department did programmers express a desire for responsibility. Firms in which more than 25 per cent of systems analysts described their work as purely technical – meaning by this the procedures of work analysis and systems design – were the mail order company and Manufacturer B. Of these two, only Manufacturer B had more than two-thirds of systems staff with a strongly expressed need for responsibility. The degree of fit between need for responsibility and opportunity for responsibility was therefore good.

Most people had a very considerable amount of responsibility in their jobs and this could be an occasional source of stress. A systems analyst from computer Manufacturer A told us, 'on every installation there is a terrible strain the month before and the month after delivery. One is trying to get it all working by the target date'. Another, who worked for one of the consultants said, 'We have the responsibility for making the systems happen. I am accountable for the success or failure of the project. The Company has made an act of faith in employing me.' The pleasure of responsibility and challenge outweighed the stresses, however. Out of our sample of 274 only eighteen individuals regretted taking up this form of work.

Advancement as an end itself had been given a low priority in the hierarchy of needs, but promotion as a means of securing responsibility was sought after by a considerable number of people, although by no means as many as one would expect to find in a more upwardly striving group. This may have been because promotion within the data processing hierarchy was quite rapid and people wished to gain experience and consolidate their own position before moving on to a higher job.

Fig. 3.9 Desire to change to a job of higher status at the time of interview (percentages)

	User organisations	*Computer manufacturers*	*Computer consultants*
Programmers	54	31	52
Systems analysts	54	42	43

In the user organisations nearly everyone wanted a higher job in EDP, but in the government department a majority (60 per cent) of those saying they would like a higher job spoke of jobs outside EDP such as 'financial adviser', 'welfare officer'. In the computer manufacturers only 15 per cent of those saying they would like a higher job were thinking of non-EDP jobs while in the consultants the percentage dropped to 9 per cent. Programmers generally wished to become systems analysts or data processing managers; systems analysts spoke of becoming data processing managers, Heads of Management Services or EDP consultants.

These results are interesting in that although a large majority saw responsibility as an important need in work, around 50 per cent in each organisation did not necessarily see promotion as the best short-term means for meeting this need. For many, promotion was a deferred need, something which it would be nice to have in the future but about which there was little haste and no compulsion to actively seek it out. Responsibility was much more related to the task in hand. The opportunity to take charge of a challenging program specification or a demanding and difficult piece of systems analysis. This is not to suggest that individuals were content to remain programmers or systems analysts all their working lives: 48 per cent of programmers did see themselves as either programmers or systems analysts in five years' time but this was true of only 17 per cent of all systems analysts. Most of the systems analysts with limited career expectations were to be found in the user group. Figure 3.10 shows what programmers and systems analysts thought they would be doing in five years' time.

Fig. 3.10 Kind of job in five years' time (percentages)

	Users	Manufacturers	Consultants
Programmers			
Similar job to now (including promotion to senior programmer)	31	20	11
Systems analyst or senior systems analyst	28	23	26
EDP manager or consultant	13	21	42
Non-EDP job	11	6	7
Don't know	17	24	14
Systems analysts			
Similar job to now (including promotion senior systems analyst)	44	6	–
EDP manager or consultant	34	68	67
Non-EDP job	20	11	11
Don't know	2	15	22

In all three groups those who saw themselves in non-managerial data processing jobs in five years were likely to be less than twenty-six years of age. Those who believed that they would be data processing managers within five years tended to carry considerable responsibility. They had generally held more than one data processing job with their present employer and so had already moved a step or two up the data processing ladder. They were all in jobs with technical, administration and human relations content and their work covered a wide range of activities.

When people were asked to say what they would be ultimately likely to become – the job they would wish to hold at the peak of their career – the picture became different again as the following table shows:

Fig. 3.11 Ultimate job ambition (percentages)

	Users	*Manufacturers*	*Consultants*
Programmers			
Non-EDP management	19	4	26
EDP management, consultancy	37	32	29
Not sure	44	64	45
Systems analysts			
Non-EDP management	32	31	35
EDP management, consultancy	27	32	27
Not sure	41	37	38

Nearly half of all programmers and systems analysts had unclear ideas regarding the job they would eventually like to end up in. Programmers in the user and manufacturer groups who had thought about this saw their future in the data processing profession, while systems analysts were more likely to opt for line management or senior management unrelated to EDP. Only one programmer in the user group aspired to becoming a director or a member of senior management and only 10 per cent of the systems analysts. In the computer manufacturers these proportions became 4 per cent and 18 per cent and in the computer consultants, 14 per cent and 24 per cent. In the manufacturer and consultant group there was a statistical correlation between age and a wish to become a director or senior manager in a function unrelated to EDP and individuals saying this were likely to be more than twenty-six years old. In the user group and the consultant group this level of ambition was also related to experience, for people actively wanting senior management jobs tended to have worked for more than three firms since they had left school. In the manufacturers, those seeking senior management positions also came into the small group who saw advancement in their career as an important personal need.

Recognition as an important need

Just as responsibility cannot be easily separated from self-development, so recognition cannot be separated from responsibility. In order to be given responsibility the abilities of an individual must first be seen and noted. Many programmers and systems analysts sought the reassurance that they were doing an effective and important job and that colleagues and supervisors were appreciating this. Material recognition usually takes the form of promotion or financial rewards but praise for a job well done can also provide a great deal of satisfaction. Systems analysts generally looked to their customers rather than their supervisors for this praise and there were many references to the pleasure felt when user departments expressed satisfaction with a new system: 'When the objective of the new system is achieved and it turns out to be the right objective; the system goes in on time and the client department is pleased.'

The firms in which more than two-thirds of programmers expressed a need for recognition of their ability were Industrial Products, computer Manufacturer B and computer Consultant C. It was also sought by a majority of systems analysts in the mail order company, Industrial Products, both manufacturers and Consultant C. Staff in the other organisations either felt they already had recognition or were not very interested in it.

In order to establish whether recognition could be achieved through promotion, programmers and systems analysts were asked to evaluate the promotion opportunities in their companies. Here the fit between need and expectations proved to be poor for some groups as the table below shows.

Fig. 3.12 How programmers and systems analysts saw their promotion opportunities in their present firms (percentages)

	Users	*Manufacturers*	*Consultants*
Programmers			
Good	37	57	56
Average	28	11	14
Poor, nil	26	24	12
Not sure	9	8	18
Systems analysts			
Good	19	64	35
Average	22	11	8
Poor, nil	46	18	30
Not sure	13	7	27

Fig. 3.13 Timing of promotion expectations (percentages)

	Users	*Manufacturers*	*Consultants*
Programmers			
Within 1 year	29	41	53
Longer	41	22	19
No idea	30	37	28
Systems analysts			
Within 1 year	24	62	20
Longer	47	13	20
No idea	29	25	60

Promotion as an indication of recognition provided an uneven fit between what programmers and systems analysts required and what their firms were able to provide. In the manufacturer and consultant groups 57 and 56 per cent of programmers respectively thought their promotion prospects in their firms were good. In the user group, where the fit was least good, this percentage dropped to 37 per cent and it can be seen from the Figure 3.13 above that only 29 per cent thought that they would achieve promotion within a year from the date of interview. Looking at individual firms a third of the programmers of Industrial Products and the government department thought that promotion opportunities were very poor. This was also true of a quarter of the programmers of Manufacturers A and B.

Systems analysts were even more pessimistic about promotion than programmers. Only 20 per cent of all user analysts thought that their promotion prospects were good, while 59 per cent of the mail order company and 47 per cent of Industrial Product analysts said that their promotion prospects were poor. The picture was less dark in the manufacturing firms. Here 64 per cent of analysts thought that their promotion prospects were good and the figure above shows that 62 per cent thought that they would get promotion within one year. Despite this optimism, 25 per cent of Manufacturer B's analysts said promotion prospects were poor. Consultant systems analysts were generally unsure about their future and there were a large number of 'don't know' replies. Even in this group only 35 per cent thought that their promotion prospects were good in their present firms. Time will show whether the more pessimistic of our computer staff were correct about their promotion prospects and the government department management suggested that their personnel had little cause to worry. Problems will arise, however, so long as programmers and systems analysts seek promotion within their own specialism and are reluctant to move into other areas of business activity.

There were some interesting statistical correlations on this promotion variable. User programmers and systems analysts who thought that their promotion prospects were average or poor were also likely to have regretted making data processing their career. Those who thought that they would get promotion within a year were as a rule under twenty-six years of age. The consultant group also showed this tendency for young men to think that they would get early promotion and for those over twenty-six to say that their promotion chances in the firm were poor or nil. In the consultant firms there was a strong relationship between thinking one's promotion prospects were good and believing recognition of ability to be important.

Salaries as part of the effort-reward bargain will be discussed in the next chapter, although it must be recognised that pay is one of management's chief instruments of recognition.

Promotion and pay are internal methods for recognising ability – that is they are awarded by the manager of the group or department to which the recipient belongs. We mentioned at the beginning of this section that systems analysts sought recognition from user departments and that receiving this was a major source of job satisfaction. These relationships between EDP and user department staff will be covered in chapter 5.

It is interesting that not all of our programmers and systems analysts gave recognition as an important need and if we accept Maslow's hierarchy of needs theory the explanation would be that they believed they had this and were therefore giving other, less well-satisfied needs, higher priority. However, little is known about the extent to which different age or occupational groups seek for recognition of their abilities in the work situation. It has been found that a desire for esteem and recognition increases as one moves down an occupational hierarchy, perhaps because there is less chance of receiving it there, and that this factor is not related to age (20). This seems more likely to be true of white-collar than of blue-collar groups and it does not fit our programmers and systems analysts for there was no correlation between occupational status and desire for recognition. Those who sought recognition of their ability from others may have been influenced by the newness of their technology. Only if their work was approved and accepted would they be able to utilise their talents to the full.

Work interest

Programmers and systems analysts were asked if they wanted to be doing interesting work *all the time* or if they enjoyed spells of routine and found them relaxing.

More than two-thirds of the programmers of three firms and the systems analysts of one, gave continual work interest as an important need. This does not mean that other programmers and systems analysts did not want interesting work, but only that their need for continual interest was not so strong.

Programming and systems analysis are both activities which can range from the comparatively simple to the extremely complex and so their interest content can vary. The dominant factor here is usually the proximity of the task to the computer hardware. In some firms systems analysts assume the largest part of systems program design, leaving the programmer with only the task of coding the programming specifications into a language which the computer can understand. In other computer departments, systems analysis is defined as something similar to work study and the programmer takes decisions on how the job shall be organised for computer operation. In all our firms, programmers were doing the larger rather than the smaller job and there was some conflict as to where job boundaries should be drawn.

Some programmers and systems analysts spoke of the opportunity for creativity as providing them with the greatest amount of work interest.

> It's when one is able to create successfully by one's own efforts; one has a sense of achievement, an ability to influence events.

> It's finding something no one else can find; solving the problem.

By work interest programmers meant the technical aspects of their jobs, whereas systems analysts were much more inclined to speak of the pleasures of helping client groups and of making users enthusiastic about computers.

Many studies have now been made of the alienative effects of some kinds of work. The fact that work is so dull that satisfaction can only be obtained from family and leisure pursuits. It is thought that for many people work becomes a barrier which must be endured in order to collect the financial reward and have the opportunity to enjoy it (5). There were no signs of this kind of attitude amongst our programmers or systems analysts. On the contrary, both groups were enthusiasts about computer technology and their own part in helping firms to utilise it. The job content of programmers and systems analysts will be discussed in chapter 6 and work interest examined in more detail there.

Employer's image

Systems analysts in five firms and programmers in one spoke of their need to work for an employer whose image and status in the community was high. But in saying this they were not always referring to the same kind of community. When the staff of Industrial Products and the government department said that they would not work for a firm which they did not believe in and consider efficient, they were thinking of the standing of their own organisations in the eyes of the public and the community in general. When the staff of the computer manufacturers and consultants said this the reference group for them was the computer community and the professional standing of their companies in this group.

It would be logical to associate an interest in an employer's image with age and length of service in a firm for, as a rule, the longer one works for an organisation the stronger one's ties with it become. This was in fact true in the manufacturers where there was an association between being over twenty-five years of age and wishing to work for an employer with a good image. But it did not apply to the users or consultants.

Systems analysts were far more concerned about company image than programmers and this raises the question whether there is something about the systems analyst's job which makes him more interested in the image of his employer. Perhaps the systems analyst has to believe in his company and its potential for efficiency if he is to be successful in selling systems change to others. If he cannot identify with the needs of his firm then his own job becomes meaningless and ineffective. The programmer, in contrast, is much more of a backroom boy. He can carry out efficient programming in any situation. We found that programmers were generally engrossed in the technical aspects of their work and had limited contact with other non-EDP groups. In contrast systems analysts moved in a wide social circle, were identified with their company's interests and wished to present themselves in a good light to other groups. An alternative explanation may lie in company selection processes. It is possible that personnel officers diverted individuals who were clearly task centred into programming jobs, while individuals who were more 'company centred' were encouraged to take up systems analysis.

Pleasant social relationships in work

Systems analysts in five of the eight firms and one group of consultant programmers stressed the importance to them of social relationships in work. Here again the explanation for these differences in the social needs of programmers and systems analysts may lie in the nature of their work and the kind of person who is attracted to this work. Whereas programmers obtained much satisfaction from solving intellectual problems, systems analysts, because of their continual contact with client areas had developed considerable social skills and had become very aware of the importance of social relationships. Also most systems analysts experienced some stress and role conflict when they were out in the field away from their own departments. It was therefore important to them to be able to return to an agreeable, supportive group when each field work project was completed. An IBM systems analyst has been quoted as saying:

> The research worker who prefers to have his own office, work by himself with no interruptions certainly is not going to make a very capable systems analyst. You have to try and picture what others are thinking, understand their situation, their relationship with their own problem, understand their problem and try to devise your own answers and understand why they are acting as they do (10).

Conclusions on psychological needs and EDP staff

In the short term almost all the programmers and systems analysts in our survey saw their psychological needs as being realised within the data processing area. The exception was the government department where 30 per cent of programmers and systems analysts wished to move into non-EDP jobs on promotion.[1] In seeking these they were following the normal government department career pattern of occupational mobility.

[1] NB. Thirty per cent of all government EDP staff in our sample wanted a non-EDP job on promotion; 60 per cent of those government department EDP staff who wanted a higher job *at the time they were interviewed* wanted these to be non-EDP jobs. Thus desire for a non-EDP job was greater in those who were actively seeking promotion.

Let us now summarise how well those needs which were important to more than two-thirds of staff in at least three firms in our survey were being met within the work situation. These needs were self-development, responsibility and recognition for both programmers and systems analysts; continual work interest for programmers only, and company image and social relationships for analysts only. All these needs were being reasonably well catered for by employers although in both the programmer and the systems analyst groups the least perfect fit between needs and provisions to meet needs was in relation to self-development and recognition.

Fig. 3.14 Fit between needs and provisions to meet needs

Programmers		
Self-development	Wanted in all 8 firms	Perceived as not entirely satisfactory in 7
Recognition	Wanted in 3 firms	Perceived as not entirely satisfactory in 2
Responsibility	Wanted in 4 firms	Perceived as not entirely satisfactory in 1
Continual work interest	Wanted in 3 firms	Satisfactory in 3
Systems analysts		
Self-development	Wanted in all 8 firms	Perceived as not entirely satisfactory in 6
Recognition	Wanted in 3 firms	Perceived as not entirely satisfactory in 2
Responsibility	Wanted in 7 firms	Perceived as not entirely satisfactory in 1
Good company image	Wanted in 5 firms	Satisfactory in 5
Pleasant social relationships	Wanted in 5 firms	Satisfactory in 5

We found that most staff had some unfulfilled self-development needs although these could be catered for by providing more or better training courses. In the consultants, the government department and the mail order company there were some doubts on whether career prospects were good enough to enable fostered ability to be exploited. We do not know whether these doubts were justified or not. One unexpected finding on psychological needs was that although most staff conformed to the Herzberg model and expressed a need for the motivating factors which he has identified, programmers in more than half of the firms were not much concerned about receiving responsibility and recognition. This raises a number of interesting questions. Did programmers believe they had these already, leading to their replacement by needs which were less well satisfied, or were there other factors at work? Was a desire for responsibility related to age, so that the young would be less interested in this than the more mature? There was no evidence to support this last proposition. But detailed examination of the research data did produce an interesting finding on responsibility. This was that in each of the firms where less than two-thirds of staff had expressed a need for responsibility, programming staff were more likely to define their jobs in purely technical terms. It seemed that people who had rather narrow jobs, without a great deal of responsibility, did not want responsibility. This suggested that a desire for responsibility came as a result of being given it and liking it.

The reasons why some programmers did not want recognition – in the sense of appreciation or promotion – were more difficult to identify. It is clear that many programmers had a high intellectual involvement in their work and if this was accompanied by a low people involvement, the satisfaction of doing the job could be sufficient. There would be little interest in ability being recognised by others. There was also a relationship between having a university qualification and a lack of interest in recognition. This might suggest that recognition was a displaced need for some programmers. The fact that they had obtained university degrees was a convincing indication to the world that they had ability. After all they had a piece of paper to prove the point. But the first explanation seems more likely, with those programmers who had university degrees being more self contained than others.

Some tentative conclusions can be drawn from this examination of the needs of data processing staff. One is that most people will only put forward as needs those things which they believe can be attained without too much difficulty. A second is that some needs such as self-development will continue to remain powerful at certain stages of a person's career, even though opportunities for their achievement are clearly being provided. A third is that other needs, such as a desire for security or financial rewards, are displaced once they have been attained. Up to now we have concentrated almost entirely on the organisation's ability to fulfil its part of the psychological contract and to provide employees with a work situation in which they can realise their most important needs. We have seen that these needs are, for most people, the Herzberg motivators – self-development, responsibility, recognition and work interest, and the hygiene factors – the image of one's employer, and the opportunity for pleasant social relationships in work. Before ending this chapter let us consider the extent to which data processing staff were meeting the demands of their firms for motivated employees who would remain as long as their services were required.

The needs of employers

All the evidence we have set out up to now shows that there was no problem over work motivation. Our programmers and systems analysts were enthusiastic about their work and keen to maintain high standards of efficiency and competence. The real problem lay in the second area, that of length of service. Research has shown that the long-service employee has two characteristics which make him desirable to his employer. The first is the fact that he is there, doing the job. If he leaves then there is the problem of replacing him. With data processing staff a tight labour market means that this is both an expensive and difficult process. Experienced staff become scarce and in great demand and both high salaries and exciting and challenging work have to be provided to attract them. Inexperienced staff can be obtained but firms then incur the expense of setting up specialised training departments with no guarantee that these staff, once trained, will stay with the company. Forty-five per cent of the programmers and systems analysts whom we interviewed told us that they were thinking of leaving their employers. This percentage was even higher in those firms where the fit between what employees were seeking from work and what they were receiving was not very good.

The second reason why the long-service employee is an attractive proposition is that as a rule he is more identified with the interests of his employer. It has been observed that as scientists advance into supervisory positions they became more committed to their laboratories (4). Other researchers have found that with tenure, the acceptance of organisational values by industrial scientists tended to increase, and that identification with a company grew as a result of length of service (6). It has been suggested that the recruitment of older people into data processing jobs could assist the development of long-service employees. Most young men between the ages of twenty and thirty are mobile whereas older people are more stable and have stronger ties with a particular locality (25).

In the user programmer group the average length of service with the present employer was eight years; the average length of time in data processing, two years. These results are weighted by the long-service employees of Industrial Products and the government department, for 82 per cent of the mail order company programmers had less than four years' service with their company. Despite these long-service records 24 per cent of Industrial Product programmers and 30 per cent of the government department programmers said they were thinking of looking for other jobs. In Industrial Products this proposed movement was a direct result of a perceived promotion blockage, for the reason most frequently given was the desire to move into a management job. The manufacturers' programmers had an average length of service with their present employers of $2\frac{1}{2}$ years, although they had been in EDP work on average for 3 years. Manufacturer B had the greatest problem here with 62 per cent of staff proposing to leave – this time to gain wider experience in data processing and to become systems analysts. Consultant programmers had an even shorter length of service, an average of fifteen months with their present firms and four years in data processing. Here 55 per cent of programmers were thinking of leaving, the majority to get wider experience in data processing or to obtain particularly interesting computer work.

User systems analysts had an average length of service with their firms of $8\frac{1}{2}$ years and an average of $3\frac{1}{2}$ years in data processing. In both the mail order company and Industrial Products 48 per cent were thinking of leaving and here again promotion was the problem, the majority saying that they would have to leave to obtain managerial jobs. In the manufacturers average length of service was 2 years 8 months, length of time in data processing, 4 years. In both of these firms more than 50 per cent of staff were thinking of leaving with the highest percentage in Manufacturer B. Systems analysts in Manufacturer B gave the same reason as their programmer colleagues – a desire for wider EDP experience – whereas systems analysts in Manufacturer A were leaving to obtain management jobs. In the consultants, analysts had an average length of service with their firm of eighteen months and an average period of 6½ years in data processing; 37 per cent were thinking of leaving, again to obtain managerial jobs.

Fig. 3.15 Length of service, intention to leave and reasons for leaving

	Users	*Manufacturers*	*Consultants*
Programmers			
Average length of service in firm	8 yr 2 mth	2 yr 5 mth	1 yr 3 mth
Average length of time in EDP	2 yr 1 mth	3 yr 1 mth	3 yr 8 mth
% thinking of leaving	36	48	57
Principal reasons for wanting to leave (%)	Wider exp. in EDP 48 Management job 40	Wider exp. in EDP 40 Management job 38	Wider exp. in EDP 48 Management job 28
	Users	*Manufacturers*	*Consultants*
Systems analysts			
Average length of service in firm	8 yr 5 mth	2 yr 8 mth	1 yr 6 mth
Average length of time in EDP	3 yr 7 mth	4 yr 3 mth	6 yr 7 mth
% thinking of leaving	41	55	37
Principal reasons for wanting to leave (%)	Management job 48 Wider exp. in EDP 43	Management job 40 Wider exp. in EDP 36	Management job 58 Wider exp. in EDP 27

It is clear that in terms of employers' needs, the desire for long-service, committed employees were in the process of being frustrated. This was due to an inability to provide the required recognition of ability through opportunities for promotion to managerial level within the data processing hierarchy. Because of this many staff were looking for other jobs. The other incentive for staff to move elsewhere was a desire for more self-development opportunities than an employer could provide: the urge to get wider experience in data processing or to work on particularly interesting computer applications. This reason for changing jobs seems to be characteristic of some of the newer specialisms where expertise depends upon being able to keep up with a rapidly developing body of knowledge. An article by Taskmaster in *Computer Weekly*, May 1967, suggests that moving from job to job is the only way for the computer man to get experience. He must avoid over-specialisation: 'For a young man this mobility is the finest way of seeing the industry from the inside, but if he has ambition he has to make sure that his jobs and moves are planned as progressive steps' (22).

Unfortunately this desire for experience on a variety of different computer installations was a need which few individual firms were able to meet.

4

The efficiency contract

In the last chapter we looked at the needs of our firms for motivated employees who would, when necessary, put the interests of their employers before their own. In this chapter we will look at one of an organisation's most important motivational requirements – that for employees who are willing to meet output and quality standards and who will accept those controls which the firm believes it must use in order to achieve these standards. In return for meeting standards and accepting controls, the employee requires an equitable financial reward and a form of control which fits with his personal disposition and values. Many of these controls will be provided by supervision and relationships between subordinates and supervisors will be extremely important in creating a good fit between what the firm is asking for in terms of efficiency and what the employee will accept as legitimate demands. Control is, of course, only one aspect of supervision and an effective supervisor will also play a major part in meeting the psychological needs discussed in the last chapter.

Once again we will need to consider how operating in a particular product market influences a firm's output and quality standards, and the extent to which product market and company culture influence the nature of management controls and supervisory style.

Financial rewards

An important factor in the success of the efficiency contract is the nature of the effort-reward bargain. This is the amount which firms are prepared to pay to secure knowledge and competence, and the manner in which they choose to reward their staff, together with expectations of staff on how much they are worth and how they wish to be rewarded.[1] Financial rewards could have been

[1] There is less variation in the methods of rewarding white-collar staff than blue and normally earnings are received as a straight weekly or monthly salary. However, firms are now experimenting with incentive bonus schemes for high-status white-collar workers such as computer personnel, e.g. the mail order company.

considered in chapter 2, on the 'knowledge contract', for the willingness of an individual to join the staff of an employer is strongly influenced by what the employer is prepared to pay. They were also referred to in chapter 3 as an indication of an employer's recognition of ability. However, an examination of pay structure and levels seems to fall most appropriately into the present chapter as the wage payment literature has always given a great deal of attention to what it calls the 'effort-reward' bargain. This is the belief that the amount of effort which an individual is prepared to exert in the work situation – i.e. his willingness to meet output and quality standards – is directly related to the amount that he is paid. Such an assumption is almost certainly too simple for the complex world of data processing where we have already seen the number of factors which affect attitudes to work. Nevertheless the perceived equity of salary levels must have some influence on behaviour.

In chapter 3, programmers and systems analysts were shown to give a low priority to financial rewards but this was not interpreted as an indication that money had little importance for them. It was taken that salaries were perceived as adequate and had been supplanted by needs which were less well catered for and therefore viewed as more urgent. With the tight labour market normally associated with data processing and the present and predicted future shortage of skilled computer staff a firm would have to provide extremely attractive non-financial work satisfactions to induce its staff to accept what they saw as an inadequate salary. The Cornmarket salary survey for 1970 shows that computer programmers had a 6.2 per cent differential *above* the national all-category median of staff employees (2). Systems analysts in the twenty-six to thirty age range had a 16.5 per cent differential *above* the national median although this dropped to 12.3 per cent in the thirty-one to thirty-five age group.

There was little difference in the salary ranges offered by users and manufacturers. In 1969 the salary range in the mail order company was from £950 to £1200 for a trainee programmer, to £2200 upwards for a senior systems analyst. In the government department it was £650 to £1610 for an executive officer, £2220 to £2720 for a senior executive officer. In computer Manufacturer A a junior programmer started at £1190 to £1780 and a senior software adviser was on £2440 to £3660; in Manufacturer B equivalent salaries were £620 to £1085 for a trainee programmer, £1000 to £425 for a junior programmer and £2050 to £3000 for a technical officer or section leader. In the consultants, salaries ranged from around £1000 at the lower end of the scale to between £3000 and £4000 for consultants in firms A and C and to £6000 for a senior consultant in firm B. It is difficult to make comparisons between salaries for similar work in the three groups as job grades and titles are organised very differently but, as might be expected, the consultants were paying considerably higher salaries than users or manufacturers at the top end of the scale.

Perhaps a better guide to salary level is the answer the data processing manager in each firm gave to the question 'Would you say that, on the whole, the earnings of the staff in your department are (*a*) about the same as, (*b*) lower than, or (*c*) higher than they could earn in other firms in your district? In the user group the head of management services of the mail order company thought that his salaries were higher than his staff could earn elsewhere, and it must be remembered that this company had a cumulative bonus scheme in operation which enhanced earnings considerably if staff were prepared to stay with the company for a number of years. The head of management services in Industrial Products believed that his salary scales were the same as those of other firms in the district. The government department data processing manager said that his salaries were higher in the more senior grades but lower in the junior grades. In computer Manufacturer A, management saw their company's salaries as being about the same as those paid by other firms in their area but managers in computer Manufacturer B thought that their firm paid lower salaries. All the Consultants said that their salaries were higher than those paid elsewhere in their area.

A summary of the opinions of managers on how their firm's data processing salary levels compared with those paid by other firms in the area is set out below. Underneath this is a summary of how programmers and systems analysts in each company viewed their salary levels.

A good fit between what a firm is offering its data processing staff financially and what these staff believe to be an appropriate level of reward can be a product of a number of factors. Of these the most important is likely to be an individual or groups' salary expectations and these, in turn, will be influenced by the perceived state of the labour market, the employee's willingness or ability to move to another job in order to obtain a better salary and the employee's evaluation of his own skill and knowledge contribution. In the user group the mail order company believed that they were paying higher salaries than other firms in the area and the small percentage of expressed dissatisfaction would suggest that this was in fact the case. Many of these staff were new to the firm and their salary expectations and aspirations were more strongly influenced by their evaluation of data processing salaries as perceived through advertisements in the Press and through professional gossip, than they were by salaries paid for other kinds of work within their company. In Industrial Products, although management thought that data processing salaries were no higher than elsewhere in the area, EDP staff, who were almost all internal recruits, were well satisfied. In the government department, where management doubted the competitiveness of salaries at lower levels, almost a third of data processing staff said that their salaries were poor.

Computer Manufacturer A paid somewhat higher salaries than Manufacturer B and although management said that the firm's salaries were only on a par with those of other firms in the area, their staff were reasonably content. It will be remembered that many of this computer manufacturer's staff derived great satisfaction from working for a firm which they believed was pioneering data processing developments. The situation was less happy in Manufacturer B. Here management perceived salaries as lower than could be obtained elsewhere, and 28 per cent of staff agreed that salaries were poor.

Consultants B and C thought that their salaries were higher than could be earned in other local firms and their staff accepted that they paid good salaries.

Fig. 4.1 Views of salary levels, programmers and systems analysts

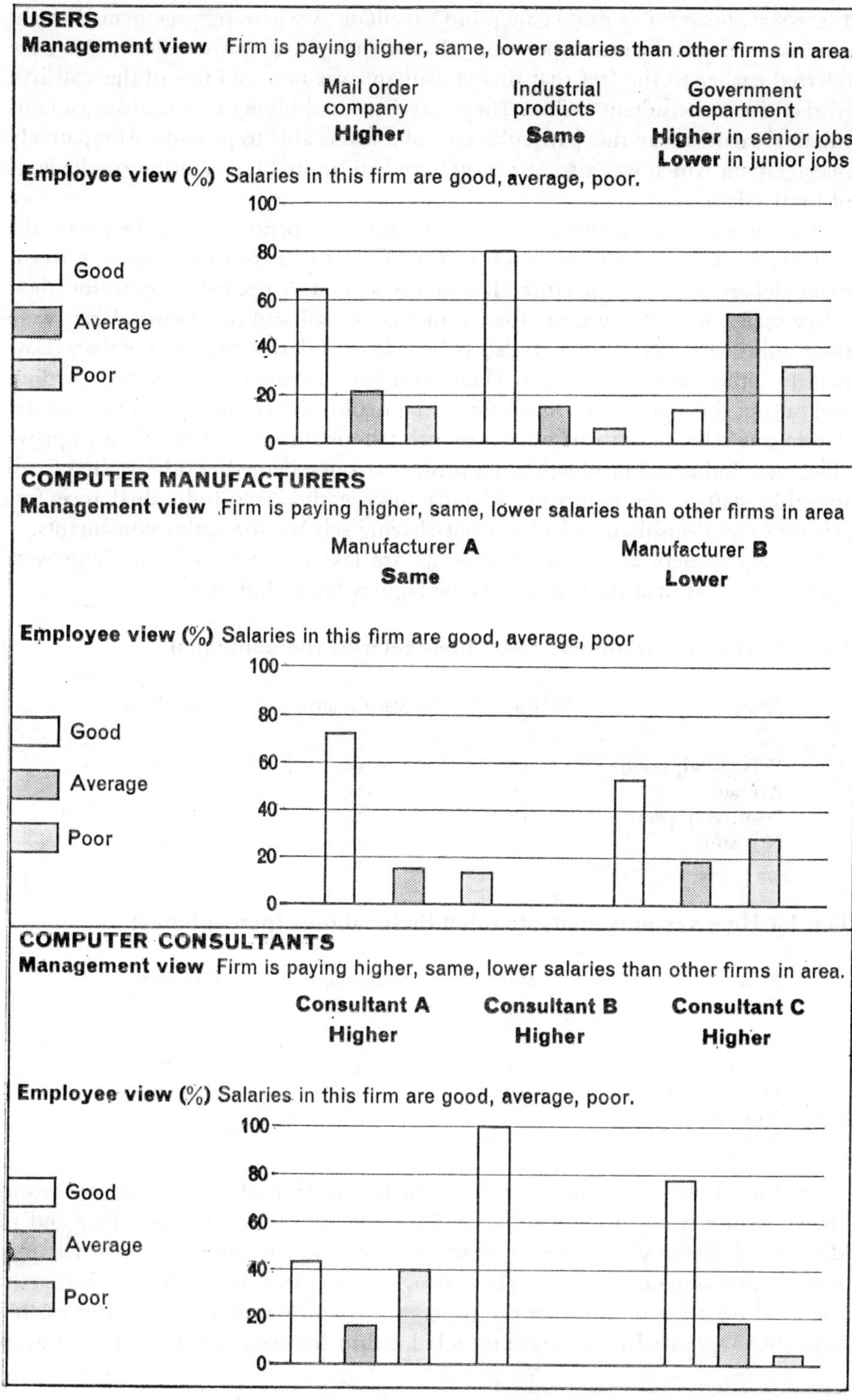

There was, however, a discrepancy in Consultant A where management thought salaries were good but 40 per cent of staff thought they were poor. We have referred earlier to the fact that this consultant was new and few of the staff had worked for a consultant before. They may have had higher expectations of consultants' salaries than this particular consultant was able to provide. Alternatively management which was also new may have had limited information on the level of local salaries.

If we accept that efficiency and job satisfaction depend to some degree on the perceived equity of the effort-reward bargain, then it is apparent that the government department, Manufacturer B and Consultant A needed to examine their salary scales. In all three more than a quarter of staff said that their salaries were poor and in two management also believed that salaries were lower than those paid by other firms in the area. There were few attempts at increasing earnings and output through incentive schemes. The mail order company had its cumulative bonus scheme but this was to reduce labour turnover rather than improve efficiency. Industrial Products had a profit-sharing scheme but this applied to all monthly staff in the company. Manufacturer A did have individual incentive schemes and Consultant B had a profit-sharing scheme for senior consultants.

If programmers and systems analysts are taken separately then there were some variations in attitude to pay as the Figures below indicate.

Fig. 4.2. How programmers rated their salaries (percentages)

Rating	*Users*	*Manufacturers*	*Consultants*
Very good, good	52	50	77
Average	30	15	14
Poor, very poor	11	24	–
Not sure	7	11	9

Fig. 4.3 How systems analysts rated their salaries (percentages)

Rating	*User*	*Manufacturer*	*Consultant*
Very good, good	54	65	41
Average	21	16	20
Poor, very poor	17	11	19
Not sure	8	8	20

On the whole programmers were satisfied with their salaries. In the user group the government department programmers were less satisfied than others and in the manufacturer group the programmers of Manufacturer B were less happy than those of Manufacturer A. These programmers placed much more stress on the need for recognition than the programmers of Manufacturer A, and in this firm there appeared to be a strong relationship between desire for recognition and dissatisfaction with salary level. We have referred earlier to the fact that this was the only firm to employ female programmers in any numbers and it is possible that the firm was paying women lower salaries than men.

It can be seen that consultant systems analysts were less happy with their pay than consultant programmers, but one firm accounted for a large part of the dissatisfaction. This was Consultant A where 28 per cent of systems analysts were dissatisfied.

Salary levels in our firms were influenced more by the state of the labour market than by the product markets in which the firms were operating. The product market exerted the greatest influence on the consultants and their need for excellence was reflected in the high salaries which they were prepared to pay to senior staff.

Work organisation

Firms vary in their philosophical approach to the means for achieving desired output and quality standards. Some organisations will try to attain these through tightly structured rules and procedures which they believe reduce the margin for misunderstanding and error, others believe that output and quality are best produced through motivating their staff to set their own targets and monitor themselves (15). Firms with the latter approach will tend to keep formal controls at a minimum. Our users are likely to vary in the extent to which they use formal controls according to whether they prefer to run their data processing departments in a structured or flexible manner. In this group the mail order company which had a manager who supported McGregor's Theory Y approach should favour the most organic arrangement. We would expect the manufacturers to organise work in a structured manner, with formal rules and procedures, and the consultants with their experienced, high calibre staff to take a looser, more organic approach. These predictions proved to be substantially correct.

The data processing managers of each firm were asked to indicate:

- how precisely work standards and work procedures were spelt out in their departments;
- how precisely the sequence of work operations was set out. Did work have to be carried out in a certain sequence or was it quite flexible?
- to what extent jobs were tightly specified.

Each of these questions had four alternatives which ranged from a very structured to a very flexible description of that particular aspect of work organisation.

Taking the three questions together the order of work formalisation was as follows, placing the firm with the *fewest* formalised procedures first.

Mail order company
Consultant B
Consultant C

Consultant A
Manufacturer B
Industrial Products
Manufacturer A
Government department

The mail order company was the only firm not to have quality standards and work procedures written down. All the consultants had standards and work procedures set out in general terms but did not find it necessary to go in for detailed descriptions. The computer manufacturer, Industrial Products and the government department set theirs out at length in procedure manuals.

Work was most tightly structured in Industrial Products, the government department and the two manufacturers where there was a certain sequence of operations which programmers and systems analysts were expected to follow. All firms avoided tight job specifications. In the users and manufacturers, jobs were specified but only within broad limits; in the consultants, jobs were seen as very flexible and likely to change from day to day.

These work characteristics fit the constraints and opportunities provided by the product markets in which the firms operated. The consultants' product market was one that made a wide variety of demands on staff talents and was likely to change from day to day. They reacted to this by adopting a considerable amount of administrative and work flexibility. The staff of the manufacturers were required to meet tight output and quality standards and so it was logical to expect staff there to work in a more structured environment. The data processing departments of the users were more distant from their product markets and influenced to a greater extent by organisational culture and by the personal philosophy of the data processing managers. The government department and Industrial Products had a bureaucratic tradition (using this word in its non-perjorative sense) and at the time of our survey Industrial Products were trying to introduce more effective work controls into the data processing department. The mail order company, although bureaucratic in its normal business operations, had a head of management services who believed in an organic approach to work organisation and who had established a flexible work environment within his own department.

Internal controls

The manner in which work is organised within a department is an important factor related to efficiency but other factors will also make a contribution. One is the nature of work controls and work checking procedures. Here data processing encounters difficulties for it is not always easy to check work where it originates and mistakes may not show up until a new system is implemented in a user area. Our data processing managers were asked to indicate how long it would be before substandard work produced by their departments became apparent. This question was not easy for them to answer and replies varied greatly. In the user group answers ranged from twelve months in the mail order company to within a week in the government department. Industrial Products, whose computer group processed data for operating departments, said that this time span could vary from one hour to two years. In the computer manufacturer group, Manufacturer A said within a week, Manufacturer B said within six months. In the consultants the time span varied from within a month to longer than six months.

Despite these divergent views on the time within which errors could be identified, all our data processing departments had systems for checking work, although these varied in rigour. In the three users, checks were made by the person doing the job, by the colleague to whom he passed the work for further processing and by the unit supervisor. Manufacturer A relied primarily on the supervisor but, as we have seen, had a tight set of work procedures; Manufacturer B had a complex checking process which included a special work checking section within the data processing department. The consultants relied on the employee himself and on his supervisor. In Industrial Products, Manufacturer B and the programming section of Consultant A all work was tested against precise specifications. In the government department, Manufacturer A and Consultant C part of the work was checked in this way but in the mail order company and Consultant B precise specifications were not seen as useful and greater reliance was placed on the individual's ability to monitor his own performance.

Another method of control is through the use of formalised communication procedures and we attempted to ascertain the extent these were used in the different firms. The greatest number of standard communication documents was found in computer Manufacturer B and these conform with this firm's other rigorous control procedures. Industrial Products and Consultants A and B also used standard documents and the mail order company was developing these. In addition the government department and computer Manufacturer B had specified communication procedures; for example, that communication to other departments should be through the department manager. A rough categorisation of the extent of this form of control in the various firms is set out below with the firms which relied *least* on formal communication listed first.

Mail order company
Manufacturer A
Consultant C
Consultant B
Consultant A
Government department
Industrial Products
Manufacturer B

Manufacturer A is the surprise here. He believed in formalised work procedures but less formal communications.

All our firms exercised a degree of control over staff performance through employee appraisal. This was carried out annually by firms in the user group and either annually or more frequently by the manufacturers and consultants. In every case these assessments were written ones and use was made of specially designed forms which asked for detailed evaluations of staff.

Looking at work organisation, controls and procedures as a whole the firms with the fewest formal rules and procedures were the mail order company and the three consultants. The manufacturers, Industrial Products and the government department preferred to run their operations in a more tightly structured manner. This fits with influences exerted by product markets, organisational culture and, in the case of the mail order company, the personal philosophy of the Head of the data processing department. The mail order company's EDP department was insulated from the firm's product market and culture by the nature of its R and D role. The preferences of the department's head thus became the major influence on organisation and controls.

External controls

Up to now we have been discussing the internal organisation and controls of the data processing areas with which we were concerned in our survey. But these were, in addition, subjected to controls applied by the senior management of their companies. All data processing managers, except those in the government department, made regular reports to their boards of directors or divisional management. In the mail order company and Industrial Products these reports were made annually, in the manufacturers they were made at monthly intervals and in the consultants at periods varying from one month to three. In the government department reports were made to a steering committee which met every three months.

In the majority of cases these were written reports which included statistical information; the exceptions being the mail order company report which discussed objectives and progress and the report of Consultant B which was presented orally to the board. Managers were asked what action top management would take if the performance of their department, in quality and output, fell below top management's expectations or if the manager failed to keep within his budget. In the mail order company, Industrial Products and Consultant A we were told that action would be of a financial nature and that some tightening of budgetary control would result. In the other firms top management response to inadequate performance was more likely to be verbal in that managers would be asked to explain what had gone wrong and to describe the corrective action they were proposing to take. Discussion of this kind took place immediately defective work was observed, whereas financial pressures would be applied at three-monthly intervals when budgets were checked against performance. The data processing departments of firms where financial controls were used tended to be operating on longer time scales than the others. For example, both the mail order company and Industrial Products told us that the results of many of their work activities would take from one to five years to show up in the firm's profit and loss statements.

Employee needs and company controls

So far we have been looking at the nature of the controls used by our firms in order to achieve what they saw as necessary output and quality standards. We must now consider the extent to which employees perceived these controls as appropriate to their personal needs for a congenial work situation. We have seen that Industrial Products, the government department and the two manufacturers organised their activities in a more formal and bureaucratic manner than the consultants and the mail order company. If this approach is to have the desired impact on output and quality then staff in these firms must accept and approve of this method of administration. Similarly the staff of the mail order company and the consultants must be the kind of people who like working in a free, unstructured environment otherwise they will suffer from anxiety and stress.

We asked programmers and systems analysts how work could be most effectively controlled. Their answers are set out in Figure 4.4.

Fig. 4.4 How can work output best be controlled? (percentage replies)

	Mail order company	*Industrial prods.*	*Government dept.*	*Man. A*	*Man. B*	*Consult. A*	*Consult. B*	*Consult. C*
Formal controls	27	74	41	47	58	72	73	46
Other methods	73	26	59	53	42	28	27	54

The less structured approach of the mail order company appeared to fit well with the staff's own philosophy, for answers to the question 'how can work output best be controlled' were in terms of 'knowing the man', using 'self control' etc. The consultants, who did not use formalised work procedures, still had staff who were in favour of formal controls. But they defined controls in a broad and non-restrictive manner. One consultant suggested that 'Quantity controls can best be achieved by the allocation of tasks which are well matched to people's abilities and by giving wide responsibilities within these tasks. Quantity – this depends on good management and motivation. Having well planned tight schedules and lots of work.' Another proposed 'Quantity controls through bar charts for each job, progress stages. Quality controls through providing proper test data, thoroughly checking documentation.' People were also asked, 'What controls are used here?' and 'What criticisms do you have of these?' Answers are set out in Figures 4.5 and 4.6.

In terms of our concept of 'fit' between what the firm was providing and what the staff were seeking, this seemed to be excellent in the mail order company.

Fig. 4.5 What controls are used here? (percentage replies)

	Mail order company	Industrial prods.	Government dept.	Man. A	Man. B	Consult. A	Consult. B	Consult. C
Formal controls	15	60	74	33	64	40	74	61
Other methods	85	40	26	67	36	60	36	39

Fig. 4.6 Do you have any criticisms of controls? (percentage replies)

	Mail order company	Industrial prods.	Government dept.	Man. A	Man. B	Consult. A	Consult. B	Consult. C
Yes	27	47	37	10	34	12	26	57
No	50	53	43	69	32	48	58	25
Other	23	–	20	21	34	40	16	18

Here there was administrative flexibility and few formal controls, together with a staff who did not wish for more controls.

The mail order company was consistent in approach. It did not have formalised work procedures, formal communications or formal controls and there was little criticism from staff regarding the absence of the latter.

The consultants did not have formalised procedures or communication but they did have formal controls; only in Consultant C was there any criticism of these. Again this fits what we know about our three consultants. Their staff had a high level of competence and therefore wished to work in a flexible manner, yet the demands of their product markets made it essential that there should be time and quality controls.

Manufacturer A was somewhat of a puzzle for it used formalised work procedures, but few formal controls and its staff were happy with this situation. Industrial Products, the government department and Manufacturers A and B all had structured work situations with standardised methods of working. There was some criticism of controls in Industrial Products and Manufacturer B, but this was directed at the nature of these controls rather than the fact that controls existed. At the time of the survey Industrial Products was using activity analysis as a way of monitoring programmer output in order to obtain some precise information on the length of time EDP projects took to complete. The routine of filling in forms to record activity was causing staff some frustration. In Manufacturer B controls were used and approved of and many grumbles were related to the fact that controls were not seen as strict or effective enough. This company had recently introduced a quality control section and this was seen as leading to improvement.

The consultants were flexible organisations with few bureaucratic rules and procedures, yet there was a strong consciousness of the need for controls in developing and maintaining quality and output standards. In Consultants B and C there was criticism of the form controls were taking and in Consultant C 57 per cent of staff had complaints. In these firms criticisms were again directed at the ineffectiveness of the controls which were used. Staff said: 'There should be more control. Management should enforce more stringent conditions on the project leaders. Management are flapping around aimlessly at the moment, ideas are not getting through.'

Fig. 4.7 Structure and control fit

Firms with flexible work organisation (few formal rules and procedures)	
Mail order company	Formal controls not wanted and not used. Fit = Good.
Consultant A	Formal controls approved of and those used by company seen as effective. Fit = Good.
Consultant B	Formal controls approved of but those used by the company seen as ineffective.
Consultant C	Formal controls only partially approved of. Those used by the company seen as ineffective.
Firms with structured work organisation (a considerable number of formal rules and procedures)	
Industrial Products	Formal controls approved of but some criticism of those tried out by the company.
Government department	The majority preferred informal to formal controls. They experienced formal controls and there were criticisms of these.
Manufacturer A	Staff preferred informal to formal controls; these were used and there were few criticisms. Fit = Good.
Manufacturer B	Formal controls approved of and used but not seen as effective.

It seems that in all these firms programmers and systems analysts were generally receiving work control of an amount and kind which they believed to be appropriate, although in four firms staff said that the manner in which these controls were operated could be improved upon. Only in the government department was there an indication that formal controls could be usefully modified and made more informal or less cumbersome. Here the complaint was that existing controls slowed activities down.

It is interesting to find that tight, effective controls can operate successfully in organisations like our consultants, where work procedures are flexible and permit a great deal of discretion. Organisational theorists tend to describe the bureaucratic situation as one with tight procedures and tight controls. Our study shows that strict controls are compatible with organic situations.

A method of regulating individual employees commonly used by industry is that of insisting that employees shall comply with certain rules concerning behaviour, one of which is that they shall come to work at a certain time and leave at a certain time. Programmers and systems analysts are perceived by outsiders as resisting this kind of conformity and seeking a considerable degree of personal freedom in when they arrive and leave work. If this is true and if the relationship between employer and employee is to be a satisfactory one, individuals who seek this kind of freedom should work for firms who are prepared to provide it. In our sample of eight firms we would hypothesise that the consultants would be most likely to do this. The answers to the question, 'How much freedom should programmers and systems analysts be allowed to have?' showed marked differences between the three groups as the Figure below shows.

Fig. 4.8 How much freedom should programmers and systems analysts be allowed to have? (percentage replies)

	Mail order company	Industrial prods.	Government dept.	Man. A	Man. B	Consult. A	Consult. B	Consult. C
A great deal	80	70	70	67	60	48	42	64

Surprisingly the consultants, who were the group with the greatest freedom in the sense that they were constantly moving around to different clients, were the most conservative about the amount of freedom which data processing staff should have. The reason for this was that they were particularly aware of the need to conform with the norms of their clients. They said: 'Data processing staff must obey normal conventions otherwise their chances of success are hampered. . . . A fair amount of freedom is essential but this must be consistent with working with clients; hence dress and manner are important.'

User programmers and systems analysts, perhaps because they felt a need to express their group identity by rejecting the conventional behaviour of their non-data processing colleagues were more anxious to throw off restraints. 'Data processing staff should have a great deal of freedom so long as the job is being done and the results achieved. No real set hours, free to take work home and stay after 5 p.m. or to have more than one hour for lunch.'

Needless to say none of our users provided this kind of freedom and all three were strict about timekeeping. The replies to this question may indicate the wish of data processing staff working in business environments to emulate what they believe to be the free and easy behaviour of the scientific backroom men of industry, rather than any real desire for freedom of this kind.

Programmers and systems analysts were also asked whether they should have to work normal office hours. Here the results were consistent in most of the firms with about a third saying Yes. Exceptions were Manufacturer A and Consultant C where a much smaller percentage thought normal office hours to be necessary and desirable.

The role of supervision in the attainment of efficiency

A key factor in the success of the efficiency contract is the supervisor. It is he who must ensure that controls operate effectively and achieve the desired result; it is he who must coordinate work activities so that output and quality targets can be met; it is he who must motivate his staff so that they willingly strive to achieve these output and quality standards. Floyd Mann (12) has pointed out that at the structural level the role of the supervisor involves the following:

- The direction and coordination of the tasks and activities of the subordinates within the supervisor's work group.
- The relating of these activities to those of other work groups at the same organisational level as his own.
- The relating of his own and these activities to those of other organisational units operating at the next higher and the next lower levels in the organisation.

In order to carry out these control, coordination and motivational activities the supervisor requires three sets of skills. He must have administrative competence if he is to be successful in his control and coordinative responsibilities. He must have human relations expertise if he is to meet the psychological needs of his staff discussed in chapter 3. He must have technical competence if he is to carry out his day to day tasks and be an effective trainer of his staff. Mann suggests that different kinds of supervisory roles require different mixes of administrative, human relations and technical skills and that a group of subordinates will require an altered supervisory approach as it progresses through different stages of its life cycle. For example, early in the life of the group, human relations and technical skill are likely to be very important. Later, as the group grows in size and becomes more complex, administrative and control skills will become increasingly dominant.

There are many descriptions of the job of a data processing manager in the computer literature. For example, Nowlan sees his administrative and control functions as follows (13):

1. Erecting and working to a set of rules and regulations regarding provisioning and general organisation.
2. Supervising current work, providing forecasts and progress reports while working to a budget, costing.

Human relations responsibilities he sees as 'the normal personnel functions necessary when any group of people are working together. Technical functions are:

1 The operating of the main production runs from data collection through to distribution.
2 A development function which may be subdivided into the inspection and analysis of new and existing applications by systems analysts; and the writing and testing of programmes for new applications as well as maintenance of existing jobs.

These activities are seen as forming a production line and it is suggested that 'a production line such as this must be costed as regards time, equipment utilisation and individual contribution in order to more easily maintain an objective picture of the unit's efficiency'.

This description of the responsibilities of a data processing manager is related only to his functions and not to the qualities and qualifications which he requires in order to carry these out. Greenwood believes that he should have a university degree, possibly in accounting, economics, mathematics, physics or engineering (6). He must be accepted within his company and this may require extensive company experience. If he is to be really effective he must have a good knowledge of the people with whom he has to relate, and know in detail how the company conducts its affairs. In addition to business knowledge and technical skills he will also require managerial skills. One facet of these is the ability to persuade and sell – to accomplish his objectives without alienating the people he must work with. It is also important for him to be able to evaluate the economic potential of particular computer-based solutions to problems; and he needs planning skills. Lastly, he requires the ability to motivate and guide his staff without destroying initiative and integrity. His staff should be able to support those things which they believe are best for the company, regardless of internal political pressures.

Nowlan sees the job of the data processing manager as similar to that of any other production manager, with a large element of day to day control of work activities and with a network of procedures and regulations to assist him in achieving his output targets. Other writers place more emphasis on his planning activities (15). Bradley sets out the decision process for a research manager and this would seem to equate very well with the development responsibilities of the data processing head (1). These are:

1 Scan environment, predict changes in this.
2 Determine logically the 'right' thing to do. Make this the first objective.
3 Formulate other objectives towards which he must commit himself and his resources.
4 Establish priorities.
5 Communicate the urgency and necessity of these objectives to subordinates.
6 Through communication continuously review and update planned action.

Before considering the administrative, human relations, and technical responsibilities of the data processing managers in our eight firms, we will look first at their management philosophies. Management theorists have suggested that organisations and managers both tend to develop certain styles or modes of operation. These can broadly be divided. First, there are managers who operate in what can be called a mechanistic mode – that is they prefer structured situations governed by clearly formulated administrative procedures and with a set of known and universally applied sanctions for deviations from accepted practice. In contrast there are organisations and managers who prefer to operate in an organic mode. These prefer a certain fluidity and flexibility in their environment so that they can evaluate the needs of a particular situation and respond in a manner which meets these needs even if this does not conform to regular practice. Wherever possible they avoid formalised procedures, rules and regulations and when these exist they are prepared to bend them. Although a manager may, because of his personality, have a natural inclination towards a mechanistic or an organic management style (this is sometimes called task-centred and employee-centred leadership) it is thought that organisations tend to mould men in their own image.[1] Therefore, a manager working in a firm or department which is mechanistically organised, with many formal procedures and controls, may be expected to have a mechanistic or task-centred philosophy. In contrast, a manager working in a looser, more organic situation, where people are expected to set and maintain their own objectives and standards may assume a more flexible, employee-centred approach to his work.

In an attempt to establish whether the managers of our data processing departments had a mechanistic or an organic supervisory philosophy we gave them twenty-four statements and asked them to indicate whether they agreed or disagreed with the sentiment expressed in the statement.[2] Twelve of these statements stated an organic viewpoint, twelve a mechanistic viewpoint. Examples of statements expressing a mechanistic point of view are:

> Always define lines of promotion clearly, and base promotion on objective criteria (written qualification, measured performance).
>
> Everyone's job should be clearly defined. People like it that way and it is more efficient.

Examples of statements expressing an organic point of view are:

> It is better to take on self-starters of whatever shape and to let them define their own jobs, than to fit square pegs into square boxes in organisation charts.
>
> Treat people *as* people and you won't have to supervise them closely; they'll do the job for you.

It will be remembered that the three consultant firms and the data processing department of the mail order company functioned in a loose, organic manner,

[1] It also equates to McGregor's Theory X and Theory Y.
[2] See Appendix C.

while the two manufacturers, the government department and Industrial Products preferred a more structured environment and had a larger number of standard procedures and formal controls. It would be logical to hypothesise that the managers of the former companies would subscribe to a flexible adaptive philosophy with few rules and procedures while the managers of the more tightly structured organisations would support a mechanistic philosophy and task centred management style. Again, if we consider our basic proposal – that firms are seeking a fit between company and employee needs and that company and worker satisfaction is a product of the goodness of this fit – then we would also expect that employees working in the more mechanistic companies would prefer a more mechanistic type of supervision.

Our findings on management philosophy broadly subscribe to our hypothesis that mechanistic companies will have managers who have a mechanistic philosophy – indeed it might be difficult for these managers to survive if they did not. If managers' answers are ranked in terms of the extent of their organic inclinations the following hierarchy emerges:

Most organic	*Score*[1]
Mail order company/Consultant B	62
Industrial Products	59
Consultant C	55
Consultant A	54
Government department	50
Manufacturer B	49
Manufacturer A	47
Least organic	

The only discrepancy in this ranking between what was expected and what emerged was in Industrial Products where the data processing manager, although working in a structured environment, appeared to have a very organic management philosophy.

The questions on management philosophy were asked only of departmental heads. Other supervisors located within these managers' departments were asked to comment on the nature of their supervisory responsibilities, on the number of staff they controlled, on those aspects of supervision which they found difficult and on the kinds of supervision which they found worked best with their staff. As the majority of these supervisors had small numbers of staff under them, their own personalities might exert as great an influence as the structure and culture of the organisation and the management philosophy of their boss. Nevertheless, we would expect to find that supervisors in the more mechanistically organised firms would be more task centred than those in the more organic, where supervisors would place a great deal of emphasis on the

[1] Three points were given for agreement with an organic statement, one for disagreement. Three points were given for disagreement with a mechanistic statement, one for agreement. Two points were given for a 'don't know' answer.

development of good relationships as a mechanism for motivation and control.

In the user group a third of all programmers and systems analysts had supervisory responsibilities of some kind but, with one exception, all of these supervisors had less than six staff under their control. In the computer manufacturer group 29 per cent had supervisory responsibilities but here many groups were larger than six in size, in some cases considerably larger. In the consultant group 44 per cent said that they had supervisory responsibilities and just under one half looked after more than six staff.

We asked all supervisors to describe the aspects of supervision they found the most difficult, anticipating that in the more tightly structured companies problems of authority and control would be referred to more frequently. This proved to be the case, for problems of this kind were described most often by supervisors in Manufacturers A and B and Industrial Products and least often (by less than one-third of supervisors) in the mail order company and in Consultants A and B. Sixty-five per cent of the supervisors in Consultant C also spoke of authority and control problems and these supervisors appeared to be experiencing difficulty in attaining required work standards.

Despite the fact that some of our firms had more formal controls than others, the consensus of opinion amongst the supervisors was that supervision, to be effective, must be loose and employee-centred. There were very few references to a production-centred form of supervision. Typical comments from supervisors were:

> One must not be strict. One must give freedom but staff must feel that they can approach one for help when necessary. As a supervisor one is only interested in the end result. They can do the work as they please.

> I am informal and give people a lot of responsibility. My staff are very intelligent and creative and so must be allowed freedom and initiative.

Supervisors were very conscious of the need for cultivating personal responsibility in their staff. Although it is often thought that bureaucracy goes with an authoritarian supervision, in specialist groups such as those described here this would seem not to be the case. A degree of work and procedural formality can still go with a loose, employee-centred supervision. It may be that in organisations which have a need for a system of formal controls, and which have departmental heads who subscribe to this structured approach, employee tolerance for these controls can best be achieved through having a first level supervision which is employee rather than task centred.

Methods which assist the supervisor

Industry is nervous about the free and easy atmosphere in many of its data processing departments and there are attempts to control employee behaviour and performance through various measuring and motivational procedures. The data processing press is very concerned with the subject of work measurement for programmers and an example of this is given in the *Computer Weekly* (18). This discusses the attempts made by one company to devise time estimates for various tasks – flow charting, coding, testing, etc. – within a major assignment. These estimates were expressed in programmer hours and when a new job was assigned the programmer concerned was asked to agree the time needed for its completion, as a whole or step by step, according to its magnitude. Once these times, in hours, were agreed they became binding on the programmers concerned, only to be altered with the agreement of the chief programmer if the job specification had to be changed, or if some unforeseen complexity came to light as work progressed. These estimated hours became the target time from which completion dates could be predicted, priorities worked out and progress monitored. One of our firms, Industrial Products was, as we have seen, experimenting with a form of work measurement for programmers which used time schedules and activity analysis sheets. Staff there agreed, in principle, with the aims of this exercise but some found the necessity for filling in forms every half hour irritating, and suggested that there was no guarantee that these would be completed accurately.

One of a supervisor's most important responsibilities is to use sound human relations policies as a means for motivating his subordinates to reach required output and quality standards. We have already discussed the psychological needs of programmers and systems analysts and it is evident that a good supervisor will be aware of the psychological needs of his staff and will see it as his responsibility to ensure that these are catered for. In chapter 3 we showed that the need to achieve was particularly strong in our data processing groups and a great deal of management literature now tells us that if this need can be directed at the attainment of specific targets and objectives then there will be harmony between the achievement objectives of both organisations and their employees.

Many of our firms used a form of management by objectives as a means for reaching standards, and there were references by supervisors to their practice of setting work targets and then monitoring their subordinate's performance to see that these were being kept. In the user firms, the supervisors of Industrial Products adopted this approach. It was also used in the two manufacturers and in the three consultants but there were no references to target setting of this kind in either the mail order company or the government department.

For readers who are unfamiliar with the method, management by objectives is based on the recognition that a desire for achievement can be used to further both organisational and individual needs and goals. One use of management by objectives is described by Frank in *Research Management* (5). This defines MBO as a process

> whereby an individual and his supervisor jointly define major areas of responsibility, identify common goals, and establish specific plans so that understanding and acceptance will form a basis for future activities. This process can also establish a basis, both by the individual and the supervisor, for a later evaluation of the planning and performance accomplishments.

Frank gives an example of the use of management by objectives with a research and development group. Here, the major emphasis in the MBO programme was on the improvement of planning and communication within the group and this was achieved through using discussion groups to set objectives and secure agreement on mutually acceptable goals. Individuals were helped to look at their work and its direction in an organised manner. Attempts to meet objectives resulted in the development of a very specific system for planning work activities and for organising results.

An effective use of an approach similar to MBO is described by Stuart (14). This was an attempt to move a data processing department from a functional to a federal form of organisation. A number of project teams were created and the members of these teams were developed as computer generalists, with an ability to perform all data processing jobs. The only significant standard was embodied in results and these were evaluated on whether they were well scheduled and delivered on target as specified. Responsibility was fixed personally. It was acknowledged before, exercised during a project, and rewarded after the delivery of a complete package. Before this method was introduced projects had been handled in the conventional manner by systems analysts, programmers, operators etc. With the new system a team handled the entire project from start to finish. This team was responsible for everything; planning the system, designing it, implementing it and operating it. Team leaders were required to ensure that team members would carry out a number of different functions within these activities. No attempt was made to impose standards from without for the team was expected to set its own standards and to see that these were achieved. This kind of system would seem to be very flexible and where data processing staff are experienced and mature, and have a need for working in an environment which they can control and structure themselves, it may work very well indeed. It would not succeed with individuals who are unsure of themselves and like the security afforded by a management which sets their objectives for them.

Research described by Locke shows that one of the most important factors determining the level of efficiency which an individual attains in work is the attitude with which he undertakes the task (10). Through experiments Locke was able to demonstrate that one way of achieving a high level of performance is through setting hard goals. He says 'irrespective of whether subjects or experimenter set the goals, the harder the goals, the higher the performance'. However, this ability to achieve difficult goals will only come about if the task is seen as legitimate and willingly accepted. Locke suggests that once a hard task is accepted, the logical thing is to try one's hardest until one decides to lower or abandon the goal'. These findings appear to support other research which shows that employee participation in decisions which affect them motivates better job performance (9, 11, 16, 17). But Locke believes that it is not employee participation in the goal-setting process which affects task performance, but the fact that goals are set at all. The same results might be achieved if supervision set the goals, providing that these goals are acceptable to the individuals who are going to strive to achieve them. It may be that employee participation in decisions on output and standards does not necessarily lead to higher output and quality standards, but achieves consensus on the efficiency level on which the group can legitimately be expected to perform.

We have been discussing the administrative and control elements of the data processing supervisor's job. Our findings show that there can be a dilemma, in organisations which like formality and structure in their work arrangements, between a desire for discipline and control through rules and procedures and the recognition of the first line supervisor that his subordinates want a loose form of supervision in which they can to a large extent control themselves. In the firms in our survey modified versions of management by objectives were generally used to solve this problem.

Supervisors sought a way out of this 'discipline versus freedom' dilemma by encouraging their subordinates to exercise self-discipline, to participate in the setting of targets and to use supervision as a resource to be called on when work difficulties were encountered.

Leadership effectiveness

Fiedler suggests that the effectiveness of a leader is a product of both the manner in which he relates to his followers and of the favourableness of the situation in which the team is operating (3, 4). He found that leaders who focused on tasks rather than on group relationships, tended to find difficulty in working with some members of their groups and obtained their greatest satisfaction from task achievement. In contrast, leaders who valued good personal relationships and personal acceptance from their subordinates paid more attention to these than to successful task completion. They were also more likely to get on with all members of their group. Looking at the situation in which the leader operated, Fiedler found that task-orientated leaders were more effective in very favourable and very unfavourable situations. Relationship orientated leaders were more effective in intermediate situations. This may come about because in favourable situations the team is not under stress. Therefore good interpersonal relations are easily developed, even without the assistance of the leader. In unfavourable situations, when the team has to accept a great deal of stress, the necessity for coping with an alien environment may weld the team together as a unit. In the intermediate situation, in contrast, those factors which assist the group to feel that it is a group may not exist and the group leader may have to play an active part in developing good personal relationships.

Ideas on effective supervisory behaviour are in a state of continual development and modification. The progression so far has been (1) examining the effectiveness of task-centred versus employee-centred leaders; (2) considering leadership style in relation to the situation where the leader and group are operating; (3) considering in particular the effect of stress situations on leader-follower relationships. A fourth theory is proposed by Hersey and Blanchard (8). They put forward a 'life cycle' theory of leadership which takes account of the degree of 'maturity' of the leader's group. This theory attempts to provide a leader with some understanding of the relationship between an effective leadership style and the level of maturity of his followers.

The emphasis of the 'life cycle theory' is on the followers, who are seen as the most crucial factor in any leadership situation. Once again the breakdown of a leader's behaviour into that concerned with tasks and that concerned with relationships is used. Task behaviour is seen as 'the extent to which a leader defines the interaction between himself and his followers in terms of well-defined roles and patterns of organisation, specified channels of communication and ways of getting jobs done'. Relationships behaviour is the 'extent to which a leader is likely to organise and define the interaction between himself and his followers in terms of friendship, mutual trust, respect for follower's ideas and consideration of their feelings'.

According to 'life cycle theory' as the level of maturity of a leader's followers increases appropriate leader behaviour not only requires decreasing emphasis on the task and increasing emphasis on trust, consideration, etc, but it should also entail a decrease in the emotional support provided by the leader. Maturity is defined as achievement motivation, relative independence and ability to take responsibility. These components of maturity are often influenced by level of education and amount of experience. Psychological age is more important than chronological age.

Life cycle theory suggests that a leader should relate to his followers in the sequence of behaviour set out below if he wishes to develop a mature group:

1 High task	low relationships behaviour
2 High task	high relationships
3 High relationships	low task behaviour
4 Low relationships	low task behaviour

With highly trained and emotionally mature staff, the last is usually the most effective leadership approach, although during the early stages of a project a certain amount of structure regarding the limitations and requirements of the project will need to be established. Once these boundaries are understood the project manager may move rapidly through the cycle to stage 4. When a supervisor has his group in stage 4, then his role should become an external one devoted to long-range planning and to interaction with the group's environment. To be effective the supervisor must be able to influence the environment in which his group operates so that the group can attain those of its objectives which require external cooperation. This theory suggests that span of control should not be a function of level in the management hierarchy but should depend on the level of maturity of the individuals being supervised.

The fit between supervisory practice and subordinate needs

We asked all the programmers and systems analysts in our firms five questions about supervision:

1 Are programmers and systems analysts difficult to supervise?

2 If yes, why?
3 What supervision works best with them?
4 What supervision do you respond to?
5 Do you get this kind?

In the user group, majority opinion in the mail order company was that programmers and systems analysts were difficult groups to supervise and control and 100 per cent of programmers and 82 per cent of systems analysts said that this was so. In Industrial Products and the government department this was a majority opinion only amongst systems analysts. Computer manufacturer systems analysts also spoke of supervision problems but in the consultant group opinion was divided, with more programmers than systems analysts seeing problems in Consultants A and B and more systems analysts in Consultant C. Reasons given for these supervision difficulties can broadly be divided into those associated with the kinds of people programmers and systems analysts are, and those associated with the nature of the work they have to do. Figure 4.9 shows the divergence of opinion:

Fig. 4.9 Do supervision difficulties arise because of the kinds of people programmers and systems analysts are or because of the nature of the work they are called upon to perform? (percentage replies)

	Users		*Manufacturers*		*Consultants*	
	Progs	*SAs*	*Progs*	*SAs*	*Progs*	*SAs*
People	50	66	50	50	56	71
Work	50	34	50	50	44	29

Users and consultant staff were more likely than manufacturers to refer to supervision and control problems which stemmed from the kinds of people engaged in computer work.

Yes, because they are brighter than most, more independent thinkers.

Yes, because they are young and intelligent and feel that they can do everything well.

They are working on a type of job which gives them a lot of scope to act as individuals.

There was unanimity in each group on the form that supervision should take and the approved approach was flexible and employee-centred. Tight, production-centred supervision was seen as inappropriate for the kind of individual associated with computer work. However, a number of people did stress that while supervision should not impose tight controls, it should encourage the setting and achieving of targets. Firms whose staff placed the greatest emphasis on the desirability of targets were Consultants A and B, in particular the systems analysts of Consultant B where 72 per cent approved of targets, and the two manufacturers. There were fewer references to the desirability of targets in the user group. Here again the explanation for this difference in attitudes towards controls may lie in the product market. Both consultants and manufacturers had to meet target dates agreed with their clients. If these targets were not met future contracts would be jeopardised. User EDP groups were, of course, subject to internal pressures to meet targets, but if these were not met sanctions were likely to be less severe.

Satisfaction with the manner in which control was exercised by supervisors was quite good and in no firm was a majority of staff unhappy with supervision, though some dissatisfaction was found in the user systems analyst group where 28 per cent had grumbles and amongst consultant programmers where 23 per cent were not entirely happy. No firm stood out as having a particularly bad fit between the kind of supervision that was being provided and the kind that staff saw as acceptable. Complaints were less about harsh supervision than about supervisory gaps such as an absence of guidance. 'Guidance is missing when you want it. In certain areas of the work no one is sure what they are doing.'

Programmers and systems analysts in all the firms regarded their supervisors as resource people who could be called on for assistance rather than as controllers who were interested only in output. Complaints were therefore about too little supervision rather than too much. In the user group those who did complain about supervision tended to have worked for their firm for less than two years and to have held only one job with the company; they were, therefore, the younger and more inexperienced members of their departments. Those who were well satisfied with supervision were longer service employees and many had held other jobs in the firm unrelated to data processing.

If we now look at the degree of fit between what the firms were providing in the form of supervisory controls and what their staff said they wanted we find the best fit in the following firms:

MAIL ORDER COMPANY	Staff wanted loose supervision; they thought they received this.
GOVERNMENT DEPARTMENT	Staff wanted loose supervision; they thought they received this.
MANUFACTURER A	Staff wanted an employee-centred form of supervision, but one which set clearly defined targets; they thought they received this.
CONSULTANT A	Staff wanted an employee-centred form of supervision with clearly defined targets; they thought they received this.

The fit was less good in the other firms:

INDUSTRIAL PRODUCTS	Systems analysts were not very happy with their supervision: 25 per cent of systems analysts wanted targets but there was a belief that supervision was not very good at setting these.

MANUFACTURER B — Programmers had complaints here. A number said that they were subjected to excessive pressure when target dates were approaching.

CONSULTANT B — Here again it was programmers who had problems. This firm had some tight programming controls and these were seen as restrictive.

CONSULTANT C — Programmers thought that supervision did not provide them with sufficiently clearly defined work structure. Work organisation was too free and easy.

These differences in employee needs show how very difficult it is to generalise about supervision. The kind of supervisory practice that works well in one firm will not necessarily prove equally successful in another. Here again product market, culture and the nature of work condition people's attitudes to supervision and influence the kind of supervision which is seen as appropriate by both management and subordinates. The product market factor had a particularly strong influence on supervisory behaviour in the computer manufacturers and the consultants, where staff had to respond quickly to the demands of their clients. This led to much emphasis on target setting by management and to an approval by staff of this method of achieving results. Cultural influences on supervision were those of the quasiscientific culture in which data processing specialists operate. Here supervisory practice followed that found effective in highly qualified specialist groups such as R and D.

First line supervision everywhere exercised a loose, permissive type of supervision and this was approved of by their staff. All these supervisors were themselves computer specialists and so they well understood the prevalent attitudes to supervision in their kind of specialist group. Not all department heads subscribed to this employee-centred supervision, however, and a number, as we have seen, had a personal leadership philosophy which preferred rules and procedures to permissiveness and adaptability. In this respect the heads of data processing departments appeared to be more influenced by the culture of their companies than by the norms of their subordinates.

Computer work is complex and diverse and because of this it is difficult to control (7). Both programmers and systems analysts welcomed the discipline imposed by the setting of targets, and this was especially the case in the manufacturers and consultants. Targets were not necessarily seen as being set by management but often by the work group itself. Attempts to measure performance, particularly in programming, were not so well received and were often seen as irritating and time-consuming. People believed that the nature of their work meant that they had to use their own judgment and initiative. They expected their supervisors not only to allow them to do this but to actively assist them through providing advice and guidance when this was required.

If we group together those firms we have categorised as liking flexible work arrangements and those which prefer formal rules and procedures and compare them, we find few differences in attitudes to supervision. Staff working for organic firms were more likely to say that programmers and supervisors were difficult to supervise and control, and they were more inclined than those in the procedural group to blame this on the nature of the work rather than on the idiosyncrasies of the people, but this was all. We might expect that staff working in a more structured environment would like a supervision which encourages the setting of targets. In fact, it was Consultants A and B that most favoured the use of work targets while the mail order company, Consultant C and the government department made the fewest references to the desirability of having these.

5

The ethical contract

In work people are evaluated both for their performance and for their behaviour when relating with others. Some organisations place a great deal of importance on their staff's effectiveness as producers and rate personal qualities such as sympathy, trust and integrity much lower. In other words they seek 'efficiency' men. Other organisations value highly employees who are as successful as human beings as they are as producers. They wish to have 'civilised' men in their work force. Organisations either seek to recruit individuals whose values match their own ideologies and culture or, if this is not possible, they develop methods for indoctrinating new employees into desired behaviour. Many of these are informal; they are not written in rule books, yet all employees know that certain ways of behaving are expected of them and if relationships within the firm are good, they accept these. Thus a firm's culture and values are passed on to new employees as much by the old hands as by the management. In turn, individuals seek employers who hold similar sets of values to their own. A man who believes strongly in the importance of personal relationships will not wish to work for an employer who values his staff only for their work output, even though he rewards them extremely well for meeting his production targets. Similarly, a man who has strong material needs and a desire for personal power will not be happy in a company whose concern for democratic values leads to personnel policies which frustrate his ambitions.

There will be a good fit on our 'ethical' variable when a company recruits or develops employees who subscribe to its ideology and values concerning behaviour and relationships in the work situation. There will be a bad fit if, for example, the company has employees who place great importance on human relationships and an ethical approach to others (however they define this) and yet are asked to work in a ruthless environment where work performance is rated above everything else. Similarly, there will be a bad fit if employees are not human relations conscious when their employer is.

The nature of values

A company can have a philosophy and set of values which appear to influence all its activities. Many firms are described by their staff and by the communities in which they operate as 'paternalistic', 'democratic', 'welfare-minded', etc. Others are regarded as 'tough', 'ruthless', 'hard men to work for'. But within this general culture there may be many differences. Banks points out that the hierarchical organisation of enterprises, with authority flowing from top to bottom and rigid functional divisions is likely to lead to serious conflicts over the purposes which the enterprise serves (3). These conflicts are found not only between management and labour, but within the ranks of management itself. Different philosophies and values may be found in the research laboratory from those found in the marketing department. The staff of the personnel department are likely to look at employee behaviour on a perspective different to that of the operational research or production departments. Where professional staff are employed they are likely to bring into the firm powerful sets of values which they have acquired through the ethical content of their training and the influence of the external professional groups with which they associate. Senior management are often heard to complain that their 'experts' have a greater loyalty to their own professional groups than they have to their employer and this criticism is frequently directed at the computer specialist.

Many people believe that society is presented with two conflicting sets of values at the present time and that a choice has to be made between these. Ellul sees a clear conflict between 'technological' and 'human' values for he believes that technology is bringing about a loss of freedom and a subversion of civilised attitudes to life (8). Here the enemy is not the machine or any particular technology, it is 'technique', or the drive to rationalise every human activity; the search for the 'one best way'. He maintains that technique tends to take over all man's activities, to 'transform everything it touches into a machine'. But not all commentators are so pessimistic. McLuhan suggests that ours is the first society in history to have the opportunity to escape technological determinism. We can now live pluralistically in many worlds and many cultures. But freedom of choice depends on our making the effort to understand the process by which technology affects our culture.[1]

Despite the hope for a better future that McCluhan holds out there is at present a considerable gulf between what the ordinary person regards as legitimate behaviour and many aspects of industrial organisation. This difference in values leads to problems such as restrictive practices, the gap between industry and the academic world, the ambivalence with which technologists are regarded by industry, and the uncertain status of personnel departments. If industry is to flourish, while providing meaningful and worthwhile careers for those who work in it, then this gap must be reduced. This can only be done by our society giving hard thought to what its preferred sets of values are. If it decides that human

[1] This discussion of McLuhan's views is taken from Silberman (28), ch. 6, p. 111.

needs must not be sacrificed to technical needs then it must create organisational mechanisms to ensure that the conflict between technological objectives and human values is kept at a minimum.

Although increasing numbers of people subscribe to liberal, democratic values which place high importance on 'civilised' behaviour there will always be differences in how the idea of civilised behaviour is interpreted. In this chapter we will examine the values of our data processing personnel; try to establish whether the EDP staff of user firms, computer manufacturers and consultants all had the same sets of values, and check if in any organisation there was a divergence between the values of the company and the values of the data processing employees.

Before we look at the philosophy and values of our firms and their computer staff it is essential to be quite clear what we are talking about when we use the word 'values'. It is also useful to consider how individuals acquire their personal philosophies of living; to ascertain how these affect behaviour; to distinguish between values and interests and to establish whether values, once acquired, remain the same throughout life or whether they change as circumstances change. Unless we look at values from this broad perspective it will be difficult to understand any variations we may find between our eight organisations in how their computer personnel believed they should relate with user and client groups.

It is clear that everyone does have values. These take the form of beliefs or standards of excellence which help us to make choices. Because of our personal values we think that some things are right and desirable and others wrong, and we are prepared to make an effort to achieve certain moral objectives or to behave in a way which we believe to be right and proper. Our values give our life meaning and direct our behaviour. It is suggested that we have religious, political, social, aesthetic, economic and theoretical values and that we share these sets of values with other individuals and groups who are similar to ourselves (1).

Our values are influenced by our social positions; for example, our educational status, age, class, or race. But they also reflect such matters as attitudes, tastes, beliefs and behavioural norms (5). One psychologist has made the interesting point that friendship is more frequently based on similarity of ideals than it is on similarity of personality (14).

We acquire our social values from the social atmosphere which surrounds us, from our families, our friends, our workmates (26). Once acquired these values are internalised, they become a part of us and produce lasting social attitudes. This is what prevents us from behaving in an unpredictable way when we meet new people and new situations. Some values, which are firmly established, continue their existence through many generations.

The extent to which we are influenced to accept particular sets of values by the social groups to which we belong depends on a number of factors. These are, first, the attractiveness of the group for us. For example, one of the groups to which we have strongest ties is the family. If we greatly esteem our parents and brothers and sisters then we are more likely to believe that their values and approach to life are correct than if we are at loggerheads with them. Secondly, we are usually influenced by the pressures to conform which exist within most groups. If our work or social groups have strong beliefs that certain ways of behaving are right and others wrong, then they will try to persuade us to accept and act by this philosophy. Thirdly, values are more likely to be associated with important than unimportant matters. There will be stronger values on moral issues, such as how to relate to a friend who falls on hard times, than there will be on trivia such as minor matters of dress or etiquette. Values are likely to be more pervasive if a group is homogeneous in social composition or personal status; if a great deal of social interaction takes place within it; if the members like each other, and if the group as a whole plays a part in setting the standards which influence its behaviour.

Values are often confused with 'interests' and it is useful to distinguish one from the other. It is thought that values refer to widely shared conceptions of the good society, the things we should strive for because they are right and desirable (20). Interests are at a lower level and refer to a desire for special advantages either for oneself or for the group of which one is a member. Values are long-term beliefs. Interests are short-term desires to protect or maximise certain advantages which a group has secured.

Whereas we are prepared to bargain with our interests, we will not, as a rule, enter into practical compromise with our values (29). Even though in the short term it may be more important to us to secure some interest advantage for a group to which we belong than it is to realise one of our ideals. However, this depends on the strength of the values which we hold. At present, we have very little information on the extent to which individuals place values before interests or interests before values. Yet it is important to know this if we are to understand people's behaviour in work. There is evidence that some individuals have stronger and more pervasive values than others and, if these values are human rather than technical, then people would come into our 'civilised man' category. It is claimed that strong values of this kind provide a system of anchors around which all social relationships are established (26). Other people operate much more in terms of expediency and short-term interests. They go with the wind and their behaviour standards can change as they move from one social group to another. Our efficiency expert who seeks high financial reward and rapid material achievement may be motivated more by personal interests than by a set of moral values. However, 'technical' men have their values like everyone else. The man who is wedded to technology and cares little for human relationships may take this position because his personal value system convinces him that this is the right approach to ensure community progress.

We know, then, that many of us have powerful values which exert a major influence over how we behave. We do not know with any precision how stable these values are. Do they, once acquired, remain with us throughout our lives or are they regularly distorted, manipulated, reinterpreted to fit our needs and desires at particular moments of time? To what extent and in what kinds of situation are they overridden by the pressures of short-term interests. This question is even more important when asked of an organisation rather than an individual or group. From where does a company acquire its business philosophy? How stable is this, what causes it to alter, and is it possible for an organisation to change its values if it believes them to be no longer appropriate?

People with strong values appear to gravitate to groups with similar values (5). But if an individual who has a specially powerful set of values finds himself in a group where he is psychologically uncomfortable he is likely to look for a more congenial set of associates. He needs such a group to reassure him of the correctness of his own behaviour. For the less committed, group membership and personal values are likely to be related. A sharing of beliefs leads to friendship, while close contact as a member of a group leads to a sharing of beliefs.

At the beginning of this chapter we referred to the fact that modern life is making many people question the correctness of some prevailing values. In particular, there is the intellectual dilemma of whether to achieve progress through the exploitation of science and technology or through the development of a more concerned and caring society. In the past two or three decades we have seen the rise of the 'rational spirit'; the belief that science can help to better the human condition (4). This has led to the development of rational values – an emphasis on scientific method and the virtues of logical thought. Today the undesirable byproducts of science are leading many people to question the rightness of these rational values and new sets of values based on the importance of personal relationships appear to be emerging. Many people are therefore caught in sets of cross pressures which cause extreme mental discomfort. A scientist may work in a group which subscribes strongly to rational values while in his social life he takes on many welfare responsibilities where human values are all-important. This sort of conflict situation causes most people psychological strain and they seek to resolve it by going along with the values of the group to which they feel most strongly attracted.

Increasingly it appears that in the future society will demand that technology is used with due regard for its human consequences. This will induce many scientists and technologists trained to accept rational values to rethink their personal philosophies. This is likely to be as true of computer technologists as of any other technical group in the firm.

Company values and philosophies

The value with which we are particularly concerned in this chapter is 'concern for human relationships'. Not in this instance the way the organisation treats its own staff, which we dealt with in chapter 3, but the way it hopes and expects its staff will relate with other groups, either inside or outside the company. Whether, as we said earlier, it wants them to behave as 'civilised men' or as 'efficiency men'. We expect to find differences in our eight organisations in this respect. We also expect these differences to be related to the product market in which each firm operates and the pressures exerted by this; to the culture of the company as a whole and, in our user group, to the culture and values of the data processing department and its manager. Because an organisation expects a particular form of behaviour from its staff it does not necessarily mean that this desired behaviour in fact occurs. Whether it does or not depends on the extent to which the firm's values and philosophy have permeated its employees: whether employees identify with their employer, accept his beliefs as legitimate and internalise these as their own. It also depends on the recruitment philosophy of the organisation; the extent to which it actively seeks out people whose personal values fit its philosophy, and its success in finding them.

One of the difficulties of the external recruitment of computer personnel is that these individuals may bring with them a very different set of values from those generally found within the company. Behavioural scientists believe that when divergent cultural backgrounds are represented among the members of an organisation, individuals will hold different cultural values and have a different approach to organisational problems from those of the local establishment (7). This increases conflict and a heterogeneity of personnel is positively associated with organisational tension and conflict. The externally recruited computer man frequently has, as we have seen, a technical background and a technical approach to problem solution. In contrast conflict can be expected to diminish if people are drawn from the same backgrounds because there is then a consensus on the way problems should be solved and the manner in which people should be treated. We would therefore expect that the mail order company computer personnel, of whom a considerable number were recruited from outside, would have greater problems in relating with user departments than the computer staff of Industrial Products or the government department. We would also expect the staff of the computer manufacturers to find it easier to relate to staff in the data processing departments of client firms than to the staff of user departments in these firms. This may also be true, to a lesser extent, of the consultants.

It is always difficult for a research worker to obtain an idea of company values and philosophy through asking questions in an interview. A true sense of a firm's ethos is much more likely to emerge through walking round and seeing how people talk and behave to each other, and by spending considerable time with the company and talking informally to staff at every level. We were able to do this in our user firms as they were taking part in a larger study of technical change, but not in the manufacturers or consultants where our information is derived from questionnaire data. Our three user organisations had very similar sets of values. They were all large and paternalistic with reputations for treating their staff with consideration and for expecting their staff to treat each other in the same way. Industrial Products had a scientific ethos and employed large numbers of technical staff. This was not the case with the mail order company and the government department, whose operations were entirely clerical.

In an attempt to obtain information on the values and philosophies of the various organisations we gave each departmental manager nine propositions and asked him to indicate which three of these he took most account of when considering the viability of a new idea. These propositions were:

1 The response of competitors to new methods arising out of the idea.
2 The departmental savings (staff or cash) likely to result from the new idea.
3 The gains in knowledge or experience arising from introducing the idea.
4 The return on investment the company might gain from the proposed idea.
5 The technical difficulties of getting the idea into operation.
6 The staff or labour relations difficulties of getting the new idea into use.
7 The administrative difficulties of getting the new idea into use.
8 The effect of the proposed idea on company sales.
9 The effect of the proposed idea on customer relations.

If we look at the factors taken account of when a new idea was being considered, we find that the following pattern emerges:

At least two, and for some factors all, of the three users indicated that the criteria which most influenced their evaluation of the idea were propositions 2, 4 and 5.

There was no consensus between the two manufacturers. Manufacturer A gave propositions 4, 8 and 9; Manufacturer B gave propositions 2, 3 and 6.

At least two, and for some factors all, of the three consultants indicated that the criteria which most influenced their evaluation of a new idea were propositions 3, 4, 8 and 9.

The influence of closeness to the product market on decision processes is shown by the fact that both manufacturers and consultants indicated the importance of the proposed idea to company sales and customer relations, whereas these were not seen as of major importance by the users. No user referred to company sales as a decision criterion, although they placed considerable weight on departmental savings. It was interesting to find that this emphasis on departmental savings was not accompanied by a similar emphasis on the effect of a new idea on staff or labour relations. Yet when staff savings are seen as an important reason for innovation there would seem to be a strong likelihood of employee resistance to the change proposal.

Industrial Products and the government department, both of whom recruited internally for their data processing departments, gave the technical difficulty of getting the new idea into operation as one of their three most important decision criteria. In contrast, the managers of the organisations employing career computer men – the mail order company, the manufacturers and the consultants – all said that this was of little concern to them, presumably because they believed that they had the technical competence to handle most problems.

Let us now make some predictions on how differences in approach and values will influence the internal and external relationship of our three groups of computer specialists.

Mail order company

Because of the external recruitment to this department and the emphasis placed on technical competence we would expect that the computer group would experience relationship difficulties with other parts of the organisation. They might be little known to the rest of the company and perhaps be regarded as strange and alien. Few of them had worked elsewhere in the firm; they did not have many friendship ties with line departments and because of this they might emphasise manipulative techniques as the best way of getting user cooperation. It is possible that they would not have a great deal of sympathy for the personnel problems of user departments.

Industrial Products

Here there should be easier relationships between the computer department and the rest of the firm. Internal recruitment meant that computer staff had worked in other departments in the company. They were likely to have friends amongst the non-computer staff and they would be reluctant to put these friendships in jeopardy. Their long service should mean that they accepted the social values of their company and were conscious of its human relations philosophy.

Government department

The comments above about Industrial Products should also apply to the government department. The situation there was essentially the same.

Manufacturer A

Staff here should be more conscious of the importance of congenial human relationships than those in Manufacturer B because they were more directly in contact with the customer. Relationships might, however, be more contrived and artificial than in the user group. The establishment of good customer relationships is likely to be seen as very much a means to an end – that of selling computer hardware. Computer personnel working for firms who are customers of particular computer manufacturers are often unsure of the true nature of their relationships with a manufacturer's staff. Are they developing genuine friendship with a professional colleague or is the other merely playing them along as part of his selling role?

Manufacturer B

Attitudes should essentially be the same as in Manufacturer A. Answers may be academic rather than based on practical experience as not many of these staff were in direct contact with the customer.

Consultants A, B, C

There should be great concern for the development of effective human relationships in this group. This will be for two reasons. First, without good customer relationships the consultant will not get any business or, if he gets it he will not keep it. Second, the consultant will partly depend on good relationships for his problem-solving success. His solutions will not be acceptable unless he is liked and respected as a person. Thirdly, we have already established that the consultants saw themselves very much in a 'helper' role in relation to their clients and this kind of role leads naturally to the development of friendships. The consultant should therefore be more concerned with genuine consultation than with techniques based on 'selling' and persuasion.

Role perception

The values of our employers, together with our own values greatly influence how we define our work responsibilities. When jobs are tightly structured and a product of precise job specifications then we may have little control over *what* we do, although we will have considerable influence over *how* we do it. With jobs which are loose and unstructured and for which the organisation has not produced tight job specifications, we will have control both over what we do and how we do it. Many data processing jobs clearly come into this last category, in particular those associated with systems analysis. *How* an individual does his job will be closely related to his personal values and the values of the organisation for which he is working. What he sees his job involving will be a product both of the way in which his department is organised and of a set of factors operating in his own personal environment. These will determine his role. By the word 'role' we mean the behaviour expected of an individual by others who associate with him. In the case of the data processing man these associates will be the management of the firm for which he is working; his data processing colleagues, and those groups who are on the receiving end of his services in user departments or client firms. Most of us occupy a multiplicity of social roles. We are citizens, fathers and mothers, husbands and wives as well as employees, managers, subordinates. Here we are only concerned with how people define their roles and have their roles defined for them within the work situation but the concept of role always concerns relationships and it is individuals, not organisations who play roles and occupy role positions (18).

There can be a conflict between role and values. If values are defined as how one thinks that one should behave then there may be a serious gap between this and how one actually does behave. This gap can make individuals neurotic or cynical about themselves as people and conflict may be particularly acute if our 'civilised men' find that they are working for 'efficiency' oriented firms. In this kind of situation the individual may have a clear idea of how he should behave in terms of his personal values, but he may recognise that it is not in his interests to behave in this way, given the attitudes of his employer. He then is under great pressure to abandon his principles in order to assist his main interest which is that of survival in a tough environment.

Conflict can also arise when the way an individual sees his role differs from the way his role is perceived by others. This may cause special difficulties for computer men whose own perception of what their job is may differ markedly from the way their role is defined by people on the receiving end of new computer systems. The greater the lack of role consensus, the greater the likelihood of misunderstanding and conflict between the two groups. Problems are increased by the fact that computer personnel are specialists for it is thought that specialisation has the effect of accentuating differences between groups (7). Specialists are more likely than others to develop vested interests and to make claims over certain spheres of work; claims which they are ready to defend against encroachment by others. They therefore define their roles in terms which other groups do not necessarily accept and which cause resentment and antagonism. If, in addition, these specialists are recruited from outside the company so that they arrive with sets of values which are different from those held generally within the organisation, then the conditions for major conflict will exist.

An important influence on how an individual defines his own role, in contrast to how others define it, is the nature of the groups which exert an influence on his attitudes and behaviour. These will be of four kinds (6). First, there will be groups with which the individual identifies and from which he derives many of his ideas and values. With computer personnel a most influential group is other EDP experts located both within and outside his own firm. Those data processing experts whose articles he reads, whom he meets at professional symposiums and with whom he associates at work. Second, there will be the groups with which he interacts within the work situation. These will include top management, members of user departments, other specialist groups and customers. All these groups are very important because they can either assist or frustrate the achievement of his personal objectives. Third, there are the groups outside his own specialism whose opinions he values and whom he respects and looks up to. For the computer man these are likely to be scientists and quasiscientific groups similar to his own. Lastly, there are those who are perhaps not intimately connected with what he is doing but who observe and evaluate his behaviour. Here the computer man is likely to have to face criticism from humanists and behavioural scientists who question the ethical validity of his emphasis on technical objectives, and from the community at large who are likely to become worried at some of the predicted social byproducts of his activities; in particular, the possibility of computers reducing the numbers of jobs available. The groups one identifies with; those which one respects, and those who observe and criticise one's activities, all help the individual to set and maintain standards of work and conduct. The groups one interacts with may be less important in this respect. Although the computer man is highly visible to users of his systems and they may actively try to change his behaviour, unless they also have the power to stop what he is doing they may not be able to influence him for he can be blinded by his own innovation objectives.

Let us now look at the various roles which an individual can assume within a work situation and establish which are relevant to the computer specialist. Studies of industrial scientists have identified five major roles that they may be expected to fulfil (30). These are: scientist, professional, administrator, employee and colleague.

The scientist role is thought to contain powerful values derived from the scientific community (17). These concern the importance of objective 'truth', the free availability to all scientists of scientific findings, a concern for objectivity in scientific activity and an organised sceptism – that is the suspension of judgment until the facts are established. The professional role is less rigorous in its ethical requirements. Here research results may not be open to all but may be shared with certain individuals in the firm. Although truth is still sought after, this is a focused rather than a general truth and there is little conflict between pure and applied science. A degree of altruism is required in that the researcher must be prepared to give up ideas to others and to see them modified. He must be able to communicate his ideas and research findings in non-technical terms and he must place his company's interests before those of his scientific discipline. His behaviour in his administrative role will depend on his status and position in the firm. If he is a manager he will be expected to get results from his staff, to be a good coordinator of his department's activities and to perform efficiently all the other aspects of a supervisor's job. In his employee role he will be required to adhere to his side of the efficiency contract by being a good producer. He will be expected to accept his status position, submit to authority and abide by the rules and procedures of the group of which he is a working member. In his role of colleague and friend he will need to show a variety of social skills. Stein suggests that these are being assertive without hostility and aggression, being aware of the needs of others, being congenial on the job and sociable off it, 'knowing his place' without being obsequious, 'speaking his mind' without being domineering; sincere in his relationships with others, honest and trustworthy (30). In other words, our idea of the 'civilised man'.

If we accept this description of the roles of the industrial scientist then it would appear that the roles of the computer specialist are similar although not identical. He is a member of a technical rather than a scientific community and therefore he will not subscribe to a value system which places high priority on the universality of knowledge, the importance of a search for truth, and the need for scepticism and objectivity. He is likely, however, to subscribe to the technical values discussed earlier in this chapter. These will include a strong perception of the importance of technology and of its advantages and a logical and rational if not an entirely objective approach to problem solving. Because of the newness of the data processing occupation it is not yet a profession, but we have seen in chapter 2 that every effort is now being made to develop both an examination scheme and an ethical code of conduct. Professionalism is therefore well under way. In his administrative, employee and social roles there would seem to be no difference between the industrial scientist and the data processing specialist.

One interesting feature about data processing departments and the staff who work there is that there appears to be a dual ideology. There are departments who see themselves in a powerful innovatory role, acting as a 'ginger' group to the rest of the firm and pushing new methods and ideas out to the rest of the organisation. These innovators want to stir things up; to work on the frontiers of knowledge. Their approach is aptly described by one of their number as 'if it works it is obsolescent'. In contrast other data processing departments see themselves as 'helpers' rather than innovators. Their philosophy leads them to be somewhat subservient to management. They have been described as the fact gatherers, the fact processers and the interpreters (23). They help management to introduce change but it is management who decides what it wants done and who takes responsibility for the implementation of change. These important value differences appear to stem from a number of factors. The 'innovator' position can appear when a dynamic data processing department is located in a conservative, slow-moving firm. The mail order company is one such example. Generally this dynamism is a product of the personality and interests of the man heading the department and of his recruitment policy, which is likely to be one of recruiting staff from outside. The 'helper' philosophy is more likely to be found in a company with a scientific ethos and a tendency to innovation in all its activities. Here both top and line management are continually scanning their environment to spot where new ideas can best be applied and they are not prepared to play second fiddle to any specialist department. The fact that this philosophical dichotomy exists between data processing departments is in itself interesting. It is difficult to think of any other function in a company where this philosophical divergence occurs.

Considerable conflict occurs in an organisation when the way people define their roles and the way these roles are seen by others bears little similarity. This leads to an ambiguous situation in which the occupant of a role does not perceive clearly what others expect of him and people on the receiving end of his activities are themselves unclear on what they should expect. Ambiguity increases with distance and so it is likely to be greatest between groups that normally have little to do with each other but come together from time to time for a specific purpose. This is, of course, particularly true of data processing personnel. In the next section we will examine both how data processing staff define their own roles and how user departments perceive them. Relationships between data processing specialists and users will not necessarily be constant. Research has shown the importance of feedback in this kind of relationship (13). If the innovator responds to user objections to his new system with a hostile counter-attack then staff in the user department will react to him in a very different manner from that which they would have adopted if he had been submissively compliant to their complaints. If he partially responds to their pressure then they are likely to increase this pressure. If he is overcome by tension and anxiety then they may lay off him. Thus a continual feedback process is going on with role expectations being continually adjusted as the relationship between the innovator and the recipients of change ebbs and flows.

Data processing people are in a peculiarly difficult situation by virtue of the nature of their functions. They must believe in change if they are to succeed, yet in doing so they may come into conflict with many parts of their organisation. Innovative roles of this kind have been described as patterned organisational deviance. They are seen as arising as a result of bureaucracy attempting to build into itself a capacity for change. One can hypothesise that data processing specialists will experience less conflict in their relationships with other groups when these groups are similar to themselves. Thus relationships with other data processing staff should be easier for them to handle than relationships with user departments.

Interaction with other groups

We found that the people with whom our data processing staff associated were different in the three groups and were not the same for programmers as for systems analysts. Figure 5.1 sets out these differences.

Fig. 5.1 Groups with which data processing staff said that they had the most contact (percentages)

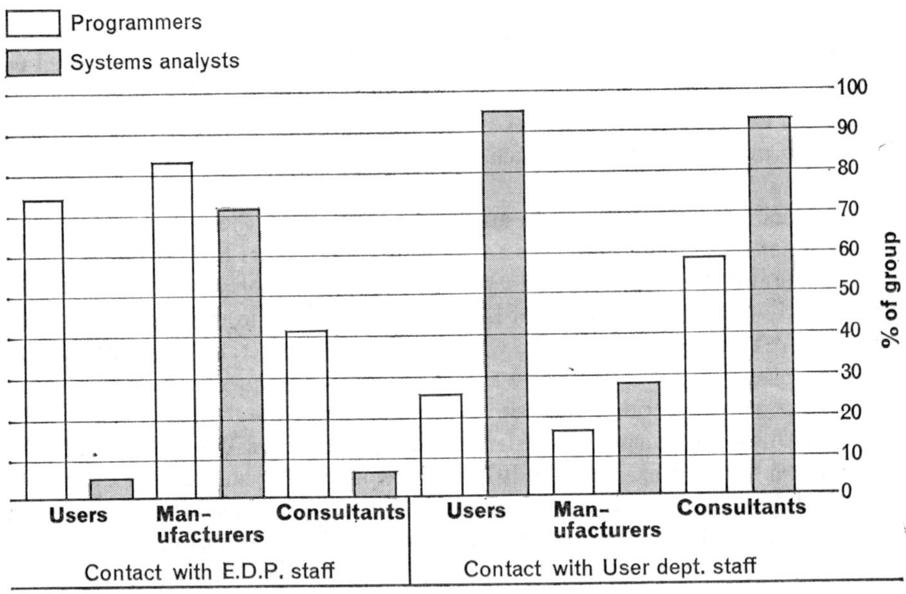

For users the heading 'EDP staff' refers to the programmers and systems analysts' own departmental colleagues. It is apparent that programmers did not have a great deal of contact with other groups in their firm whereas systems analysts worked in close association with the staff of departments where new systems were being introduced. In the manufacturers 'EDP staff' contacts were with customers. All the staff we interviewed in Manufacturer A had some client contact whereas this was only true of 50 per cent of the staff of Manufacturer B. Staff who did not have client contact have been excluded from the figure above. Both computer Manufacturers show a similar pattern with programmers and systems analysts associating with client data processing staff rather than with client User departments.

In the consultant group, programming staff were more likely to have contact with client user areas but we have already pointed out that with consultants the demarcation between a programmer and a systems analyst is blurred. Systems analysts followed the user group pattern and had most of their contacts with user departments in client companies. Our analysis shows that whereas the majority of programmers interacted generally with their own kind, as did the systems analysts of computer manufacturers; the systems analysts of both the user firms and the consultants associated most frequently with departments which were introducing computer systems. They therefore had the difficult and delicate task of relating with groups whose culture was different from their own and who might question the value of the new EDP systems which they were putting in. We would expect to find more recognition of the human relations difficulties of introducing technical change in these two groups than elsewhere.

Their success as innovators will be closely related to their ability to communicate lucidly with people who do not think in the same terms (13). The innovating role is always a stressful one; the innovator is primarily interested in the creative, non-routine aspects of his job, yet his implementation responsibilities may be routine rather than creative and will require skills of administration and human relations which he may not possess. To get their systems in and working systems analysts require cooperation from users, yet this cooperation may be reluctantly given. When innovators encounter a lack of support their reaction may be to remove themselves from a stressful situation. Unfortunately the computer innovator cannot do this as his survival depends on the successful implementation of his ideas (13).

When we consider the nature of their contacts, our hypothesis that the systems analysts of users and consultant's will interact in a more personal way than the systems analysts of manufacturers appears to be supported.

Fig. 5.2 The form that contact with other groups takes (percentages)

	Selling systems and ideas; supplying and getting information	*Discussion and problem solving*
Manufacturers	69	31
Users and consultants	31	69

Parsons suggests that when we interact with others we have to solve three different varieties of problems (21). The first is establishing the kinds of relationships which will enable us to achieve our personal goals; this he calls instrumental interaction. The second is relating with people for the intrinsic satisfaction that this provides; this he calls expressive interaction. The third is relating with people so as to secure the coordination of activity of a number of different groups; this is integrative interaction. Systems analysts in our three groups will be concerned with all these kinds of relationship, but the interaction of manufacturers' staff will largely be of the instrumental variety, whereas that of user and consultant systems analysts should be directed more to the development of integrative relationships if they are to be effective innovators.

Because innovators have a vested interest in change, while groups on the receiving end of innovation may be more concerned with the preservation of stability, one would expect many systems analysts to experience a conflict of loyalty between the interests of their own firm or department and the interests of their clients. We found that this conflict of loyalty did exist but it was experienced less by systems analysts working for Consultants than by those working for User firms or Manufacturers.

Fig. 5.3 Number of systems analysts in each group who experience conflicts of loyalty (percentages)

	Conflict	*No conflict*
Users	49	51
Manufacturers	49	51
Consultants	29	71

User systems analysts who did experience a conflict of loyalties tended to resolve these by siding with the client department rather than their own.

> There are times when your responsibility to the user department overrides everything else, even though it means attacking people in your own department.

> I would forget my own department if I really thought that we were wrong and the user was right.

Manufacturers' staff, as might be expected, were more likely to resolve any conflict by looking after the interests of their employer.

> I am in the client's firm to implement company policies and to make a profit for my company.

However, this did not mean that they were not anxious to do their best for the client.

> What is for the customer's benefit may be good for our company too. Keeping the customer happy is good for our reputation.

Consultants appeared to experience less of this kind of conflict, because their values made it natural for them to put the interest of the client first.

> If one is true to oneself then the client comes first, and one's own company too in the long run. The consultant must do what *he* thinks is right.

> One's responsibility to the client is the most important thing.

ORDER NUMBER

PO NYAATP08

BOOK NUMBER

8606703

BAY NUMBER

135-8

AUTHOR	Mumford, Enid
TITLE	Job Satisfaction and Computer Specialists
DESCRIPTION	

A source of human relations problems in all three groups was the fact that user departments and client groups tended to perceive computers and computer usage in a way that differed markedly from the approach and outlook of the data processing specialists. The majority of systems analysts in all three groups referred to problems arising from these different perceptions.

User group systems analysts spoke of their own long-term perspective compared with the short-term view of the client department.

> They are concerned with their own problems. We look at problems from the outside.

> Users don't know what happens outside their own departments and don't care. Even departmental heads can only see their own part of the system.

> Our aims are different. Most users want to do a day-to-day job. The pressure on them is such that they cannot look for better ways to do it.

Computer manufacturer staff referred more to the inability of the client to understand computer technology; its opportunities and restrictions.

> They can't understand computers and launch in at the deep end.

> They don't understand the problems and think that any information they get from a manual system they can also get from a computer system.

Consultants spoke of the difficulties of 'problem definition' – the inability of the client to define his own problems with any clarity.

> People have nebulous ideas of what they want. They do not think through the details.

> We are the professionals who have to battle through red tape to get to the problem.

> Often the client has an image of 'the ruthless consultant bringing the computer in'.

The social values of a group are likely to show up clearly when they are asked about their behaviour to other groups. Observers suggest that relationships between departments or groups with different functions can be characterised by the responsiveness of one department or group to the needs of another, the accuracy of information exchange and the attitudes of one group to the other (32). We would expect the attitudes of systems analysts to user groups to become clear when they answered the question, 'How do you get people to accept innovation?' Our earlier analysis of the relationship of attitudes and values to the product market, culture and technology of an organisation and to the training and background of the individual would lead us to hypothesise that there will be considerable differences between the three groups in their attitudes to innovation strategies. The users and consultants are likely to place more importance than the manufacturers on attitude change and they will seek to secure user commitment to their systems through education and involvement. In contrast the manufacturers with their powerful market pressures may believe more in the efficacy of a rational approach, 'proving that the computer can be of value'; in a straight marketing approach based on persuasion or, if these fail, on hard line approaches such as coercion or 'buying' a new system in. In the user group the mail order company EDP staff may have a different approach from the other two users for their technological backgrounds may lead them to be impatient of an educational/participative approach.

This hypothesis proved to be correct as the table below demonstrates.

Fig. 5.4 Answers of systems analysts to the question: How do you get people to accept innovation? (percentages)

	Through education and involvement	*Proving it to be of value, 'selling' or coercion*
Manufacturers	33	67
Consultants	76	24
Industrial Products and Government department	74	26
Mail order company	35	65

The answers of programmers to this question will be more academic as few of them have had any experience of implementation, yet they should still reflect the values of their companies. This indeed proved to be the case as user and consultant programmers showed the same tendency towards education and consultation, while manufacturer programmers prefer to demonstrate the computer's effectiveness and to use marketing tactics. In the programmer group there is no longer any difference between the mail order company, Industrial Products and the Government department.

Answers to the question 'How do you get people to accept innovation?' are likely to be given in ideal terms – that is in relation to situations where change is relatively easy and no significant resistance is encountered. Unfortunately computer personnel do not always meet this kind of situation and opposition to new computer systems can be intense and bitter. When this kind of reaction is encountered then the computer man with values which differ from the group whose activities he is attempting to computerise is likely to use more coercive methods. Coercion will be particularly tempting if the computer group believes that it has considerable power to get others to conform to its requirements. By power we mean the capacity of a group to impose its will on others, despite the opposition of the second group. Because of the tenuous and dependent nature of their relationships with clients, neither the manufacturer nor the consultants would be in this position. Computer personnel in user firms may see themselves in a power situation and this perception could be more prevalent in the mail order company than in the two other user firms. Figure 5.5 sets out the answers to the question 'What action would you take to overcome resistance to change?'

There is little difference between the groups in their answers. The hard-line men who would resort to coercion were the programmers of the mail order company and of Industrial Products. These groups perceived the potential power

Fig. 5.5 Answers to the question: What action would you take to overcome resistance to change? (percentages)

	Educate, involve	Coerce. 'sell'	Withdraw, would not allow it to happen
Systems analysts			
Users	32	32	36
Manufacturers	42	34	24
Consultants	42	12	46
Programmers			
Users	34	48	18
Manufacturers	53	21	26
Consultants	53	19	28

of their own departments but, because they had little to do with implementing new systems, they had not learnt that these tactics are rarely successful in practice. One told us, 'the user cannot resist, he can only be reluctant'. Systems analysts attached to consultants spoke of their unwillingness to let such a situation arise.

> I would not let it get to this stage. The secret of good systems analysis is to let functional management believe that it is their system. I would never design a system that is not acceptable. This is the way systems analysts fail. It is not *your* system, it is *their* system.

In the answers above, 'education' in the sense of getting people to understand what computer systems are all about and 'involvement', allowing groups who will be affected by new computer systems to participate in the decisions associated with their creation, have been grouped together. If the answers which refer to involvement are separated out a rather disturbing picture emerges.

Fig. 5.6 Answers to the question: How do you get people to accept innovation? (percentages)

	Involve in planning and decision-taking	Other answers
Users	13	87
Manufacturers	4	96
Consultants	15	75

The replies to the question 'What action would you take to overcome resistance to change?' showed a slight move towards involvement on the part of Manufacturers and Consultants but a move away from it by user firms.

Fig. 5.7 Answers to the question: What action would you take to overcome resistance to change? (percentages)

	Involve in planning and decision-taking	Other answers
Users	4	96
Manufacturers	9	91
Consultants	20	80

Clearly few of our programmers and systems analysts believe in associating democratic processes with the introduction of major technical change.

Answers were generally in terms of 'getting the other side to think as we do'.

> Do not blind with science. Discuss their problems; gain their confidence so that they are on your side when you present computer solutions.

> Joke them into something early on, and then introduce it.

> Cover every aspect of the system in your explanations and carry out a public relations exercise with everyone who is likely to be affected so that they will have a degree of confidence.

A surprising feature of these answers was that many of them were given by young men – a group normally associated in the newspapers with movements for increasing community participation in decision-taking. It is interesting to speculate why our young computer innovators, who are undoubtedly a group who will bring major changes to society, are so little appreciative of the logic and benefits of democratic processes. In many instances this undemocratic approach contrasted with the value system of their own companies. For example, both the mail order company and Industrial Products had long-established systems of worker–management joint consultation. It also contrasted with statements made by their own department managers. When asked the best technique for getting people to accept innovation all except one placed participation – in the sense of involving people in joint problem solving and joint decision-taking – top of their lists.

It is probable that this reluctance of the computer man to involve others in his new systems, or even to perceive the need for doing this, is a major reason for the conflict that so frequently develops between innovators and those on the receiving end of innovation. Interdepartmental conflict arises when visits and questions from EDP staff are seen as interference rather than considerateness, and when attitudes of distrust exist between the departments.

This reluctance on the part of computer men to use a democratic approach may be due to their wish to retain command over the situation in which they are operating. They appear to believe that if they can do this then their system will go in essentially as they have designed it. There will be no need to compromise by having to accept what are to them the misguided and ignorant opinions of the user. When problem solving takes place and more than one group is involved power tends to be shared through the decision process. A situation develops in which both sides put their points of view and a joint solution is eventually arrived at. From the computer man's point of view a solution conceived in this way may force him to meet group opinion by abandoning some of his technical objectives. Bennis tells us that change typically involves risk and fear (4). Any significant change in human organisation involves rearrangement of the patterns of power, association, status, skills and values. Yet, he says, 'change efforts sometimes are conducted as if there was no need to discuss and work through these fears and worries'. He highlights the problem when he says that 'most change strategies rely almost totally on rationality. But knowledge about something does not lead automatically to intelligent action. This requires commitment as well as truth.'[1]

Behavioural scientists maintain that individuals brought up on a rational set of values are badly cast to play the intricate human roles now required of them. Their ineptitude leads to systems of defence being developed which interfere with the problem-solving capacity of the organisation. Bennis, pursuing the same argument, points out that acceptance of change depends very much on the relationship between those responsible for bringing in the change and those on the receiving end. The more profound and anxiety-making the nature of the change, the closer and more collaborative the relationship required between innovators and users. He suggests that change will be resisted to the extent that the user possesses little or incorrect knowledge about the change, has little trust in the innovating group and has little influence in controlling the nature of the change.

Bennis sets out the values which he believes a successful innovating group should hold. These emphasise *openness, collaboration, consensus, team leadership* and *authentic relationships* based on mutual trust and agreement. It would be interesting to know the number of computer groups who both hold and practise these values.

When innovation is not based on collaboration and joint involvement in decision-taking then one would expect to find some disgruntlement in user departments and a considerable difference in the way the innovator group sees itself and the way it is seen by the recipients of the new systems. One might find a situation where users claim to know little of innovator group activities and, whereas the innovators believe themselves to be skilled in human relationships, they are seen by the user groups as having poor skills in this respect.

We have no information on how our manufacturers and consultants were perceived by their clients, but because the interviews with user firm programmers

[1] Computer men who have read this paragraph, argue that they are being unjustly accused and that the responsibility for democratic processes lies not with them, but with line management. They have a point here. Nevertheless in situations where line managers are unused to handling major change, it is not unreasonable for them to look for guidance to the experts whom they see as bringing change to their departments.

and systems analysts formed part of a larger study we do have information on how computer personnel were perceived by other groups in our three user firms. All clerical staff about to be affected by major new computer systems were asked if they thought that the computer department had a good reputation. In the mail order company, despite the imminence of the changeover and the fact that a large number of girls would be affected by it, there was almost total ignorance concerning the computer department. Only five girls out of forty-five were prepared to comment and of these three said that they thought its reputation was good, two that they thought it was poor. In Industrial Products there was a mixed sex labour force and men were more aware of the computer department's existence than women. Fifty-three per cent of women had no knowledge of the computer department, again in a situation where computer personnel were working in their department. Of those that did know, a half said that their reputation was good; a half that it was poor or average. Three-quarters of the male clerks did know about the computer department and the majority saw its reputation as good. In the government department, 50 per cent were again unable to express an opinion and of the remainder there was an even division between those who saw its reputation as good and those who were critical of it.

This remarkable lack of contact on the part of ordinary office staff with the group which were just about to make a major change in their work situation shows alarming deficiencies not only in consultation, but in straightforward communication. In all three user situations staff commented bitterly upon the inadequacy of management communication.

Clerks were asked how they felt about the way their firm introduced new systems of work and if their comments were adverse they were asked a follow-up question on what mistakes it made. Overwhelmingly criticisms referred to communications. In the mail order company we were told:

> They don't give us much information. They don't tell us what is going to happen. It just happens and then we are told about it.

Similar comments were passed in Industrial Products.

> They don't tell us about changes in time. This computer has been talked about for years but we don't really know anything about it except what we have picked up through rumours.

In the government department there were fewer remarks of this kind and girls spoke more of the ways in which communication could be improved.

> They just give you a book to read. There is little explanation of the new things that are happening.

A possible reason for these defective communication practices is that while the personnel department might be regarded as the group which should assume responsibility for communication during periods of change, relationships between the computer specialists and their personnel departments were often bad.

All heads of computer departments were asked to indicate on a seven point scale their relationships with those departments in their companies with whom they might be expected to work closely. The scale was as follows:

1 Relations are excellent – there is complete cooperation.
2 Relations are very good.
3 Relations are better than average.
4 Relations are average – we get along even though there are problems of achieving cooperation.
5 Relations are not very good.
6 Relations are poor – cooperation is difficult.
7 Relations are extremely bad – there is no possibility of cooperation.

The mail order computer manager rated his relations with personnel as average. Industrial Products said that theirs were 'very good', and the government department put theirs as average. Both the mail order company and the government department got on better with their accounts departments than with their personnel departments. Yet it would seem that if due notice is to be taken of the human problems of introducing computer systems, particularly those associated with consultation and communication, then very close cooperation is required between computer and personnel department staff.

Poor communication when introducing change seems to occur more as a result of a lack of knowledge of information needs and an absence of clearly defined responsibility for communication than through a deliberate withholding of information. The obstacles to effective interdepartmental communication have been described as physical barriers, difficulties in synchronising contact, lack of knowledge of one another's work, and lack of interpersonal skill (32). Clearly the two first do not apply to computer men as they are normally working for long periods in the department which is seeking information. Lack of knowledge of another's work should not apply either as it is the systems analyst's job to find this out so that he can design an improved system. Interpersonal skill is certainly an important factor but it may be that subconsciously the computer man hopes to get his system through without argument if he does not say too much about it, or if he adopts a marketing approach of eulogising its advantages while glossing over its disadvantages. The sociologist finds this tendency to 'sell' systems rather than to discuss their merits and demerits, particularly those relating to people, hard to understand. All his research experience tells him that this approach leads to misunderstanding, a lack of involvement on the part of the user and even a subsequent hostility to the new system. An explanation for the systems analyst's unwillingness to take account of human needs is provided by Martin and Norman in their book, *The Computerised Society* (16). Discussing systems analysis they suggest that 'man as a system component provides so much variety that he is always difficult to analyse. . . . The human element is therefore treated as unequal, random, obstinate, and very significant.'

This may be true of advanced computer systems though it seems more than likely that in the lower levels of systems design man tends to be disregarded as a design variable for to include him would make the task of the systems analyst too difficult. Woodward also provides a reason why selling and persuasion play such a large part in user acceptance of computer systems (33). She suggests that whenever there is a conflict of goals within an organisation and the goals of one group are not seen as desirable or feasible by another group, then persuasion will be used in the decision-making process. If, after this persuasion, the proposed goals are still not viewed as desirable then decision making will shift into a bargaining mode. Because the introduction of a computer system is often accomplished without much participation in the decision process by user management, our experience suggests that when persuasion does not work there can be a shift towards authoritarianism on the part of the innovating group.

The systems analyst, like most other people wishes to work for an organisation whose values fit his own. Because his values are of a technical/rational kind he should find little difficulty in conforming with the norms and philosophy of his employer if he works for a computer manufacturer or consultant. His difficulties are likely to be greater if he works for an organisation whose business is something other than selling computers or computer problem-solving expertise, for his values may then come into conflict with those held by the rest of the organisation, particularly the user departments into which he is trying to introduce his new systems.

Essentially the computer man derives his credibility in his firm from the fact that he is seen as an expert. But even experts are without influence if they cannot engender trust and acceptance in those who use their specialist knowledge. Hedley describes the problems caused by a conflict of values in one of the firm's which he studied (10, 33). Here the computer unit had the technical objective of introducing a centralised management information system. User companies reacted to this with anxiety as they perceived a loss of individual control over their affairs. Responsibility for decision-taking was not clearly formulated and the people responsible for systems analysis made policy decisions about the various controlling factors almost without being aware that they were doing so. As a result there was a danger of long-term decisions being taken in terms of their appropriateness to system design rather than in relation to more important criteria. Because the value position of the systems analysts was never questioned real control tended to shift to the system designers and away from the user areas.

The real clash of values in our user firms arose because of an unwillingness or an inability on the part of systems analysts to recognise the importance of the human factors operating in the user areas. These factors were of two kinds. Firstly, there was user anxiety about the amount of say they would have in the design and control of the new system. They wished both to be told clearly what was going to happen and to have a say in any decisions that were taken on the nature of the new systems. Secondly they had fears concerning the consequences of the new system for their job security and for their job satisfaction. Would they be made redundant or have to do jobs which had lost a great deal of their intrinsic challenge and interest? Many of these fears arose because they viewed the computer experts of their firms as technical men who took little note of human needs. They had certain expectations of their computer experts and too often their computer experts conformed to these expectations.

Factors which influence attitudes and values

Figure 5.8 sets out those factors in the computer man's environment which are likely to influence his personal values and hence his relationships with user departments. The way he perceives his role will be influenced by his education, previous job experience, the nature of his EDP training and the attitudes both of his firm and of his own occupational group. Our analysis of the attitudes of user group programmers and systems analysts provides some interesting information on how these factors influence an individual's views on how to get innovation accepted. Thus people with a university education and a science degree were more likely to describe coercive and manipulative methods. It was apparent that their university experience had not endowed them with democratic values. We have also seen in an earlier section of this chapter how computer men who were recruited externally were influenced more strongly by the technical ethos of their own specialist groups than they were by the human relations emphasis of their company. Individuals who were aware of the importance of establishing good human relations through providing opportunities for user involvement tended to have worked in a number of jobs in the firm and these previous jobs had not been associated with data processing. They told us that career advancement was not important to them and that they had joined the firm because they approved of its community image. In contrast the externally recruited men were university graduates, they were young, and they had joined the company because they were attracted by the data processing opportunities which it offered. Most of these young men were in the mail order company. Perhaps because of their youth and inexperience they were rated low on efficiency by their supervisors.

The job needs of data processing specialists also affect their relationships with user departments. The most important needs here are a desire for status and approval. If these needs are fulfilled solely within the data processing group, then their determinants will be technical expertise and problem-solving skill. But if status and approval are sought in user departments then they will not be awarded unless technical knowledge is allied to human relations skill.

Career aspirations will also influence relationships with user departments. If the data processing man wishes to make data processing his career and believes that he can best do this by spending only a limited period of time with his present company; then he may have little interest in developing good relationships throughout the organisation. But, if he hopes to make his career there and intends to move out of the data processing function into line management then a good technical reputation will not be enough.

Fig. 5.8 Factors influencing the relationships of EDP staff with user areas

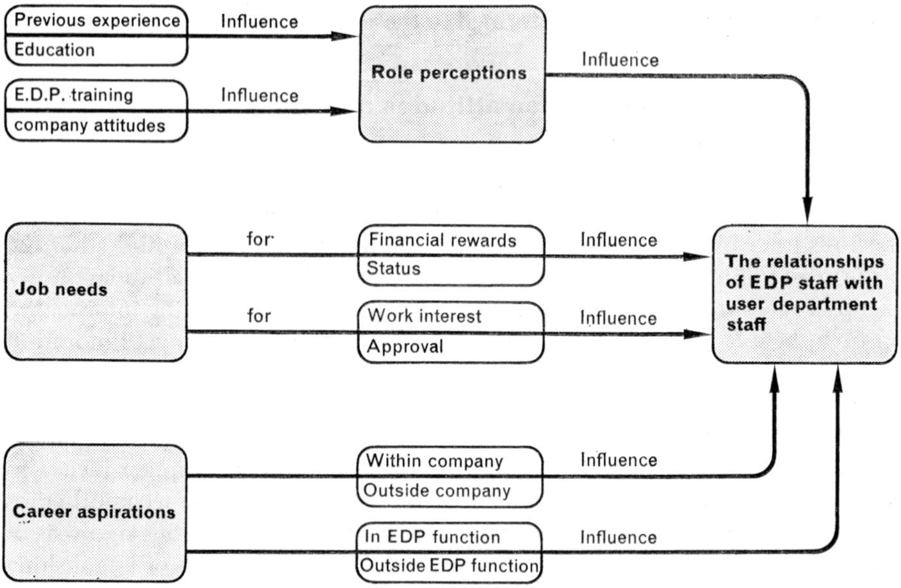

Humanistic values

A more humanistic approach to computer introduction requires the computer man to shift his value position and recognise that human values are as important as, if not more important than, technical values. But it also requires that both he and his employing organisation change their behaviour when coping with technical change. Three things are particularly important here. First, his innovator role must be clearly defined so that what he does conforms with what people expect of him. Second, he must develop techniques of systems design which enable him to take account of human needs and not to ignore these because he believes human variables are too complex to be catered for. Third, senior management in the firm should consider the structural position of the data processing department in the organisation and consciously develop linking mechanisms which assist its integration with other departments. Let us look at each of these factors in turn.

First, the computer man's personal value position. Many writers in the computer Press draw attention to the communication gulf existing between data processing specialists and other members of the firm. Ross, writing in *Computers and Automation* (24), points out that numerous surveys and research studies have come to the conclusion that the need for management participation and direction is a prerequisite of any successful EDP application. He suggests that the so-called 'communication gap' between manager and computer man is often cited as the number one reason for the underutilisation and poor performance of computers. Speaking from the value position of the computer man, he sees the solution as 'changing the manager's behaviour to the extent that he both appreciates the potential of the computer and the problems of computer personnel and has learned to use the computer to solve his managerial problems'. No mention here of the computer man changing his attitudes and behaviour in any way. Ross continues this theme in other sections of his article. He quotes a well-known data processing consultant as saying: 'The problem is to change the psychological outlook – the behavioural pattern of the executive and the manager to the extent that they can talk to the systems analyst when he comes into the department.' There is little recognition here that the data processing man's success may depend, not on the line manager becoming more conversant with his language, but of his becoming more understanding of the problems and needs of the line manager. The success of his technology depends on the willingness of the line manager to use it.

The reluctance of the computer man to understand or take account of the value system of the line manager is partly a product of the location of power. Power is recognised by both managers and sociologists as an important factor explaining the relationships between individuals and groups. Unless there is a balance of power between the line manager and the data processing specialist there may be small inducement for the computer man to change his behaviour. It has been argued that if the strong party in a relationship cannot be effectively threatened then there will be no incentive for him to accommodate the interests of the weaker party (22). If the computer man does not understand or sympathise with the interests of the user group; if he operates from a technical/rational value position and if he has high power derived from the sanction given to his activities at Board level, then there may be little legitimate action that the line manager can take. But he is likely to be hostile to the new computer system and his morale and that of his department is likely to be at a low ebb.

If computer innovation is to continue to thrive then it seems important to bring the value position of the computer man somewhat closer to that of our 'civilised man', so that he no longer defines his role in purely technical terms. The mechanisms for doing this exist but perhaps need to be made more explicit. First, internal rather than external recruitment, appears to give computer personnel a set of values closer to the general ethos of their companies. Second, much more could be done in the education and training of systems analysts to stress the importance of human values. Sackman, a computer man who is also a psychologist, puts the desired position very well when he discusses what he calls 'Humanistic automation'. He says: 'Humanistic automation is the elevation of human intelligence and the enhancement of social well being achieved through the use of computers. . . . Humanistic automation provides a general ethical basis for the design of systems to meet human needs and serve social well being' (25).

We have seen in chapter 2 that few computer courses train the systems analyst in any depth in human responsibilities.

Clarifying the systems analyst's role will also assist him to get his value position clearer. At present the job of the systems analyst seems to be shrouded in ambiguity. One reason for this is that he often appears to cut himself off from information on how he is perceived by the members of the user department in which he is operating. Behavioural scientists have pointed out that self-identity – seeing clearly who we are and what we are doing, depends on a precise and meaningful feedback from those around us (13). How are others evaluating us? How satisfied are they with what we are doing? Our research into the reactions of employees to new computer systems has shown that the members of an affected department may be filled with anxiety and distrust about what is taking place, yet the computer man either does not notice their reactions or he dismisses them as being typical of 'a lot of stupid clerks'. Sackman, who would like to see all new computer systems treated as scientific experiments and their introduction carefully monitored at both the technical and human level says, 'All system events are potential experiments and potential candidates for providing useful system feedback, and as such, should be linked to an analysis system capable of selectively sensing, filtering and acting upon significant data' (25).

Systems design

One way of reconciling the value differences between computer technologists and their clients is through a more ethical approach to systems design. By ethical approach we mean the taking account of human needs and values when designing computer systems. This approach is not new in job design. The Tavistock Institute in Britain and the Graduate School of Business Administration in the University of California have made major contributions to thinking on this subject (11). But the greater part of the research undertaken so far is directed at redesigning existing jobs so as to make them more satisfying for the individual worker. The challenge for the computer systems designer is somewhat different. His problem is that of creating new jobs within his overall systems design which are both individually satisfying and provide satisfying forms of group interaction. There is little evidence that any computer systems analysts are as yet using this approach. One of the reasons for this is that a great deal of systems analysis thinking is derived from work study principles, and work study is commonly associated with job specialisation.

In an attempt to increase the skill and effectiveness with which jobs are performed it is usual for the work study man to analyse them into their component activities (11). Yet there is little evidence that the most effective way to organise the performance of a task is to break it into small pieces. This approach leads to jobs which are simpler than workers are capable of doing and hence a great deal of boredom and frustration in work.

One reason for user dissatisfaction with computer systems is the fact that while a great deal of thought and expertise goes into the design of the technical part of the system, little if any attention is paid to the design of the human part of the system. This becomes merely a byproduct of the technical system and entirely determined by the technical system. This lopsided approach is due to the fact that computer men have little understanding of the concept of sociotechnical systems. They do not appreciate that all but the fully automatic system requires interaction of some kind between man and machine and that it is therefore logical to view technology and people as part of a unified system and to design accordingly. The only way of ensuring that both the technical and social parts of a system are under control is to recognise that there is always some freedom of choice in the way a system can be designed and to consciously work for solutions in which both technical and social variables are organised so as to be compatible with each other.

At present there are two constraining factors which make a sociotechnical approach to systems design difficult. First, few computer technologists in this country have received any training in the behavioural sciences and this makes it difficult for them to identify social needs and incorporate mechanisms to cater for these into their design procedures. It may be that we should not expect them to do this and that there is a place for the behavioural scientist in the systems design team. Secondly, there is as yet no training in the human aspects of job design incorporated into systems design courses. This would appear to be a major deficiency in view of the considerable changes that can occur in task structure as a result of the new computer systems. The author is developing a method to enable computer systems to be designed in both human and technical terms (19). Its use requires the following resources and procedures.

1 The acquisition by systems designers of some knowledge of the contribution of the behavioural sciences to theories concerning people's attitudes to their work and motivating factors in work, and to behavioural theories of job design. The recruitment of people with behavioural science backgrounds as systems analysts could help here, or professional sociologists or psychologists could be attached to the systems design team.
2 An emphasis on communication and consultation rather than on authority, when designing and introducing computer systems. Many systems designers try to ensure user acceptance through a marketing approach. Vigorous efforts are made to persuade a manager and his staff that they do need the proposed system and that they will benefit from its introduction.
3 The selection of social and technical objectives which meet both the needs of the firm and the needs of employees. Some weighting can be permitted here. If a computer system is being designed for a user area where there are serious industrial relations problems, then the necessity for meeting the social requirements of the situation may demand a system which caters for social variables at the expense of technical ones. Similarly, if technical objectives are seen as of pressing importance then they can be weighted more strongly than social objectives, although the firm must recognise that it will incur a financial cost through adopting this policy and should compute the extent of this cost.
4 A careful comparison of available social and technical means for reaching these objectives in terms of their effectiveness and cost.
5 The careful monitoring of the implementation process to check that the new

system is not deviating from desired technical and social objectives. To check also that these objectives remain valid ends and do not require modification to meet change in the firm's or department's environment, or unanticipated employee reaction to the new system.

6 After the system is in operation a careful evaluation of the extent to which technical and social objectives have been correctly formulated in terms of organisational and employee needs. Also, an assessment of the appropriateness of the means used for the attainment of these objectives and an estimate of how these means could have been improved on. Lastly, a general appraisal of the success of the new system as an example of sociotechnical systems design.

A model of the suggested systems design approach is set out in Fig. 5.2. This requires the careful identification of the range of technical and social options which are available to the systems designer to solve existing problems and to meet the technical and social objectives which he and the firm should have set themselves. Next, technical and social options which are incompatible with each other must be excluded. This should leave a range of sociotechnical solutions all of which will come some way to meeting required objectives although not necessarily to the same extent. Some may meet technical objectives rather better than social objectives. Others will have the reverse effect. Here the firm's values will come into play and it will take a decision on the basis of a number of factors. These will be:

- Its own value position – whether it wishes to give technical or social objectives the highest priority.
- Any constraints which operate in its situation which force it to give a particular technical or social constraint a high priority.
- An evaluation of the resources required for the attainment of each solution and the availability of these resources.
- A cost-benefit analysis of each solution, which is related to the objective of introducing the new system.

This approach should lead to the design of systems which cater for people's needs in work and which incorporate job design principles directed at increasing employee satisfaction with their work situations. It must be stressed, however, that people's needs in work cannot be met without a rigorous preliminary investigation to discover what these needs are. This should be carried out at the same time as the first systems investigation into the technical needs of the user department.

The approach set out above may be difficult to implement because of a scarcity of behavioural science skills. The author therefore sets out a second approach which she calls Systems Adjustment. This accepts the technical side of the system as given but systematically translates it into human terms so that its impact on task structure and work relationships becomes apparent. She then asks two questions: 'What are the human disadvantages likely to arise from this

Fig. 5.9 Arriving at a sociotechnical solution

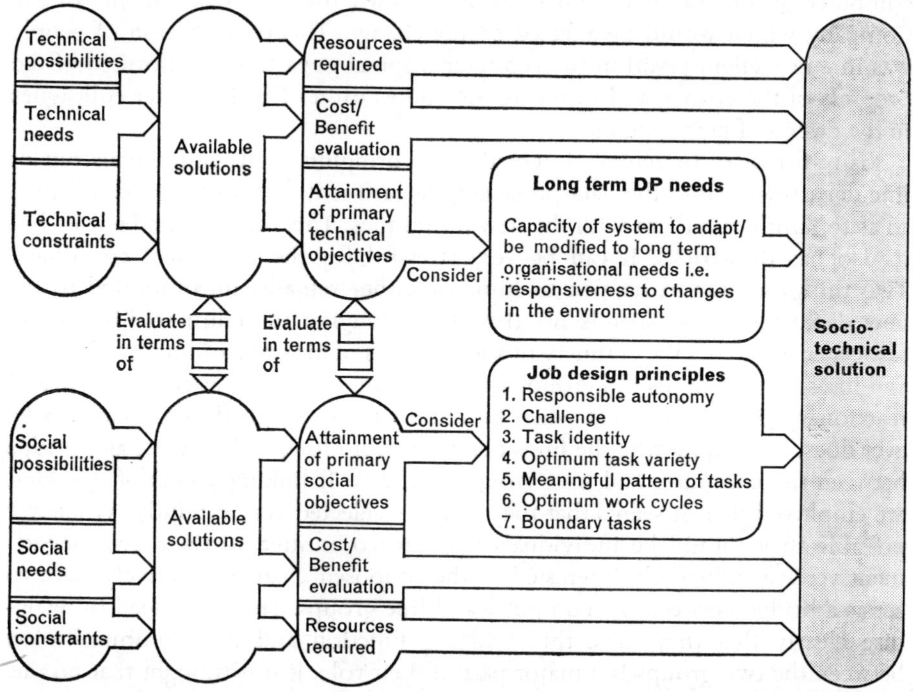

system which must, if possible, be avoided? What are the potential human advantages which, if recognised, can be exploited? She then examines the system in detail to ascertain the extent to which it can be manipulated so as to avoid disadvantages and exploit advantages. The methods for sociotechnical systems design and system adjustment are both written up in *Systems Design for People* (19).

This conscious building of human needs into systems design should go a long way towards bridging the value differences between computer specialists and the user groups with whom they interact. At present many user groups, especially managers, feel that they are being taken over by an impersonal technology. There is a belief that 'the computer is going to control everything and there is nothing that we can do about it'. Rosemary Stewart, after a visit to the United States to study the use of computers there wrote in *Management Today* about her interview with one manager who said, 'There is uneasiness among the people here. They know that they are building a monster and they don't know how to control it' (31).

Integrating mechanisms

Lastly another approach which can help to reduce the value differences between computer specialists and other groups in a company is through the careful building of integrating devices which form part of the structure of the company.

There are a number of ways of achieving this kind of integration. When a major computer system at the Detroit Edison Company USA, was introduced, the computer group was made up of people drawn from all departments in the Company which would be affected by the change. This cross-section of people was in an excellent position to keep their original departments informed of the progress of the change and to secure the cooperation of their former colleagues in the design of new systems.

Many firms try to achieve integration by bringing single individuals out of line departments into the data processing department for short periods of time, so as to familiarise them with the new techniques. This practice has benefits but it also has drawbacks. It can be very stressful for the individual concerned. Two things appear to happen to him. He either remains uncommitted to his new department and spends his time there longing to return to his normal associates or catches the enthusiasm and attitudes of his new computer colleagues and loses interest in his old group whom he comes to regard as conservative and reactionary. This means that when he returns to his original department, if he ever does, he dislikes what he finds there and is no longer able to act as a bridge between the computer and user groups (12, 27). If linking agents of this kind are employed then it seems that they must be selected very carefully. Whenever possible they should be individuals who are committed to their own department yet are sufficiently interested in the proposed change to actively want to act as a bridge between the computer and line groups. They also need to recognise clearly that they have this bridging function and that communication between the two groups is a major part of their role. If it is thought that no one inside the organisation can successfully play this very difficult role then it is quite possible to use an outside consultant to perform this service. One of the functions of the consultant has been described as that of acting as a linking agent. 'He can serve to link people or groups that need to be brought together. He can arrange confrontations of people and issues and promote effective interpersonal communications' (9). Bennis suggests that the professional behavioural scientist can act in this linkage role (4), and maintains that this type of consultant can help innovating and client groups to identify their missions and values and to set mutually compatible objectives. He believes that the behavioural scientist can effect a change in values so that human factors and feelings come to be considered legitimate. In order to do this it is necessary to improve the interpersonal competence of managers; achieve increased understanding within and between groups and develop team management and good conflict resolving mechanisms so that problems may be quickly handled. He maintains that one criteria for evaluating the success of an innovating group should be the extent to which it is successful in establishing good relationships based on mutual trust and confidence.

Some writers prefer a structural solution to this problem. They recognise the value differences between innovating groups and line departments and suggest that these can be reduced by introducing formally organised linkage mechanisms such as interdepartmental project groups and committees (15). This kind of linkage can be particularly effective if it is geared to conflict resolution and flexibility, for example, to increasing the degree of openness with which conflicts are aired and hammered out in departmental meetings. These researchers believe that attitudes will not change unless the power ratio is changed also. Thus managers in user departments must feel that they have an influence over the decisions that are being taken.

Conclusions

This chapter makes the point that job satisfaction requires compatibility of values. That is, the data processing man will normally want to work for a firm whose values fit his own. If he places a high priority on good financial rewards, on efficiency, on 'getting things done', then he will seek an employer who thinks in the same way. If, in contrast, he comes within our definition of 'civilised' man, he will want an employer who evaluates his staff for their personal qualities of integrity and for their ability to relate with others in an ethical manner.

Computer specialists working for manufacturers and consultants should have fewer problems here than those working for user firms. These employers have reputations for being 'tough', 'humane,' etc, and their reputations are well known within the data processing profession. Computer specialists working for user firms are in a much more difficult position, however. They are likely to find themselves in a serious conflict situation when the technical values of their departments are at variance with the desire of user departments to have their needs as people recognised. The solutions to these problems are threefold. First, to make computer people very much aware of the social consequences of their work so that their own value position approaches more closely the values of user departments. Second, to persuade systems designers to design systems in sociotechnical terms, so that human needs are systematically catered for in the design process. Third, to introduce integrating mechanisms into organisations faced with change so that the close association of both innovative and user groups can lead to the development of a common set of values.

6

The task contract

Another aspect of the contractual relationship between employer and employee is the nature of the work the employee is called upon to do. The employer requires the employee to perform a particular set of tasks while at the same time the employee has certain expectations concerning the kind of tasks he can legitimately be asked to undertake. The fit between these two is clearly an important element in job satisfaction yet until recently surprisingly little attention has been paid to the relationship between job content and job satisfaction and motivation. Job content has been perceived as dictated by the requirements of technology, hence it was thought that little could be done about it, that it was not a manipulatable variable (22). This may still be true of many blue-collar jobs – though the author maintains that technology is not as deterministic as management and system designers like to believe; but it is by no means true of white-collar occupations, particularly those held by specialists such as computer technologists (2, 15). With these highly talented personnel it is particularly important to ensure that the nature of the work they are called upon to do fits with their personal needs for variety, interest, control and a set of tasks that has meaning and importance. There are, as yet, few technological constraints within a data processing department, though these may arrive as the technology develops. Work can be organised in a variety of different ways and still meet management's requirements for efficiency, quality and productivity (2, 4).

It can be hypothesised that if work is too specific for specialist groups – with limited responsibility, tight job specification and considerable routine – then the fit between what the employer hopes to receive from the employee and what the employee is seeking from his work will be unsatisfactory. Specialists such as data processing personnel are likely to produce of their best if they operate in situations where work is flexible, challenging and responsible.

Any meaningful analysis of work activities as a factor in job satisfaction must be based on current theories concerning the relationship between job satisfaction and work content. These theories can then be applied to the work of our computer specialists through an examination of the tasks they performed and their attitudes to these. We shall examine the major differences between the work content of programmers and systems analysts and attempt to identify those parts of their work that they found most and least satisfying, and those skills which they saw as necessary for its successful performance. We shall also ascertain whether there were differences in the work content of people employed by users, manufacturers and consultants. Lastly, we shall check whether any firm in our three groups experienced problems because there was an unsatisfactory fit between the tasks provided by the employer and the tasks which the employee, ideally, wished to undertake.

Ideas on work content and job satisfaction

The importance of work content as a determinant of job satisfaction has been noted by many behavioural scientists including Cooper, Herbst, Vroom and Herzberg (1, 5, 22, 6, 7). Yet despite this recognition few attempts have been made to analyse jobs in such a way that their elements can be identified and categorised. The most sophisticated attempt so far has been by Cooper (1). He has built on the ideas of those psychologists and sociologists who have been interested in task structure and developed a method for classifying jobs in terms of their intrinsic characteristics (21). This analyses work in terms of four categories which he calls *physical variety, skill variety, task structure* and *goal structure.* By *physical variety* Cooper means the amount of physical differentiation which occurs within a job: the number of operations the worker performs, the number of tools he uses, the different physical locations he moves between and the number of other workers he interacts with in order to complete his tasks satisfactorily. By *skill variety* he means the application of different kinds of skill and knowledge to task problems. The more ill-defined and uncertain a job is, the more the worker has to use a variety of skills in order to complete it. If a job has skill variety it also has interest potential; it should therefore be more challenging and significant than a job which provides only physical variety.

The difference between physical variety and skill variety is the difference between job enlargement and job enrichment. Job enlargement in its least satisfactory form requires the worker merely to perform a series of simple jobs instead of just one. Critics of the approach argue that five dull and boring jobs strung together offer few advantages. In contrast, job enrichment aims to introduce a greater skill variety into work by asking the worker to develop and use a number of different kinds of skill and knowledge. Psychologists tell us that most individuals value a degree of autonomy in their work – a task or series of tasks over which they have control and can organise in their own way. Cooper suggests that autonomy increases job satisfaction because it also increases skill variety. Autonomy signifies control and choice by the worker, but choices can only be made if there are a number of alternatives to choose from. By *task structure* Cooper means the shape of tasks. The fact that all meaningful tasks have a clearly defined beginning and end and a set of activities in between, which help the successful attainment of the task objectives. A task is likely to be satisfactorily structured if it makes a clearly discernible contribution to the total product. A girl packing baby food and seeing the finished goods taken away for distribution to shops and chemists may experience more satisfaction than a girl clerk who spends her days adding up what to her are meaningless figures. In some tasks involving much time and effort and resulting in a visible piece of work, completion may be characterised by a retrospective, proprietary survey of what has been done. The individual looks with pride on what he has accomplished. In other intrinsically interesting tasks satisfaction will come from doing the job and when the task is completed there may be a feeling of regret.

Cooper distinguishes what he calls *goal structure* from goal content. By goal structure he means the act of setting or being set targets which are both clear and difficult; by goal content, the personal product of work, the fact that by working one secures a desirable objective such as money, status, security. Much of the literature on job satisfaction focuses on goal content and discusses the kind of extrinsic rewards that the individual seeks to attain through his work. This approach is known as 'instrumentality theory', with work seen primarily as an instrument for achieving other desired things. Any consideration of goal structure as opposed to goal content requires an examination of achievement motivation and a recognition of the fact that many people derive satisfaction from setting and attaining targets, particularly if these are self-imposed. The more difficult a task the more pleasurable it can be to complete it successfully. When a goal becomes easy to attain it is likely to be replaced by one that is more difficult. Cooper suggests that goal structure is related to output. Greater effort is achieved through the setting of exciting, difficult goals.

The ideal job for many people, particularly those who seek satisfaction from the work they do, will have physical variety, a degree of skill variety which uses and extends the individual's knowledge and talents, a task structure which produces a set of activities that make a visible contribution to the final product of the organisation, and a goal structure which leads to the setting and attainment of challenging targets. Cooper's analyses is a useful one because it summarises the contributions of a number of writers on the subject of job content and job satisfaction. Most of these focus their attention on skill variety as the most important element.

Herzberg's approach, applied in this country by Paul and Robertson uses an increase in skill variety as a way of enriching jobs (17). Here the employee is given the opportunity to use a wider variety of skills in his work should he wish to do so. He may be provided with opportunities to participate in the selection and recruitment of staff, in career development and in staff assessment; or, he may be allowed to assume some financial responsibility for his work through being allocated a budget or responsibility for customer credit arrangements. These opportunities are provided but there is no compulsion on the individual to accept any of them if he feels happier with a narrower type of job. This job enrichment approach contrasts with some forms of job enlargement in which the physical variety variable is the one that is manipulated and individuals are given a larger number of tasks to perform without these tasks necessarily requiring the use of additional skills.

Other researchers have brought a different perspective to bear on the problem of providing job satisfaction via work content, and have concentrated more on the goal structure variable. Locke discusses the relationship between job satisfaction and job performance and emphasises the importance of setting targets.[1] He suggests that when an individual aims for a goal and reaches it, he experiences pleasure and satisfaction, and when he fails to reach it he experiences displeasure or dissatisfaction. He also suggests that most people do try to set themselves targets. He says:

> At some point in the performance of a task an individual will almost invariably try to attain some specific standard of proficiency or attempt to reach a particular quantitative and/or qualitative goal. . . . When an individual sets himself a goal or task, reaching that goal is ordinarily experienced as pleasurable and failing to reach it is experienced as unpleasurable (12).

Locke believes that the amount of pleasure an individual feels when he reaches a goal or solves a problem depends on the importance of success to him and on how he defines success. If his goal is 'improvement' then success will be seen as an ability to improve on previous performance. Individuals will vary greatly in the difficulty of the goal they set themselves. Thus an output level that would make one man extremely happy might leave another highly dissatisfied. Individuals and groups may differ in their qualitative goals as well as their quantitative goals. Some will pursue quantity at the expense of quality, others will be temperamentally incapable of this and will always give high priority to quality.

Researchers also draw our attention to task autonomy and control as a factor leading to job satisfaction. Cooper includes this factor in his skill variety category, arguing that to control one's own work requires the use of additional high-level skills. But this appears to be such an important element in job satisfaction that it seems preferable to consider it separately. Essentially control means the use of judgment on what goals to set and what methods to use in order to reach them. Paul and Robertson build this factor into their job enrichment experiments by reducing supervision, providing opportunities for decision taking and extending responsibility (17).

This summary of ideas shows that a great deal of research has been done on those elements of job content which best meet the needs of people who seek satisfaction from work activities, and the one's discussed above – skill variety, goal structure, control and Cooper's fourth factor, task identity – appear to be the most important. But it is recognised that the application of this knowledge is made difficult by the fact that all people do not want the same things. Needs vary greatly from individual to individual and a degree of skill variety that satisfies one person may produce an extremely boring job for another. Similarly, as we have noted above, the kinds of goals that people wish to set themselves and to

[1] This point has also been discussed in chapter 4 when we referred to Locke's views on the importance of supervisory target setting.

attain may vary widely in both their quantitative and qualitative aspects. The same is true of work control – a degree of autonomy welcomed by one individual may cause intense stress in another. A further problem is that we cannot easily identify those jobs where work content is structured in such a way that it appears to satisfy the needs of the majority of their occupants. It is here that our programmer and systems analyst data should provide us with useful information.

Work content and job satisfaction in our firms

When examining the nature of the task contract in our firms – that is the extent to which the kind of work provided by employers met the needs of their employees for variety, interest, challenge, etc, – one thing stands out immediately. This is the apparent success of employers in providing their data processing staff with the kind of work they enjoyed. The answers to two questions show this clearly. These questions were, 'Have you ever regretted your decision to become a programmer (analyst)?', 'If yes or no why is this?'

Fig. 6.1 Degree of satisfaction with work choice (percentages)

Have you ever regretted your decision to become a programmer (analyst)?

	Yes	No	No answer
Users	13	87	–
Manufacturers	4	91	5
Consultants	3	93	4

If you have no regrets why is this?

	Likes the work	Other answers (Career prospects/ potential of computers)
Users	65	35
Manufacturers	50	50
Consultants	73	27

People who said they liked the work expressed great satisfaction with its interest and variety:

> The work is interesting and varied and I am my own boss.
>
> I am never bored or idle, all the jobs are different.
>
> What more could one ask for? It is intellectually satisfying and interesting. One is in the midst of innovation. One meets people who are controlling the situation everywhere.
>
> My only regret is that I did not move into the work earlier.

There must be very few jobs in industry which evoke this unbounded enthusiasm. It seems that data processing provides a continuously challenging work state for those people involved in it and many experts believe that this is the most satisfying factor in work. Leavitt suggests that people tend to program their activities so that these become routine, and then to complain that their work is uninteresting (10). They ask for the certainty of highly detailed job specifications and then complain about 'deskilling'. He believes that where tasks can be made challenging, they should be, and that this process provides greater satisfaction than the much recommended 'participation' in taking decisions and defining objectives.

Let us now look in more detail at the jobs of programmers and systems analysts, using whenever appropriate Cooper's categories of physical variety, skill variety, goal structure, control over work and task identity. This analysis may throw some light on those aspects of data processing work that makes it so interesting and stimulating.

Physical variety

This heading refers to the number of different tasks performed as part of the job and the opportunity for changes of location in the performance of these tasks. Clearly data processing specialists perform a very great variety of tasks in their work. These range from defining problems, producing methods for problem solution which are based on the use of a computer, implementing the systems they have designed and ensuring their successful operation once implemented. This is the totality of the data processing area in most firms but we have seen that these functions are split between programmers and systems analysts with the systems analyst, as a rule, taking on a larger number of different tasks than the programmer. Most research on the relevance of physical variety to job satisfaction has been carried out on shop-floor workers, but there is little or no evidence that merely increasing the number of tasks a worker has to carry out improves his satisfaction with his job (21). In computer work physical variety appears to have little significance. We have already seen that although the programmer has a somewhat narrower range of tasks than the systems analyst, he is likely to obtain just as much satisfaction from his work as the latter. The number of subsidiary tasks which make up an individual's job content therefore seems to have little bearing on job satisfaction. A study of laboratory technologists by Hall and Lawler showed that there was no association between working on a wide range of tasks and job challenge (3). Challenge came from involvement, creativity and the stretching of abilities.

The same may be true of changing one's physical location through visiting different departments either in one's own firm or in client firms. The opportunity for moving around and meeting people is frequently described as a source of job satisfaction by groups such as clerks who have little intrinsic interest in their work, and by contestants in the Miss England beauty competition whose general aspiration seems to be 'travel'. But it was never given as a source of job satisfaction by any of our computer technologists. If anything, many manufacturing and consultant staff found that it was a disadvantageous aspect of their work. The necessity for travelling around to different clients was often tiring and stressful and seriously interfered with family and social life. Being 'out in the field' meant that they were removed from the social situation of their own office and on occasion they could feel isolated and insecure. The physical variety variable therefore seems to have little relevance for the job satisfaction of programmers and systems analysts.

Skill variety

Cooper points out that the fact that a job has skill variety means that it has interest potential; it should therefore be more challenging and involving than jobs low on this dimension or containing mainly physical variety. Cooper quotes Ryan as saying:

> While we know little of the nature and conditions of interest, there can be little doubt of its importance in efficiency. Common observation indicates that work of an interesting character is not only more rewarding, but also less costly to the individual. It may be that greater improvements in efficiency can be obtained through increase in interest than in any other manner (18).

We have seen that our programmers and systems analysts did stress the interest factor in their work as a major source of satisfaction and the nature of this interest can be deduced from an examination of the kinds of skills that they told us they were called upon to use. These can be allocated within the categories which we used in chapter 2 to describe the skill and knowledge needs of our eight organisations.

1. Mental skills such as a capacity for logical and analytical thinking, problem-solving ability and imagination and creativity.
2. Technical skills associated with the use and development of computer hardware and software, together with business skills and knowledge.
3. Management and human relations skills such as a capacity for leadership and administration and skills in communicating with colleagues and subordinates.
4. Lastly, skills or more properly, attributes, deriving from a person's temperament – the ability to concentrate, persevere, work with thoroughness, etc.

Replies to the question 'what are the principal skills required in your job?' could be fitted into all these categories, although programmers and systems analysts differed in the number of references they made to each kind of skill: see Figure 6.2.

In the user group, systems analysts were more likely to refer to management and human relations skills and programmers to temperamental attributes and mental skills. In the manufacture group systems analysts were more likely to refer to technical and business skills. In the consultant group programmers were

Fig. 6.2 Principal skills required

		Percentage of total references to all skills	
		Programmers	Systems analysts
User Firms	Mental skills	44	32
	Temperament	32	18
	Management and human relations	12	36
	Technical and business knowledge	12	14
		100	100
Manufacturers	Mental skills	38	28
	Temperament	28	16
	Management and human relations	23	32
	Technical and business knowledge	11	24
		100	100
Consultants	Mental skills	39	18
	Temperament	28	13
	Management and human relations	18	43
	Technical and business knowledge	15	26
		100	100

more likely to refer to mental skills and to temperament. Systems analysts were more likely to refer to management and human relations skills and to technical and business knowledge. The greatest skill differences between programmers and systems analysts were therefore found in this group. This is curious in view of our earlier remarks in the homogeneity of the consultant group. It may be that although they believed themselves to be homogeneous this was more a state of mind than a reflection of similar task activities.

Cooper defines skill variety as task uncertainty and response uncertainty, and considers it in terms of a number of different job aspects. The first is what he calls 'object variety' – the number and complexity of the different problem areas associated with a particular task. Second is 'required interaction' – uncertainty of the demands made by people an individual is required to interact with in order to complete the task. Third is 'responsibility' which covers three factors: First the factor that Elliott Jaques has named the 'time span of discretion' – the length of time before a person's work is checked and any substandard work is identified (8, 9); second, the difficulty in the task of applying remedial action if unexpected problems occur; and third, the expense of errors in time, cash or damage terms.

Some idea of the number and complexity of the problem areas associated with the work of programming and systems analysis can be derived from looking at job descriptions. The computer technologists in our sample gave detailed descriptions of their work in terms of its technical administrative and human relations content and many described their work activities in terms of all three of these categories.

Fig. 6.3 Job content (percentages)

	Job described as			
	Technical only	Technical and administrative or technical and human relations	Technical administrative and human relations	Total
All programmers	44	36	20	100
All systems analysts	12	46	42	100

Many programmers saw their skills being used only in technical areas, while systems analysts saw their skills as having a technical, administrative and human relations orientation. In all three groups – users, manufacturers and consultants – those who saw their jobs as primarily technical tended to be under twenty-one while those who described activities which were technical, administrative and involved dealing with people were likely to be over twenty-six years of age. The fact of working for a user, manufacturer or consultant appeared to exert little influence on the distribution of work activities within the three categories. Consultants, however, had no systems analysts who saw their work as solely technical.

This breakdown gives some indication of the content of programmers and systems analysts jobs, but a better estimate of the number and different kinds of skills required in programming and systems analysis can be derived from examining the activities that people referred to when describing the technical, administrative and human relations aspects of their work. Let us consider programmers first.

Programmers

If we begin by looking at *technical* job content a measure of skill variety can be obtained by distinguishing conventional programming activity from other activities which programmers may perform and which require different kinds of skill and knowledge. Conventional programming is defined here as covering the functions described by Papetti (16). These are:

- Detailed planning of programs.
- Study of diagrams and flow charts and their documentation.
- Drawing up the sequence of instructions making up programs.
- Testing the programs on the computer, correcting them and making adjustments.
- Documentation of the programs.
- Maintenance of the programs and software.
- Revision of the programs as a result of changes in processing requirements.
- Operational responsibilities associated with the provision of a data processing service.

In addition to these functions some programmers had responsibility for certain aspects of systems analysis and systems design; others were required to have a wide knowledge of computer hardware, software and applications; others again undertook customer liaison in order to familiarise themselves with customer programming requirements. These programmers can be categorised as having specialised areas of skill and knowledge. A further small group were engaged in research and had responsibility for the development of new programming applications.

If we now analyse the activities of programmers in our firms the pattern emerges as shown in Figure 6.4.

Fig. 6.4 Activities of programmers (percentages)

		Conventional programming	*Specialised areas of skill, knowledge and responsibility*	*Research and Innovation*
Users		94	6	–
Manufacturers	A	26	68	6
	B	75	25	–
Consultants	A	22	–	78
	B	34	66	–
	C	64	28	8

These very different percentages require some explanation. In our user firms we interviewed the commercial programming groups who were generally engaged in routine programming activities. Both Industrial Products and the government department also had specialised programmers who did not come within the scope of our survey. In computer Manufacturer A programmers were concerned with sales-customer liaison and many were required to have extensive knowledge of the Company's hardware and software and to be able to advise customers on the nature of their data processing problems. These responsibilities required the majority of programmers to have a range of skill and knowledge wider than that found in the user group. In computer Manufacturer B, in the section where interviewing was carried out there was less direct contact with the customer and programming activities were more comparable with those found in the user group. The three consultants differed from each other in the kinds of skills they required of their programming staff. Consultant A was a research-based organisation and programmers there were working on highly innovative aspects of data processing. For example, the design of information retrieval systems, including on-line retrieval, on-line patient monitoring for hospitals, computer-aided systems analysis, etc. Consultant B's programmers had considerable customer contact and many of them had to have a wide knowledge of equipment and computer applications. Consultant C's programmers also had this kind of knowledge although it appeared to be located in a numerically smaller group.

Once again it must be stressed that consultant programmers and systems analysts were hard to distinguish from each other.

If the interfirm differences are ignored it can be seen that there is a progression in programmer skill variety from user group to consultant.

Fig. 6.5 Progression in programmer skill

	Conventional programming knowledge	Specialised areas of skill and knowledge	Research
Users	94	6	–
Manufacturers	50	47	3
Consultants	40	31	29

It is dangerous to generalise from these results that consultancy work always offers more skill variety than that of manufacturers and users. It would be strongly argued by both our computer manufacturers and at least one of our user firms that some of the more specialised staff working in their research and development sections would have just as much skill variety in their jobs as those of consultants. Nevertheless the trend is probably correct and it is reasonable to expect to find more people with a large amount of technical skill variety in their jobs working for consultants than working for users. It must be emphasised that these differences in skill variety were in no sense a source of job dissatisfaction. In the user, manufacturer and consultant groups the vast majority of programmers had never regretted their decision to make data processing their career and were enthusiastic about their work. The fit between the amount of skill variety that programmers were looking for and the amount provided by the firm seemed everywhere to be a good one.

In our original discussion of skill variety we pointed out that Cooper saw it covering three things: *object variety* – the number and complexity of problem areas in the task; *responsibility*, and *required interaction* with others which contained an element of uncertainty. Responsibility is impossible to define in the present context as we have no way of knowing how employers weighted the different tasks they required their programming staff to undertake. Interaction with different groups as a factor in skill variety is quite easy to evaluate. Here we found that in the user group required interaction was usually within the programming group or with the systems analysts group. In the manufacturers, in addition to interaction with internal groups, there was also interaction with clients – particularly in Manufacturer A. In the consultant group many programmers had considerable contact with clients. Interaction with others as one aspect of skill variety therefore increased as one moved from user to consultant.

It can be seen that there are considerable variations in the number and kind of technical skills found in the programming group with consultant staff generally using the greater variety of skills. Let us now see whether a variety of skills were required in the programmers' *administrative* activities. An examination of programmer's descriptions of the administrative content of their jobs shows that, in fact, administration is not an important aspect of programming. In the user group the most common form of administration was related to responsibility for a small group of subordinates. There were also a few references, but not very many, to the necessity for documenting programs and to other aspects of the planning and organisation of programming work. In the manufacturer group program documentation *was* administration for the majority of programmers. In the consultant group the programmers of Consultants A and B said that they had little or no administrative responsibilities and the programmers of Consultant C referred again to documentation. The stress laid on program documentation by the computer manufacturer's programmers suggests that it was in this group that most emphasis was given to this activity. In general, administration was not an area which provided much opportunity for the exercise of a number of different skills.

Programmers were asked to indicate how much and what kind of human relations skill they required in their work. It can be argued that those EDP staff who have to interact with non-data processing departments in their firms or with customers in other firms will operate in a more uncertain environment and require a broader range of human relations skills than those who merely relate with data processing colleagues. With the manufacturers and consultants, success in customer relationships is a major factor in success in business. In all three groups the successful implementation of EDP projects depended on effective human relationships with user areas. Set out in Figure 6.6 are the groups where programmers told us their human relations responsibilities were primarily located.

Fig. 6.6 Programmers, human relations responsibilities (percentages)

		Own department only	User departments in own firm	EDP departments and user departments in clients' firms
User firms		90	10	
Computer manufacturers	A	–	–	100
	B	67	–	33
Consultants		57	–	43

Programmers working for computer manufacturers and consultants have to liaise with the customer and therefore require human relations skills. This was especially true of computer Manufacturer A's programmers who all claimed to have some customer contact. They said:

> This is a difficult area for us. The programmer is the link man between the systems analyst and the client and the machine. He has to explain machine faults in a way

that both the systems analyst and the client can understand. Therefore he must use a great deal of tact.

Systems analysts

The job of the systems analyst is tremendously varied and provides opportunity for the use of many complex skills. Papetti defines it as covering the following activities:

1 Ascertaining existing manual or mechanised procedures and their documentation.
2 Analysis of the requirements and automation possibilities of the procedures ascertained.
3 Definition of the new organisation procedures and their documentation.
4 Design of the processes for automatic data processing and their documentation.
5 Definition of the programming systems for the implementation of processes designed.
6 Training of personnel in the organisational units concerned in the new automated procedures.
7 Starting up and implementation of the new automated procedures.

The systems analyst has therefore to use his observational and analytical skills to understand the workings of the manual system. He has to weigh up the deficiencies of the manual system and decide how it can be improved, using the potential of the computer to assist this improvement. Once he has formulated a solution to the problem he must design the new processes and procedures which forms part of this solution and, on occasion, define the programming requirements of his new system. He must ensure that staff in the user department are trained to operate the new system and he must see that the new system is successfully implemented.

Because these steps are so comprehensive and complex it was difficult to spot differences in the technical skill variety of systems analysts working for users, manufacturers and consultants. Descriptions of the technical content of their jobs given by user systems analysts fitted well into Papetti's definition: 'I am looking at the present organisation of work in user departments and trying to find better, more advantageous ways of running these departments. I then implement these new systems.'

Systems analysts working for computer manufacturers also described the technical content of their jobs in these terms but, like their programmer colleagues, they spoke a great deal about their need for considerable hardware and software knowledge, and about their advisory role. 'I must have a fairly high level of understanding of equipment and its limitations. I need a good knowledge of those computer applications which are relevant to industry's requirements.'

Once again the consultant group came out as having a wide variety of technical skills. There were references to the need for management science and operational research expertise; for management ability and for the knowledge and experience to deal with many different kinds of applications. The Consultant A systems analysts described in detail the highly innovative local government, hospital and other projects on which they were working.

> The technical content of my job varies from project to project. I must determine a client's requirements, design computer systems to meet these requirements and get hardware specifications from the computer manufacturers. I must evaluate the computer manufacturer's proposals. I must also control and direct the work of the systems analysts; produce time tables and progress the work; manage a team of people, and do public relations work with the clients.

Whereas programmers had laid claims to few administrative skills, many systems analysts saw these as a major part of their activities. One told us: 'I am an administrator. I implement new ideas and call on my experience of previous situations.'

In user firms, systems analysts saw their administrative responsibilities as covering four principal areas. The first was the organisation of their own work; the second, the management of the work of a team of systems analysts; the third, project administration covering every aspect of the implementation of a new computer system, and the fourth, documentation such as the production of proposals, reports, contracts and information for the customer.

Although major differences in the technical skills required by systems analysts have proved difficult to identify, administrative differences were much clearer, as Figure 6.7 below shows.

Fig. 6.7 Administrative skills required by systems analysts (percentages)

	Own work only	*Managing EDP team*	*Project Administration*	*Report writing etc.*
User firms	37	30	15	18
Manufacturers	24	19	22	65
Consultants	21	28	39	12

Few user systems analysts had a great deal of administration, other than organising their own activities and looking after a small team of analysts. Manufacturer's staff described the greater part of their administrative responsibilities as preparing documents of one kind or another for their customers. Consultants, in contrast, said that their administration was primarily concerned with project management and control. This was particularly the case in Consultant B, whose staff were encouraged to assume a DP management role when working with clients.

All systems analysts gave the same degree of emphasis to their human relations skill area. This involved encouraging users to look at their work from new angles, maintaining good relationships, 'selling ideas' and generally communicating what they were trying to do in a meaningful manner. Many systems analysts saw 'human relations' as the most uncertain, difficult and important part of their work.

> This [human relations content of job] is very important. It involves introducing new methods to traditional people and selling my ideas.

> It is a most important area. We work with top management and have to be able to communicate and to assist in the formulation of objectives and rational methods of managing. We have both a line and staff role when we are in a client company.

This analysis of the variety of skills required by programmers and systems analysts shows clearly that both specialisms require a multitude of skills and the use of these appears to be an important factor in job satisfaction. Indeed when asked 'What aspects of your work do you find most rewarding?' both groups tended to answer in terms of the totality of work operations.

> When one is able to create successfully by one's own efforts. One has a sense of achievement, an ability to influence events [a programmer].

> It is succeeding with a project, selling it and having it go like a bomb. Pleasing people and saving time and effort.

Programmers tended to stress the technical aspect of their work and as one moved from user firm to consultant there appeared to be an increase in technical complexity. This was not true of systems analysts and the greatest difference between those working for users and those employed by consultants was the amount and kind of administrative responsibility they were required to assume. All systems analysts placed great stress on their need for human relations skills and we have analysed the differences between the groups when discussing 'values' in chapter five.

Goal structure

This section discusses targets and objectives as a source of job satisfaction.

Cooper points out that a great deal of the literature on job satisfaction has seen work goals as extrinsic to the job itself. The theory has been that people derive satisfaction from their work, not because of what they do, but because it provides them with money, or security, or status, etc, (22). But the worker may be primarily interested in the work itself and in doing the job to his own satisfaction, according to his own or his manager's time and quality standards. If this is the case then his most important goals are intrinsic to the task itself. This may be especially true of highly qualified workers who take a pride in their own skills and abilities, and who are interested in self-development and self-improvement. Earlier in this chapter we referred to the fact that the setting of hard goals may be the greatest spur to higher performance (12). Provided the worker accepts these goals as legitimate and is interested in self-improvement, they will be more effective than financial incentive schemes or supervisory exhortation. There is some evidence to show that the setting of goals and targets works best when these are set by the worker himself, they are difficult but possible to attain, and when they form part of some conscious self-development plan. Experiments in industry with shop-floor targets set by management have shown that after their initial stimulus to higher production, interest in them can soon wane.

When we asked programmers and systems analysts which aspects of their jobs gave them the most satisfaction it was invariably stages of the job that were described and there were few references to byproducts such as independence, money or status. Programmers and systems analysts spoke with enthusiasm about the successful design of programs and systems, the successful production of output from a program or the successful operation of a system. Sometimes this last was translated into social terms and described as 'getting results for the user department'.

Fig. 6.8 Answers to the question, What aspects of your work do you find most rewarding? (percentages)

	Successful program/systems design	*Getting output from program/system*	*Seeing project in successful operation*	*Extrinsic objectives (independence etc.)*	*Other answers*
Programmers	19	49	19	3	10
Systems analysts	13	13	50	3	21

Many of the replies in the 'other answers' category were about 'establishing good relations with the user departments', which could itself be viewed as a target.

A further check that important rewards were intrinsic rather than extrinsic to the job is provided by the answers to the question, 'Why have you no regrets about taking up programming/systems analysis?' Here, it will be remembered, the vast majority answered in terms of 'liking the work' and only a comparatively small number talked about personal prospects or the future potential of computers.

Although it was apparent that targets were set sometimes by management and sometimes by the programmer or systems analyst himself, there was little criticism of the fact that they were used. Any criticism was directed at the fact that targets were not realistic, or that the monitoring to see that they were achieved was not effective. There was a general desire for high standards of work and many individuals had joined their employing company because it had a good reputation in the data processing world. In all three groups management used targets as a means of work control, but these tended to be time rather than quality targets. Deadlines were set for various stages of the system to be completed. Quality targets were set by individuals themselves and appeared to be a product of a wish to meet personal and group quality standards. They were related to such things as a desire for professionalism, a need to demonstrate competence both to one's colleagues and to user departments, and a belief that a high level of skill must be developed in data processing if it was to make its necessary impact on society.

Targets will only act as a motivating factor if there is feedback which indicates when these have been attained. Data processing appears well set up to provide this kind of feedback. Thus the programmer knows as soon as he runs his program whether it has been successfully constructed and the systems analyst knows as soon as his system is implemented whether it has been correctly conceived. Feedback is much faster for the programmer than for the systems analyst and one might therefore expect that he would find the setting of targets of more value. This was certainly true of quality targets as our last figure shows that getting successful output from a program was an important element in a programmer's job satisfaction. The same could not be said of time targets, for many programmers complained that deadlines were a major source of stress in their jobs.

The systems analyst's principal source of feedback was not the computer but the customer and with large projects results might not be seen for several years. Considerable satisfaction could, of course, be derived from the interaction between systems analyst and user as the system was being developed and from the user's acceptance that the systems analyst was working on the right lines. But this kind of feedback implies that the user knows with some precision what the systems analyst is trying to achieve and in our experience this is often far from the case. Systems analysts did derive a great deal of satisfaction and pleasure at the end of a project when the user indicated that the system was a success.

Systems analysts said:

> When you put something in and someone says 'It's one hundred per cent what we want'. This doesn't happen very often but it has happened.
>
> It is succeeding with a project, selling it and having it go like a bomb. Pleasing people and saving time and effort.
>
> It's achieving a successful installation.

There were many comments of this kind from systems analysts. All indicated that their most important job satisfaction came from designing good systems; knowing these were successful from seeing them in operation, and hearing user department staff confirm that they were an improvement on the work systems they had had before.

Task identity

The consideration here is the belief that work output has visibility and importance.

What we have said up to now supports Cooper's suggestion that an important element in job satisfaction is goal structure – the fact that targets are set and can be seen to be achieved. The comments of programmers and systems analysts which we have just quoted also support his contention that a third important factor is what he calls 'task identity' – the shape and logic of a task. Meaningful task identity will appear when tasks have a clear beginning and end; when there is a straight course to the desired goal, without the necessity for backtracking; when the goal can be achieved in a reasonable period; when successful attainment of the desired goal is apparent both to the person undertaking the task and to others; when the completion of the task assists self-development and user performance, and when the task offers opportunities for retrospective satisfaction. The fact that the work endures means that the individual can boost his morale from time to time by observing its continued success. This can happen each time the programmer runs the program he has created and each time the systems analyst passes through the department using his system and sees that it is still working successfully.

If we look at the comments of the programmers and systems analysts on those aspects of their work which provide them with the greatest satisfaction we find that many of these things are referred to. Using the Herzberg methodological approach all programmers and systems analysts were asked to describe 'an event or period of time at work which provided you with a great deal of satisfaction'. It is impossible to give all these comments but a representative sample has been selected. Programmers said, for example:

> When we first went live and saw the results coming out successfully. Anything that happened after that, although alterations could be upsetting, didn't really matter. Also I got a rise at the same time and this made me feel that my work had been appreciated.

Here we have successful completion of the task and attainment of the quality goal together with feedback on the success of the task through observation and through the pay rise.

> As a programmer I wrote a program which benefited the programming section as a whole and did this without a specification. Its outcome is that senior programmers now have a comprehensive breakdown of all programming activities. It was a useful exercise; it could be sold to other departments. I used my own initiative and this was satisfying.

Here we have an individual commenting on the satisfaction arising from doing a challenging task which stretched his abilities and required initiative, yet at the same time had a valued end product.

> My most rewarding experience was when I finished part of a payroll project. I worked alone for ten months – it was very complex. It was described in the *Computer Weekly* as 'the most complex and varied payroll ever attempted by computer'.

Again we find the satisfaction of a clearly defined task with an end product which produces recognised success. A success which is discernible not only to the individual doing the job but also to the outside world.

Systems analysts gave similar answers again stressing the importance of producing a successful end product.

> I get most satisfaction from small jobs because big ones are never finished. I had one for a traffic department. It saved work and the people there were pleased.

This comment illustrates one of the difficulties endemic in the work of the systems analyst. The fact that many of his jobs are so large that the satisfaction of seeing a totally completed job may only occur at long intervals.

> There have been many events which gave me satisfaction because I enjoy my work. The highlight I think was devising the method of pricing we are using on this project. Three of us sat down and after three weeks of brain storming came up with a system that would price anything. We had the satisfaction of developing a team spirit; also we gave a Seminar to the Sales Office on the new system, which went like a bomb.

Here again we have a difficult and challenging task successfully completed; one which provided pleasant and stimulating group interaction and also feedback on its success from the user.

> My most rewarding event is the successful implementation of a computer system and its productive running after a period of concentrated effort. This success is 1. personal and 2. a company achievement with which one can identify. People look up to you if you say you are in the computer industry.

This systems analyst worked for a computer manufacturer and saw his achievements as providing success for his company.

Although most emphasis was placed on the successful completion of a total system, people indicated that they could also achieve a great deal of satisfaction from stages along this route. For example, producing a preliminary report.

> We had a meeting this week. My proposals were accepted with minor amendments The report was seen as being of a high standard.

> Last year I enjoyed putting in a 306 at Brownings. After developing the system we ran a series of lectures for clerks to explain it. This was marvellous and the people at the lectures enjoyed them. We did this a month before the system went live.

It is interesting that all the events described by programmers and systems analysts as providing them with most satisfaction were related to the task itself. Almost all the replies to the questions, 'Can you describe an event or a period of time at work which provided you with a great deal of satisfaction?' and 'What aspects of work do you find most rewarding?' were in terms of work content, particularly the end product of a particular task – for example, producing a program or implementing a computer system and seeing it work successfully. Figure 6.9 sets out the percentages for each group.

Fig. 6.9 Aspect of work providing most satisfaction (percentages)

	The task itself	*Other factors (money, social relationships, etc)*
Programmers	92	8
Systems analysts	94	6

There were hardly any references to the rewards of receiving money, status, recognition, advancement, pleasant social relationships or any of the other factors referred to in the literature on job satisfaction. Computer programmers and systems analysts are clearly a group with a high level of job satisfaction but this satisfaction is derived primarily from the nature of the work they are required to do and from the visibility of the end product. In chapter 3 we showed that in terms of the Herzberg variables their declared needs were for self-development, responsibility and recognition. It is clear from their descriptions of the rewarding aspects of their work that they were receiving these and that computer work provides considerable opportunity for an individual to develop feelings of personal achievement.

It is always dangerous to generalise from the behaviour and attitudes of one group. However, these results do suggest that the research at present taking place into job design is likely to prove of considerable value. Computer programmers and systems analysts are a highly satisfied group. They derive their greatest satisfaction from their work and this appears to be because it meets Cooper's criteria of skill variety, goal structure, task identity and rapid feedback. These in turn allow them to fulfil their needs for achievement, self-development, recognition and responsibility. Readers might now argue that we are looking at the needs of a well-educated, highly intelligent group who are unrepresentative of most employees. To some extent this is true, but not entirely. Many of the programmers and systems analysts in our sample had not had a university education and had worked in offices or clerical jobs before transferring to the data processing department. Yet the kinds of satisfaction they derived from their work were exactly the same as those of their colleagues who possessed university degrees. Although the consultant group was recruiting staff with higher educational standards and more data processing experience than the user group, the satisfaction of the two groups was identical. Programming and systems analysis appear, although this has happened by chance, to meet an ideal standard of task structure and job design. It would be well worth investigating whether the application of the job design principles discussed here would lead to a similar degree of satisfaction in other occupational groups. Data processing is an area where the philosophy of the job reducers and job simplifiers – the followers of Taylor – has not been accepted; although there are already indications that some managements are attempting to achieve better work control through splitting up EDP activities into small, specialised sections (20). This research demonstrates very clearly the undesirability of allowing such an approach to develop. It is clear that these are lessons to be learnt from the organisation of data processing activities and at a time when increasing numbers of people are being made to do boring and meaningless work, it is exhilarating to find one group of specialists whose work seems ideally structured to provide job satisfaction.

Boundary problems

The work of the Tavistock Institute has thrown a great deal of light on the problems of group formation and group interaction. Research by Miller and Rice has shown the importance of the boundaries which delineate one group from another and give group members a sense of identity and feelings of 'belonging' and security (13). These boundaries do not exist in any physical sense, they are discontinuities either of task, time or space, between one set of work activities and another. For example, if a work group assembles a component and then passes it to another work group for painting there is a task change and hence an activity boundary between the work of the assemblers and the work of the painters. Again if a group carries out part of an activity on the day shift and another group finishes it off on the night shift, there is a time boundary. Boundaries of this kind which separate one group from another are seen as having beneficial psychological effects when they lead to systems of activities in which workers are primarily related to each other through the requirements of task performance and task interdependence. Many work groups have their activities so badly organised that the work of one group merges into the work of the next and there is no clear division of activities and hence no clear task boundary. This kind of situation can lead to low morale and to conflict as the groups fight about who does what or which group is responsible for faulty and negligent work.

Miller and Rice suggest that it is natural for large units to split up into small units and that undifferentiated large groups do not usually survive very long. Beyond a membership of around twelve, groups tend to split into subgroups. When we look at our data processing staff we find that in all eight organisations they tended to work as members of small groups or teams under a team leader. They therefore organise themselves in the way which the Tavistock researchers believe to be functional. Problems usually arise when one group has to interact with another. This involves crossing group boundaries and establishing new sets of relationships which extend further than the generally cosy relationships of an individual's own immediate work group. The setting up of relationships with another group involves the drawing, at least for a time, of new boundaries. This carries with it the danger that these new boundaries may prove stronger than the old and may be destructive to the original group. They therefore represent a threat.

The well structured group with a clearly defined boundary round its activities not only performs efficiently, it also provides a situation in which good interpersonal relationships can be developed. When the members of one such group have to interact with other groups in the course of their own work, their own group provides a refuge into which they can withdraw from time to time. This is particularly important for systems analysts whose relationships with user departments and client firms are often of a stressful and demanding character. A major responsibility of line management, according to the Tavistock thesis, is the maintenance and control of work group boundaries. Management must see that any transactions across boundaries are related to the performance of the primary task and do not threaten the group by disturbing too greatly its internal relationships and patterns of behaviour.

Herbst makes the point that all organisations need mechanisms for what he calls 'variance' control' (4). That is for detecting when work or social processes are deviating from their required paths and causing problems because of this. It must be someone's responsibility to spot that something is going wrong; to find out what is wrong; to devise methods for getting rid of the trouble; to use these methods, and to check that the disturbance has been successfully removed. Variance control would seem to be particularly important when groups with different interests have to work in close association. There is frequently a great deal of misunderstanding between groups on who has responsibility for what and on how they should relate with each other in order to fulfil these responsibilities.

Data processing groups normally interact with a number of other groups both within and outside their own firms. Two important points of interaction are between programmers and systems analysts and between data processing staff and user departments or client firms. Both of these sets of relationships can be difficult and difficulties are likely to be increased if task boundaries between the different groups are not clearly defined, leading to uncertainty on how work responsibilities shall be allocated.

An absence of clearly defined task boundaries was seen as a problem by 29 per cent of programmers and 36 per cent of systems analysts. However, another group, made up of 15 per cent of the programmers and 14 per cent of the systems analysts, suggested that problems arose not because the boundaries between one group and another were too vague, but because they were too clear cut. The reasons for their opinion given by those who suggested that an absence of boundaries caused problems are set out in Figure 6.10.

Fig. 6.10 Problems caused by an absence of task group boundaries (percentages)

	Work difficulties between programmers and systems analysts	*Management is unable to define our jobs clearly*	*User/client interface problems*
Programmers	83	–	17
Systems analysts	31	14	55

Programmers told us;

> Our DP Department is lax about the programmer/systems analyst division. It can be infuriating when programmers are working on a new job and they are asked to change an old job for an analyst. We might be better off if we were all together in one section. It would end ill feeling when things go wrong.

> Some systems analysts don't know where to fix the line. You can't define things too much for the programmer. He has no chance to develop creatively.

Programmers' complaints were principally about the poor job specifications they received from systems analysts which led to the necessity for program corrections at a late stage in the development of the program. They also spoke critically of a lack of clear divisions between the work of the programmers and systems analysts so that there tended to be a confusing area of job overlap.

Very few systems analysts referred to difficulties in working with programmers, their boundary problems were almost entirely with clients. One user systems analyst suggested that these problems were of the systems analysts' own making.

> These are problems within yourself. You know how far you can go but the O and M spirit rises when you see inefficiency. You have to ignore this but it is difficult. There are tramlines in other jobs, you know when you are stepping outside them. We do not have these.

A manufacturer's systems analyst claimed that he enjoyed the risks involved in having unclear task boundaries.

> There is the problem of knowing to what degree to spoonfeed the customer. Should one do the customer's work because there are inefficient staff at the customer's end. It is this that makes the job interesting.

This kind of opinion was common amongst the group who had not seen an absence of clearly defined task boundaries as presenting problems.

> It is the only thing which makes the work interesting.

> Not having boundaries produces the kinds of problems which many people enjoy. A lack of guidelines is interesting. Although from a management's point of view the situation may not be so good because the work is not sufficiently confined.

> I like having things this way. It is a help. One can try things on one's own initiative which might otherwise be restricted.

These comments rather conflict with the Miller and Rice position that clearcut task group boundaries are a good idea. However, whereas systems analysts regarded an absence of boundaries as a good thing because it permitted them a larger area of discretion in which to spread themselves and try out new ideas – to use greater skill variety, in fact – the user department manager's point of view might have been different. Our evidence suggests that many line managers prefer to collaborate with EDP personnel in a situation where the boundaries are clearly set and there are prescribed limits on what the innovator can and can not do.

It is clear that for many people the fact that systems analysis has a large discretionary element in it adds to the satisfaction provided by this kind of work.

Job dissatisfaction

Although the pressure to produce a good end product and to meet high standards of performance – both of which came from the individual himself – aided job satisfaction, there were other pressures in the data processing task situation which were not so positive. Chief among these was the strain of meeting deadlines. Sixty-five per cent of programmers and 51 per cent of systems analysts gave deadlines as their major source of stress and no other negative aspect of work activity was given anything like this degree of emphasis.

Fig. 6.11 Reasons for finding job stressful (percentages)

	The need to meet deadlines	*Other reasons*
Programmers	65	35
Systems analysts	51	49

Typical comments from programmers were:

> If you've got a deadline and you can't meet this. People start pushing you and the whole thing becomes a nightmare.
>
> Once a programmer gets a problem there are stresses. There is pressure to get the job out and the program won't work and takes a lot of runs to get right.
>
> It is the pressure on important jobs. One is the link between absolute disaster and success. This is extremely stressful and one gets hypertension.

With manufacturer and consultant programmers, pressure very often came from the customer.

> A customer wanted a large number of programs and I had to work ninety hours a week non-stop to provide them.
>
> It is working right through the night when clients demand very quick returns on program testing.

Programmers blamed some of this deadline pressure on unexpected snags occurring in programming, but more often the cause was seen as poor estimates of the time a program would take to complete. Programmers suggested that data processing managers gave users time estimates for jobs which were little better than guesswork and then found that they were being held firmly to these by a user who had organised his work to fit in with them. The necessity for giving users more accurate time estimates was one of the reasons why Industrial Products had made its programmers keep detailed records of their programming activities.

Systems analysts working for manufacturers and consultants were particularly subject to deadline problems. We were told:

> On every installation there is a terrible strain the month before and the month after delivery. One is trying to get it all working by the target date.

> It is the sheer volume of work and the time schedules one has to work to, and the number of people one is working with and for. For example, we may have three to four different projects on the go at one time. One has always to be prepared for the unexpected. it's a chaotic existence. One needs a 'butterfly' mind to cope. One that can jump from problem to problem.

This time pressure seemed to be the most disadvantageous aspect of the data processing work. Hall and Lawler in a study of Laboratory technologists found that the pressures most frequently reported by this group were 'time', 'quality' and 'financial responsibility' (3). Time pressures were, as with our computer personnel, related to deadlines for reports, products and proposals. Typically these deadlines were externally imposed either by customer or by higher management. Hall and Lawler concluded from their study that time pressure produced neither involvement nor performance. It caused much tension but had little or no positive utility. If anything it appeared to spoil quality by eroding the individual's assessment of his own work.

Quality pressure was a very different matter and related both to individual job involvement and organisational performance. It encouraged the professional to satisfy his need for competence in his work and provided for job challenge. This kind of pressure was generated by individuals themselves and did not come from management. Each individual had a need to conform to the perceived norms of his group by establishing a reputation as a high quality worker.

The conclusions of Hall and Lawler support the relationship described in this chapter between job design and job satisfaction. The work of our programmers and systems analysts was of a kind that generated pressure on an individual to aim for high quality and to contribute to organisational goals. It did this because it provided the necessary degree of skill variety, goals and targets, task identity and personal control to induce pleasurable feelings of challenge, responsibility and a belief that the individual was successfully developing his talents.

Hall and Lawler also found that a degree of financial responsibility acted as a motivator. Those researchers who dealt directly with customers felt that they were helping their own firm to achieve its financial goals. We did not find this in the user group whose financial accountability was somewhat indirect, and it was not an overt factor in the manufacturer and consultant groups. Here the establishment of good customer relations was perceived more in terms of preserving the reputation of the manufacturer and consultant for quality and service than of ensuring his financial viability, although clearly the one was greatly dependent on the other.

Our study has provided evidence that for data processing personnel a task structure that includes skill variety, good task indentity, clear-cut work goals with effective feedback and personal control over work activities provides high job satisfaction and considerable work motivation. One might also expect it to produce high work performance although here the evidence is harder to muster. Clearly our programmers and systems analysts believed that their work achievements were contributing very considerably to business efficiency and they were delighted when their programs and systems were praised by those departments and clients who used them. However, we have no objective evidence on how efficient and well designed these systems were. Few users would have been able to evaluate their computer system against alternative systems that might have been introduced to solve their particular problem. Locke points out that there is no necessary relationship between job satisfaction and subsequent performance (12). The fact that an individual likes his job may mean very little in terms of how he does it. He may like it because he has set easy goals for himself and attained them, or because he likes his co-workers, or because the work interests him. Thus high satisfaction may be unrelated to high production. An individual can value working at a task or engaging in a certain type of activity regardless of his degree of success or proficiency at it or any extrinsic reward obtained from it. Such tasks are what we would describe as 'interesting'. They are sets of activities which an individual likes to engage in for their own sake.

We have some evidence that this was true of our programmers and systems analysts. When the data processing managers of two of the user firms and one computer manufacturer rated their staff in terms of their creativity and efficiency on a five point scale, ranging from very low to very high – we found that a considerable number of programmers and systems analysts were rated low on these two factors. This occurred despite the unanimous enthusiasm for data processing amongst staff. Those programmers and systems analysts who had a narrow approach to their work and who described it in purely technical terms tended to fall into this category of poor performers. This was a group who did not perceive the skill and knowledge potential of their work and who were not very competent in the skills they did use.

Those who did not see their job as stressful were also rated low on efficiency, although not creativity, suggesting that in the eyes of their supervisors they avoided stress by not getting too involved in their work. This group contained many who told us they were seeking security rather than advancement; who were not very interested in self-development and who placed a high importance on their personal lives. Altogether a group who did not fit in with their own managers' ideas on correct work attitudes. There were also statistical relationships between those who were rated low on efficiency and creativity; those who were thinking of leaving their present employer, and those who were uncertain about the appropriateness of their present salary level.

Programmers and systems analysts who were rated high on creativity and efficiency were very much company men. They had joined their firms because they approved of their community image and once there they had never considered leaving. They did not think that programmers and systems analysts should be allowed a great deal of freedom and they saw having the right temperament as the essential attribute for success in data processing.

Locke suggests that job satisfaction is a product of high performance rather than a determinant of it and our data would support this conclusion. It must be remembered, however, that performance evaluation is a very subjective matter and there may be little uniformity between an individual's assessment of his own performance and his supervisor's assessment.

Conclusions

The analysis contained in this chapter shows that the nature of programming and systems analysis and the structure of tasks that comprise the programmers' and systems analysts' work responsibilities are major determinants of job satisfaction. The way data processing jobs have developed has led to a set of tasks that broadly conform with the ideas of Cooper and others on how jobs should be designed if they are to provide job satisfaction and motivation. We have seen that our data processing personnel sought self-development, responsibility, recognition and interesting work and they believed that their jobs provided them with all of these. They were able to direct their activities towards clear-cut and difficult objectives with a visible end product and this was another source of satisfaction. They also had the psychological uplift of knowing that they were working with a new and rapidly developing technology which they believed was making a major contribution to business efficiency. They were very much what psychologists call 'integrated workers'. These are people, generally of middle-class origin, who are personally involved in their work and have aspirations of upward occupational mobility. Work has meaning for them and they expect to derive important satisfaction from it. They like their work when, as in the case of the specialists we have examined here, the satisfactions they seek are in fact provided.

Shepard suggests that these kinds of people are imbued with the middle-class work values of variety, autonomy, control etc, (19). In contrast, he claims, blue-collar workers have few expectations. They view their jobs instrumentally – as a vehicle for securing the means to engage in non-work pursuits. Money is their aim and personal involvement is negligible. They are what sociologists call 'alienated' and they shun autonomy, responsibility and higher status. It is thought that this condition of 'alienation' is not just a product of the work people do but also of attributes they bring with them into the work situation and which are a result of their early social conditioning.

This point of view seems unduly pessimistic as it leads to the logical conclusion that there is little point in redesigning the jobs of manual workers to make them more interesting for nothing will be achieved by doing this. Few manual workers' jobs, outside the traditional and new crafts, incorporate the job design elements which Cooper believes lead to job satisfaction. There is therefore little evidence that providing these elements would be a waste of time and some evidence from the job enrichment work of Herzberg and others that an increase in the job satisfaction could result; providing always that there is a good fit between organisational and worker needs on our other four variables – the use of skills and knowledge, psychological needs, controls and the effort reward bargain and social values. It is likely that our present educational system is creating a different set of expectations in young people from those held by their fathers, and that dull and routine work will cause them intense frustration which will not be compensated for by high earnings. Well-designed jobs may lead to both increased satisfaction and increased performance for it is thought that the relationship between satisfaction and performance becomes more positive as the level of skill required by the job increases (11).

The belief that one is performing meaningful work – the task identity factor – is seen by Cooper as an important motivator and source of job satisfaction and our data would certainly support this. However, the survey described here was carried out in the late 1960s when considerable euphoria surrounded computer applications. More recently, with the deteriorating economic situation of the early 1970s, there has been much criticism of computer applications both in terms of their utility and their financial viability. These adverse reactions, together with some redundancy amongst computer personnel, may have led to a reduction in confidence and a survey today might show less enthusiasm for the work and more uncertainty about the advantages of some of the EDP systems which have been produced. Up to now the criterion of success in computer technology has been that a new system has led to an improvement in existing work processes. Whether this happens or not can be assessed by the non-professional, for example, the line manager or the company director. Increasingly these computer users have been expressing doubts about the extent of the improvement that has resulted from new computer systems. There have been suggestions that computer people focus their attention too much on the technical consequences of their work and do not pay enough attention to the business consequences and to the human consequences of computer systems (14). This new questioning form of feedback may be making the computer man think more carefully about the nature of his role and responsibilities and is perhaps causing him to be a little less confident in the correctness of some of the changes he produces. However, this is speculation and our survey evidence portrays a group of enthusiasts, with a great liking for their work and considerable confidence in the virtues of what they are doing.

All that remains to be said here is that computer work as performed by our programmers and systems analysts appears to possess almost ideal job characteristics. Our evidence fully supports the conclusions of the experts in job design who plead for more jobs structured in terms of skill variety, task identity, autonomy, clearly perceived objectives and targets and effective feedback. We cannot generalise and say that because this kind of task structure meets the needs of computer technologists it will also meet the needs of all other groups. But it seems well worth while to continue and extend the research that is going on into the principles of job design in order to test the hypothesis that what holds good for computer technologists also holds good for other occupational groups.

7

Job satisfaction and organisational health

In chapter 1 we described how the relationships between an organisation and its employees can be viewed as a series of contracts. These contracts are not normally written down or even made verbally explicit but they nevertheless exist and govern the expectations that both employers and employees have of each other. If there is a good 'fit' between the attitudes and activities that the organisation requires of its employees and those that they are willing and able to supply, and between the needs the employees seek to fulfil in work and the willingness and ability of the organisation to meet these needs, then the satisfaction of both management and subordinates should be high and the organisation should be internally healthy and viable.[1]

In the previous chapters we have been examining the attitudes of computer specialists to their work while at the same time attempting to identify their needs as individuals together with the needs of their employing organisations. The latter are seen as being influenced by pressures exerted by the environment in which the organisation operates, such as product market, and by internal culture, technology or administrative function. In this final chapter we shall summarise our conclusions on the success of the five contractual relationships – the knowledge, psychological, efficiency, ethical and task structure contracts – for both data processing personnel and the three employing groups, users, computer manufacturers and consultants.

We have seen that whether job attitudes are positive or negative – that is, whether individuals are satisfied or dissatisfied with different aspects of their work situation – is a result of their weighing up their needs, expectations and aspirations in work against their actual work experience. If the fit between what people seek from work – and this may be a very complex set of wants – and what they actually receive is a good one then it can be said that they have *high job satisfaction*.

[1] In sociological terminology the first 'fit' can be described as employee *role behaviour* meeting organisational *role requirements* and the second as employee *need dispositions* being catered for by organisational *need provisions*.

But, although job satisfaction is clearly an important factor in organisational health it must be accompanied by a degree of cooperation and an identity of interest between the organisation and its employees, and by efficiency and profitability. High job satisfaction can be found in poorly managed enterprises and without the concepts of cooperation, efficiency and profitability, the organisation will have difficulty in surviving. Hence the importance of the good fit between what the organisation is requiring of its employees and what they are motivated to provide. If this fit exists then it should lead to *effective working relationships*.

In these days of rapid changes in consumer demand and in technology, the slow-moving organisation will find its markets slipping away and its plant becoming obsolete. A third most important factor in organisational health is therefore the ability of the organisation to respond rapidly to those changes in its external environment which can affect its ability to survive and prosper. There should be a good fit between the speed at which environmental factors alter and produce new pressures and demands and the adaptive capacity of the organisation. When this fit exists there will be requisite *organisational flexibility*.

Lastly, the organisation will be unable to adapt successfully unless it has the internal resources in skills and knowledge to enable it to do this. When the fit between the required adaptation and the availability of resources to facilitate this adaptation is good we have *organisational development*.

Thus the healthy organisation requires *job satisfaction*, *effective relationships*, *organisational flexibility* and a capacity for *organisational development*.

The four fits described above are summarised below.

FIT 1 Between individual needs, expectations and aspirations in work *and* the individual's work experience

= JOB SATISFACTION

FIT 2 Between organisational needs (translated into role requirements from staff) and the ability and motivation of the employee to meet these needs

= EFFECTIVE RELATIONSHIPS

FIT 3 Between environmental demands *and* the ability of the organisation to respond to these

= ORGANISATIONAL FLEXIBILITY

FIT 4 Between the amount and kind of required adaptation *and* the availability of resources within the organisation to enable it to adapt successfully in the short and the long term

= ORGANISATIONAL DEVELOPMENT

Fit 1 and Fit 2 above, when combined, form the fit between *organisational and employee needs* on the five contractual variables and the diagram below sets these out in simplified form for our computer specialists. Fit 3 and Fit 4 have not been considered in detail in this book, although they have formed part of the investigations of computer-based change carried out by the Computer Research Unit at Manchester Business School and will be examined in a subsequent publication.

Fig. 7.1 Individual needs and individual experience = Job satisfaction (Fit 1)

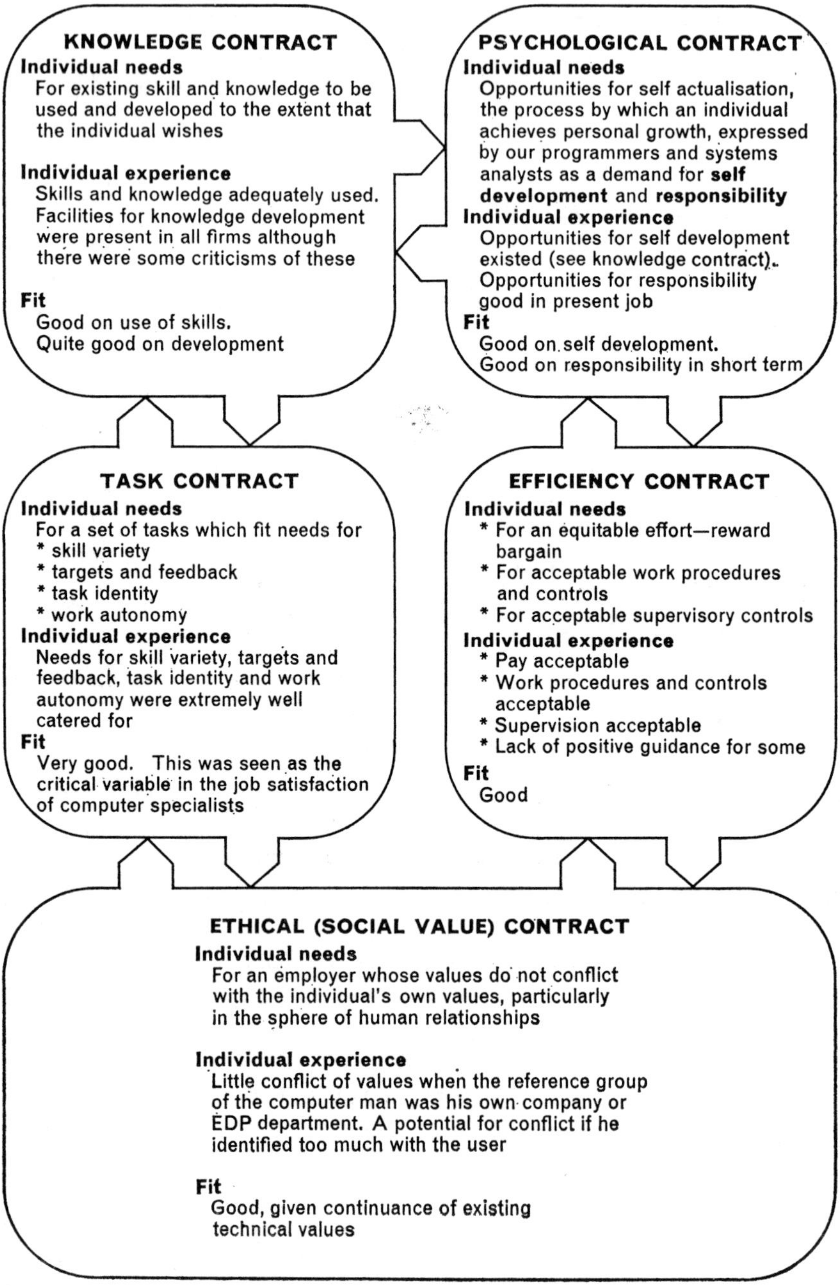

FIT 1 Individual needs and the individual's work experience = Job satisfaction

At an early stage in this study it became clear that other researchers had approached the subject of job satisfaction from many different angles and that while existing literature contained much valuable information this suffered from a lack of integration. Yet it was impossible to examine job satisfaction without a theoretical framework by which to systematically examine those needs and experiences which influence attitudes to work. This theoretical framework was derived from the writings of Talcott Parsons, although in the interests of clarity and simplicity Parson's analytical categories have been renamed and redefined. Parsons' theoretical approach was valuable because it could be applied to both individual and organisational needs and because it provided a means for integrating earlier research into job satisfaction. The needs of the individual in work were placed in the following five categories:

1. KNOWLEDGE NEEDS

The need of the individual:

- to have utilised, to the extent that he wishes, the skill and knowledge which he brings with him when he joins his employer.
- to have this skill and knowledge increased – again to the extent that he wishes – through the work he does for his employer and for this improved level of ability to be utilised.

2. PSYCHOLOGICAL NEEDS

For all or some of the following needs to be met:

- self-development
- responsibility
- recognition
- advancement
- status.

These have been described as motivating factors, which, it is believed, lead to feelings of job satisfaction when catered for.
Also:

- pleasant social relationships
- job security
- a firm or department with a good image and reputation
- the opportunity for pursuing his private interests, e.g. social and family life.[1]

[1] Some of these factors can be legitimately placed in our other contractual areas depending on the orientation of the individual and how he defines his needs. For example, for some people job security is a psychological need, for others it is an economic need.

These are hygiene factors which, it has been suggested, if not present lead to feelings of job dissatisfaction.

These psychological needs are the factors found by Herzberg to exert a significant influence on attitudes to work, although they have been modified to suit the logic of this research (4, 5). For example, when we examined the Herzberg factors in chapter 3 we included work interest as a motivator and salary as a hygiene factor because Herzberg had done this. Clearly salary fits more appropriately into our efficiency contract and work interest into our task structure and we have transferred them there. The factors which we now include as likely psychological needs are all extrinsic to work; that is, they are byproducts of work, achieved through doing work but not forming part of work activities. Not everyone will have the same number or mix of psychological needs and variations will occur which are related to age, sex, family and educational background and occupation.

3. NEEDS IN RELATION TO THE EFFICIENCY CONTRACT

That the organisation in striving for efficiency should:

- provide an equitable effort-reward bargain. That is, ensure that the individual receives the financial reward for his services that he considers appropriate. and also, should not:
- impose quality and output standards and controls upon the individual of a kind that he considers unreasonable.

4. ETHICAL OR SOCIAL VALUE NEEDS

The need of the individual to work for an organisation whose philosophy and values do not contravene his own.

5. TASK NEEDS

The need to perform a set of tasks which fit personal needs for:

- physical variety
- skill variety
- well-defined targets with feedback to show that these targets have been attained
- task identity and autonomy.

All these are intrinsic to the task itself and concern the skills and decisions associated with producing a product which in turn relate to the manner in which work is organised and the technology that is associated with it. When people speak of wanting 'interesting work' it is these intrinsic factors to which they are usually referring.

Let us now review our findings on the needs of programmers and systems analysts in the user, manufacturer and consultant groups and decide how successfully each category of individual needs was being catered for by the employing organisation.

Knowledge needs

Middle-class occupations as a rule offer more satisfactions than working class and white-collar workers with specialist skills and knowledge acquired through training will have certain expectations on how these should be used (2). They will suffer frustration if they believe that their talents are being underutilised. New specialist groups, such as computer personnel, who are associated with a recent and complex technology and whose skills are a scarce and valuable commodity are likely to be particularly concerned that their knowledge is put to proper use.

We found that programmers and systems analysts *did* want their talents to be used in a manner they thought to be appropriate and that this wish was well catered for in all three groups. There were no complaints of knowledge underutilisation. On the contrary, they expressed great enthusiasm for the work that they were required to do and made many approving comments on its challenge and complexity. Opportunities for developing further skills and knowledge were provided by employers through internal and external training courses and our User group, which tended not to recruit data processing staff who had a great deal of EDP experience, relied on such courses and on-the-job training to bring their own specialists up to the required skill and knowledge level. At the time of our survey the British Computer Society was in the process of introducing its professional examinations but these had not yet become a recognised method for acquiring data processing skills.

The fit between needs and experience on this knowledge variable was therefore good. There was no major divergence between how programmers and systems analysts thought that their talents should be used and how they perceived that they were being used. They spoke enthusiastically about their work and there was a general belief that they were being intellectually stretched.

Psychological needs

Programmers and systems analysts differed somewhat in their psychological needs. The only need that more than two-thirds of programmers in all eight firms indicated was important to them was *self-development*. There was little agreement after this and no major differences between the three groups. For example, although a majority of programmers in four firms said that responsibility was important to them these firms were spread between user, manufacturer and consultant groups.

There was greater consensus within the systems analyst group. More than two-thirds of systems analysts in all eight firms expressed a need for opportunities for *self-development* and more than two-thirds in seven firms expressed a need for *responsibility*. In both groups the factor in our list of Herzberg variables that was least sought after was job security.[1] This was almost certainly a consequence of the looseness of the labour market at the time of the survey and the unsatisfied demand for programmers and systems analysts.

Self-development

Self-development means different things to different people although always in relation to an idea of personal growth. Some individuals may seek to become wiser and more imaginative; others to improve at exercising authority and taking decisions; others to achieve breadth of learning and an interdisciplinary approach; others again to increase particular areas of specialist knowledge. The interpretation of self-development made by the individual is greatly influenced by his personal environment and the groups of which he is a member (2). He seeks to live up to what is expected of him by those groups to whom he looks for status and approval.

Our programmers and systems analysts saw self-development in terms of increasing their specialist skills and knowledge and so there was an overlap between the knowledge and psychological contracts. If the knowledge contract was unsatisfactory then psychological needs could not be met. With occupational groups seeking other forms of psychological satisfaction in work this overlap would not occur.

The fact that self-development emerged as the most important psychological need re-emphasised the importance of the knowledge contract and of the organisation being able to provide its EDP staff with opportunities to increase their skills and knowledge. It seems likely that with specialist groups of this kind the ability to learn and go on learning is an important element in job satisfaction. We have seen that the mechanics for assisting the desired form of self-development existed in all three groups. All employers offered training to their data processing staff and in the user group almost all programmers and systems analysts had been on short courses of some kind. Some had participated in as many as seven or eight different kinds of course.

Similarly, in the manufacturers and consultants there were plenty of educational opportunities and here also many individuals had taken a large number of different EDP courses. The exception was Consultant A, which was newly formed at the time of our survey. This consultant now provides excellent training facilities both for its own staff and for the staff of clients. The training provided for programmers tended to be narrower than that provided for systems analysts and this was understandable for in most firms programmers were at an earlier stage in their careers. Programmers tended to have taken programming courses only – although the government department was an exception here – whereas systems analysts had been on a wide variety of EDP courses.

Despite this excellent course provision more than 50 per cent of staff in all

[1] It will be remembered that salary, which came bottom of the need hierarchy, is seen as an economic need and is discussed in the efficiency contract.

three groups were intending to take further courses, and this intention to continue self-development was particularly strong in the manufacturer group. Programmers were interested in learning additional languages while systems analysts wished to broaden their areas of knowledge and acquire skills in real time applications, communications and management science subjects. Most programmers and systems analysts saw these courses as a means for developing the talents they already possessed, adding to their market value and helping them to keep up with a rapidly accelerating technology.

In the user group labour turnover was generally low and so data processing staff were to a large extent dependent on their employers for further EDP training. In the manufacturer and consultant groups labour turnover was high and length of service comparatively short and it seemed that people were using the loose labour market of the time as a method for gaining additional data processing experience.

Self-development, for most people, was restricted to data processing and related topics. There was little interest in acquiring a knowledge of business subjects such as finance or marketing, and surprisingly little interest in the skills of management.

The fit between the demand for opportunities for self-development and employers' provisions to enable this self-development to take place was good, but not as good as programmers and systems analysts would have liked. There was some criticism of the manner in which courses were organised; teaching was seen as mechanistic and unimaginative with too much reliance on textbook material, and course standards were often regarded as low. The fact that the quality and level of teaching was criticised in this way is yet another indication of the strength of the motivation to learn amongst programmers and systems analysts. It is not easy to think of other occupational groups which are fired with this enthusiasm for more and more knowledge. The reaction of many staff to company courses is one of reluctance and a feeling that they are wasting time away from the job. Users, manufacturers and consultants were able to provide the necessary training facilities and required time off, and this was appreciated, but they were not seen as entirely successful in what was taught and how it was taught. A common problem here was the difficulty of finding competent teachers. Individuals were not prepared to teach others if by doing this they restricted their own opportunities to learn and thus impeded personal self-development.

Responsibility

Responsibility, the need that came second, was also well catered for, at least in the short term. In each group a third or more programmers and systems analysts had responsibility for the work of colleagues within their departments. Most described their work in broad terms, indicating that it had technical, human relations and administrative content, although programmers had little administration. Comments about responsibility never took the form that there was too little of this, rather that on occasions there was too much, particularly when deadlines for new systems were approaching.

Opportunities for obtaining increased responsibility through promotion were less satisfactory although for many people these were a long-term rather than a short-term need. In all three groups 50 per cent or more of programmers and systems analysts were not anxious to move into more senior jobs at the time they were interviewed. Those higher status jobs which were seen as desirable were invariably located within the data processing function. The exception here was the government department where 60 per cent of those saying they would like promotion spoke of moving outside EDP into other clerical functions. In this they were no doubt following the normal civil service tradition of moving from one specialism to another as part of a planned progression up the promotion hierarchy.

Although many people were interested in responsibility, this was perceived as a product of work rather than a span of control. It was defined as being responsible for a difficult and important programming task or a challenging new system, and not in the traditional sense of running an office and controlling large numbers of staff. The fact that half our programmers and systems analysts were not interested in immediate promotion did not mean that this was not an eventual objective. Many of them saw EDP management as their ultimate job ambition, and a fair proportion hoped to be in EDP management jobs within five years. The percentages with these aspirations are set out in Figure 7.2.

Fig. 7.2 Aspiration to promotion (percentages)

	Users	*Manufacturers*	*Consultants*
Kind of job in five years' time			
EDP manager or consultant			
Programmers	13	21	42
Systems analysts	34	68	67
Ultimate job ambition			
EDP manager or consultant			
Programmers	37	32	29
Systems analysts	27	32	27

There are some interesting differences here. User programmers were the group most likely to see EDP consultancy or management as the pinnacle of their career, although only 13 per cent saw themselves achieving this within five years. This conservatism was not related to age, for in Industrial Products and the government department programmers were a mature group. Two-thirds of systems analysts in both the manufacturer and the consultant groups hoped to be EDP managers within five years, but more than half of these did not make this their ultimate job ambition; they hoped to later move into senior non-EDP management.

In the short term the fit between the programmers' and systems analysts' need for responsibility and the amount of responsibility they carried was good. But there were likely to be problems in the future as people sought to increase their responsibility through promotion to EDP management. Figure 7.3 shows the percentage of programmers and systems analysts who viewed their promotion prospects with misgivings.

Fig. 7.3 Promotion prospects in present firm poor or nil (percentages)

	Users	*Manufacturers*	*Consultants*
Programmers	26	24	24
Systems analysts	46	18	30

The highest percentage of people who saw future promotion problems in their firms was located among user and consultant systems analysts. Only in the manufacturer systems analysis and consultant programming groups did *less than* 25 per cent see their promotion prospects as poor.

Needs relating to the efficiency contract

Pay

The attitudes of occupational groups to their earnings are complex and often difficult to interpret. Research has suggested that there are major differences in the way blue-collar and white-collar groups regard the relationship between work and their pay packets. Thus manual workers have been seen as holding an instrumental orientation towards work, regarding it as valueless in itself but a means for securing money by which to meet domestic and leisure needs. In contrast, the professional white-collar worker has been viewed as deriving a great deal of intrinsic satisfaction from his work activities with financial rewards often of secondary importance to the pleasure of performing a worthwhile task. There is evidence to support these propositions, but they are so general as to be of little use in assisting an understanding of attitudes to pay (3, 12). Although the blue-collar worker is likely to have a different mix of needs in work from the white-collar worker it is clear that the satisfactions he derives from work are by no means all economic. Women workers, for example, enjoy the opportunities for social interaction that the work situation provides. Manual workers, generally male, with a desire for power may derive considerable satisfaction from waging a 'war game' with management and the organisation of a strike can provide as much satisfaction as its successful financial conclusion.

Similarly, professional groups may focus all their attention on pay at times when they believe that their salaries have fallen below expectations of what they should legitimately receive. We have recently seen this happen with teachers and nurses, all of whom are said to derive considerable intrinsic satisfaction from the work which they perform.

A further complication is that the importance an individual places on his earnings level is likely to vary throughout his working life. Young unmarried men, whether working on the shop floor or in the office, will have a less pressing need for money than married men who are buying houses and starting families (10). Again, for some people earnings are less a way of meeting economic needs and more a vehicle for proclaiming personal status; for others they are the means for securing the basic necessities of life.

Little importance was placed on salary by our programmers and systems analysts and when they were asked to indicate which of the Herzberg factors were important to them money was the one that fewest people sought. We interpreted this primarily as a reflection of the high salaries that were being paid at the time rather than as a lack of interest in financial rewards, but attitudes may also have been influenced by the youth and unmarried state of many programmers and by the fact that status in the EDP world was not indicated by salary level but by knowledge and expertise. For all these reasons the fit between what people perceived to be a fair salary and what they received was generally good. The loose labour market for programmers and systems analysts meant that employers were afraid that they would lose their best EDP specialists if salary needs were not met.

Some dissatisfaction with salaries was found in the mail order company at the time that the labour government was imposing its earnings freeze, but as soon as this was eased the firm moved into its cumulative bonus scheme and this provided considerable financial reward to individuals who were prepared to stay a number of years with the company. There was also some dissatisfaction with salaries in computer Manufacturer B and in Consultant A. But, despite these exceptions, more than three-quarters of programmers and systems analysts were not dissatisfied with their pay levels and more than 50 per cent were actively satisfied. Thus the fit between personal evaluation of financial worth and the level of earnings paid by employers was generally good.

Work procedures and controls

Specialist staff do not normally suffer from the imposition of rigid bureaucratic procedures and controls and our programmers and systems analysts were no exception. The mail order company and the three consultants had organic modes of management and kept formal rules and procedures to a minimum. The manufacturers, Industrial Products and the government department preferred to take a more structured approach and set out many of their work instructions in documentary form but, despite this variation in management practice, there were few complaints from staff on this issue and it was apparent that people did not think that they were being subjected to unnecessary rules and regulations.

The fact that there was little formalisation of work procedure did not mean that there were no work controls. All firms had methods for ensuring that quality standards and time targets were met although these varied in their degree of formality. The only firm where a majority of staff came out strongly against the use of formal controls was the mail order company where management preferred to use informal methods. In the consultants there was considerable flexibilty of work procedure allied to the use of formal work controls. Criticisms here were not about the fact that these controls existed but rather that they were not effective. It seemed that programmers and systems analysts, although they operated in a flexible, organic, work environment, still welcomed the security of a formal control mechanism against which performance could be measured. Although consultant staff would not tolerate much interference from management on how they did their work, they welcomed checks to help ensure that the end product was produced on schedule and to the required quality standard.

This finding is interesting as management literature often assumes a continuum from bureaucratic forms of management with specified work methods and tight controls to organic management with the employee devising his own methods, setting his own standards and devising and operating his own controls. The fact that our programmers and systems analysts approved of personal control over work methods but liked the security of formal management control over the end product suggests that this kind of procedural mix provides specialist staff with freedom and security at one and the same time.

Supervision

There was unanimity on the preferred form of supervision. In all three groups, good supervision was described as flexible and employee centred, and tight, production orientated supervision was viewed as inappropriate for computer work. However, many people again stressed the need for work controls and said that this flexible form of supervision should be associated with the setting and achieving of targets. This desire for supervisory target setting was particularly strong in the manufacturers and consultants; less so in the user group where staff were more protected from the urgent pressures of the product market.

Satisfaction with the form that supervisory control took was good and in no firm were a majority of staff fundamentally unhappy with the supervision they received. Complaints were about too little supervision, reflected in a lack of positive guidance, rather than too much. The supervisor was viewed as a resource person or enabler, whose function was to help the programmer or systems analyst to perform his job more effectively. Complaints about lack of supervision came mainly from the younger age groups – people who perhaps lacked confidence and felt the need for a degree of guidance in their work. But the chief general criticism of supervisors concerned their inability to set realistic work targets. This led to rushes at the end of jobs when it became plain that the time estimate given by the supervisor to the client had in fact been too optimistic.

The fit between supervisory behaviour and employee needs was therefore generally good. Programmers and systems analysts liked the permissive approach of supervision although there was some discontent over the supervisors' poor work scheduling. As with work controls it seemed that computer staff were seeking freedom allied with security. But whereas a permissive approach was universal with first-line supervision, who would have found it difficult to relate with their high powered specialist staff in any other way, this form of employee-centred supervision was not always subscribed to by the individual heads of EDP departments. They tended to be more influenced by the overall culture of the company than their first-line managers. They too sought to feel secure and a number said that they preferred rules, standard procedures and controls to permissiveness and adaptability.

Ethics and social values

In chapter 5 we suggested that an often unrecognised factor in job satisfaction is the need for the philosophy and values of the employing organisation, and particularly the employee's own departmental group, to broadly fit with the individual's own set of values. If this fit does not exist then the individual may find himself in situations where he is expected by his employer to act in ways which he believes to be morally wrong.

Individuals may wish to work for an organisation which fits their value position in the majority of its practices. Alternatively, they may not care too much about the philosophy of the organisation as a whole so long as the ethics and values of their unit or department are broadly in accord with their own. Values are brought by the individual to the job and also moulded on the job. They are formed through his early experiences in the family, and at school and university, and influence how he believes he should treat the people with whom he associates and how he wishes to be treated by them. Traditional values are of an acceptance of authority and loyalty to the organisation. These are now being challenged as inappropriate to modern needs and our new technocrats are seen as being more influenced by technical values than by either traditional or people-centred values. If this is true then they are likely to have relationship problems with other parts of the organisation where values are conditioned by other influences.

It has been pointed out that scientific and technological advance is the notion which has shaped western society, virtually dominates it today, and shows signs of extending its dynamic to the whole of human society (3). Progress is equated with things that are bigger, newer and faster and the modern catchwords are 'efficiency', 'competitiveness', 'growth' and 'technical change'. But, while most people accept this philosophy in principle if not always in practice, these new values are interpreted in different ways in different parts of the organisation. Thus, while the computer man sees the computer as the means to achieve progress, the line manager may prefer a different method for attaining the same objective. One with which he is more familiar and feels more secure.

We had hypothesised that there were likely to be value differences between users, manufacturers and consultants. Whereas computer specialists working for users might not be too concerned about the overall philosophy and culture of the firm, they would be very identified with the culture of their own department. In contrast, in the manufacturer and consultant firms closeness to the product market was likely to influence the values of the company as a whole with the result that they would be market-dominated concerns, the manufacturers selling a visible product and the consultants providing a problem-solving service.

The only firm in which there appeared to be a major divergence between the values of the data processing department and the rest of the company was the mail order company where computer specialists were generally recruited from outside and brought with them an innovating philosophy which was shared and reinforced by their departmental colleagues. They viewed themselves as a ginger group and the rest of the organisation as conservative, slow moving and resistant to much needed computer developments.

In the user and manufacturer groups programmers associated mainly with programming colleagues in their own, or in the case of manufacturers, in client data processing departments. In the consultant group this was less the case and consultant programmers had client contact with both EDP and non-EDP staff. But we found major differences in the interaction of the systems analyst group as the figure below shows.

Fig. 7.4 Groups with which systems analysts had the most contact (percentages)

	EDP staff only, in own or client firm	*User department staff in own or client firm*
Users	5	95
Manufacturers	72	28
Consultants	7	93

It can be seen that the systems analysts of manufacturers were much less in contact with non-data processing staff than the systems analysts of other groups and were therefore less likely to have to work with people whose values differed radically from their own.

We also found differences between the attitudes of staff working for manufacturers and attitudes in the user and consultant groups. These differences concerned the nature of relationships with others when new computer systems were being introduced. The computer manufacturers, who were talking to their own kind, relied primarily on a selling or information providing approach. The user and consultant staff, who had greater contact with people with little or no knowledge of data processing technology, spoke much more of joint discussions and attempts at a mutual problem-solving approach.

Conflicts of values of a kind that might affect morale were more likely in the

o

user group than in the manufacturers or consultants. User group systems analysts had to work closely with user departments in their own organisations, many of which had little understanding of, or enthusiasm for, computer-based innovation and saw the EDP department as a new power centre against which they had few sanctions. The policy of internal recruitment in Industrial Products and the government department helped here by creating a group in the EDP department which had absorbed company culture over many years, were identified with company values and had many ex-colleagues and friends in line departments.

Surprisingly, the percentages of programmers and systems analysts who said that they experienced conflicts of loyalty between the interests of their own departments or companies and the interests of user departments or clients was the same for both users and manufacturers – 49 per cent. Less conflict of this kind was experienced by consultants and only 29 per cent said that they had been in situations which caused them to feel a conflict of loyalties.

Whether there was a good fit between the personal value position of the individual programmer and systems analyst and that of the organisation by which he was employed or the groups with which he interacted depended on which of these he took as his principal reference group. If this was his own EDP colleagues or the data processing staff of client firms, then he was less likely to experience a serious clash of loyalty and values, for the group to which he looked for influence and approval operated from a value position similar to his own. If, in contrast, he made non-EDP staff his reference group, and user and consultant programmers and systems analysts would be more inclined to do this than those employed by manufacturers; then on occasion he might find himself torn between the technical interests and values of his EDP colleagues and the needs of user departments for social and work stability and mental and economic security.

A good 'fit' on values therefore depended on the individual's principal reference group. This could be one of the following:

REFERENCE GROUP	CONFLICT POTENTIAL
1 Own or client EDP department	little potential conflict of values
2 Own company as a whole	little conflict if working for manufacturer or consultant. Some potential for conflict if working for a user, between EDP technical/rational values and the traditional values of the firm. (The avoidance of this form of conflict was assisted in Industrial Products and the government department by internal recruiting.)
3 User department	A potential for conflict here if the computer man's identification with user interests impedes the speedy realisation of

the EDP department's interests. (For example, if the computer man wished to obtain the user department's complete understanding of and agreement to all changes before proceeding.)

Career intentions are likely to be an important factor in how the individual selects the reference group with which he identifies most completely. Those computer specialists intending to move into line management, a small number as we have seen, might be more responsive to user department worries and more anxious to establish and maintain good long-term user relationships. Their future lay with the user department and not with the EDP group.

For the majority of programmers and systems analysts in our eight organisations, the fit between their personal values and the values of those groups with which they most closely identified was good. The potential for a conflict of values was less for staff working for manufacturers and consultants. The reference group for the staff of manufacturers was their own company and they accepted its working ethos. The consultant staff saw little conflict of interest between the needs of their own firms and those of their clients. In the user group computer staff working for Industrial Products and the government department tended to have worked in other parts of the organisation before moving into EDP and so accepted organisational philosophy and culture. In the mail order group the computer staff were a tightly knit group who saw it as their function to introduce change and innovation into a conservative firm. They therefore regarded their lack of identification with overall company values as functional to their own objectives.

Two aspects of the data processing value system struck us very forcibly while carrying out this research. The first was the speed with which recruits to data processing were indoctrinated with, and accepted, EDP group values. Many programmers and systems analysts had worked in line departments on conventional clerical activities before moving into EDP. Yet once associated with this new, technical, value system old values appeared to be rapidly forgotten. Earlier research in a bank had also drawn our attention to this rapid change in values (6). People who had been bank clerks for many years, once transferred to EDP, rapidly became technocrats, impatient with the resistance to change of their old colleagues. Similarly, in the present research, it was not unusual for members of line departments to be placed temporarily in the EDP group to act as link men for new systems that were being introduced. We found that many of these became so imbued with technical values during their stay that they were incapable of performing this linking role and became totally identified with the values of the computer personnel.

The reason for this rapid acceptance of EDP values appears to be the power of the technical ethic. This is able to capture people's enthusiasm and to make them feel, perhaps for the first time, that they are associated with work that is exciting and worth while. It can be argued that these technical values are being seriously challenged at present but this is not occurring, as a rule, in the organisations which use computers.

The second interesting feature of the EDP value system is the fact that the computer man is himself totally acceptive of it. We found everywhere that most computer people sought to mould the values of others to their own and there was little attempt to identify and reconcile differences of interest or to accept that there was a viable alternative point of view. If this approach is successful it makes innovation easy for the innovator because it removes any opposition. But as the sociologist Alan Fox has pointed out it requires control over the market in ideas and the suppression or avoidance of inconvenient opinions and attitudes. It may succeed in the short run but it is unlikely to assist the long-term acceptance of computer technology which depends on a realistic assessment and management of advantages and disadvantages. Too often resistance to change is still interpreted as a failure of communication rather than understood as a legitimate conflict of interests or values.

Task requirements and task needs

On all the variables we have examined so far there has been a good fit between the work needs and work experience of programmers and systems analysts, and the fact that this fit existed has been put forward as a contributory factor in their high level of job satisfaction. But we have also suggested that with specialist groups such as computer personnel a key factor in job satisfaction is the nature of the work that individuals are required to do. This is because the work values they have acquired as a result of their family backgrounds, education and training have led them to see work activities as an enriching experience through which they can meet challenges, overcome obstacles and develop aptitudes (3). Researchers have suggested that this perception of work as leading to self-fulfilment only applies to groups which have already satisfied basic physical and economic needs. It is also thought that it only applies to occupational groups which have these expectations of work and that shop floor groups whose environment has conditioned them to expect little from work other than financial reward may not respond when management attempts to make their jobs more interesting and responsible. This attitude is found in the officials of blue-collar trade unions who still see their principal bargaining area as the financial interests of their members rather than the quality of their working lives.

The higher level jobs such as doctors, lawyers and other professional groups have always organised their work activities in such a way that they have been able to do their job efficiently while at the same time deriving a great deal of personal satisfaction from the activities which they were performing. The shop floor worker, in contrast, has been on the receiving end of a management philosophy which has equated efficiency with work specialisation and simplification. His work has therefore increasingly lost challenge and interest and he has come to accept this, often building his own job satisfaction out of anti-management activities such as restrictive practices and shop floor militancy.[1]

When we began this research we hypothesised that the computer specialist would be closer to the professional man than to other, lower, occupational groups and that a major source of job satisfaction would be the nature of the work he was called upon to perform. In order to test this hypothesis, in chapter 6 we looked at the tasks of our programmers and systems analysts in terms of the job characteristics of physical variety, skill variety, goal structure and task identity. Our analysis of the comments of programmers and systems analysts on each of these aspects of their work showed that their jobs were high on skill variety, provided the opportunity for both the setting and attaining of work targets, and had a clear identity which, in turn, provided the individual with considerable work autonomy and control.

When we asked programmers and systems analysts to say what they liked best about their work it was always the tasks they were required to do which they described. They did not pay nearly so much attention to the factors which we have categorised as forming part of the knowledge, psychological, efficiency and ethical contracts. From their remarks it seemed reasonable to conclude that the task contract was the most important factor in their level of job satisfaction and that the fit between needs and experience on this variable also contributed to the good fit on the other variables. The nature of their work and the way in which it was organised meant that they believed their skills and knowledge to be adequately used. Its skill variety assisted their demands for self-development and responsibility. Its autonomy freed them from tight work controls and its rapid technological progression fitted their innovative value system. Added to this the scarcity of their talents in the labour market at the time the survey was carried out led to financial rewards which they regarded as very reasonable.

The success of the task contract in meeting individual needs was demonstrated by the fact that in the user and consultant groups, two-thirds of all staff said that they had no regrets about making data processing their career because they 'liked the work'. In the manufacturer group there was rather less unanimity with 50 per cent saying this, and the other 50 per cent referring to career prospects and the future potential of computers.

A major source of satisfaction in the task was the visibility of the end product and the fact that work had clearly defined stages *en route* to this end product. Thus 50 per cent of programmers spoke of the satisfaction of 'getting successful output from a program', while 50 per cent of the systems analysts spoke of the pleasure of 'seeing a project in successful operation'. Work was therefore seen as important and meaningful and a further source of satisfaction was the belief that the completion of a program or systems project led to an increase in Company efficiency.

[1] There is some evidence that automation is reversing this trend towards greater work simplification by eliminating the more routine kinds of work (11).

Conclusions on the FIT between individual needs and expectations and individual work experience

To summarise, on all our five variables, with certain minor exceptions, the fit between needs and experience was good. The dominant variable appeared to be the task contract and the success of this contributed to the good fit on the other five variables. The result was a group of enthusiasts who were highly identified with the work they were doing and motivated to perform well and to continually strive to improve their competence. Our original hypothesis, that we were observing a group with a high level of job satisfaction was supported by the research evidence.

FIT 2 Organisational needs and the ability and motivation of the employee to meet these needs = Effective relationships

Commercial organisations in order to survive have a need for efficiency, profitability and growth, particularly if they are in a market situation where the demand for their products is increasing. Service organisations must also be efficient, exercise effective financial control and be able to expand to meet the needs of their clientele. In order to achieve these things both kinds of organisation require staff whose skill and knowledge level meets their production requirements; staff who are motivated to cooperate with management interests in the production process, and who will provide the firm with some labour stability by being prepared to stay with it for a number of years. Factors which influence the demand an organisation makes of its staff in order to meet these efficiency, financial and growth needs are the product market in which the organisation operates and the influence this has on what is produced; the technology which it uses to assist its productive processes, the administrative structure which it creates to link together the network of roles and relationships necessary to its efficient functioning, and the organisational culture which it has developed as a result of the objectives it has been set up to serve, together with its history, leadership and ethos.

Knowledge requirements

An organisation's total knowledge requirements are influenced by the factors listed above but the requirements of the data processing department will also be affected by the organisation's data processing experience – whether the department is new or established – by the kind of use the company is making of computers and its development plans for this technology; by its training expertise, and by the philosophy of those responsible for the recruitment and selection

Fig. 7.5 Organisational needs and the ability and motivation of the employee to meet these needs = Effective relationships (Fit 2)

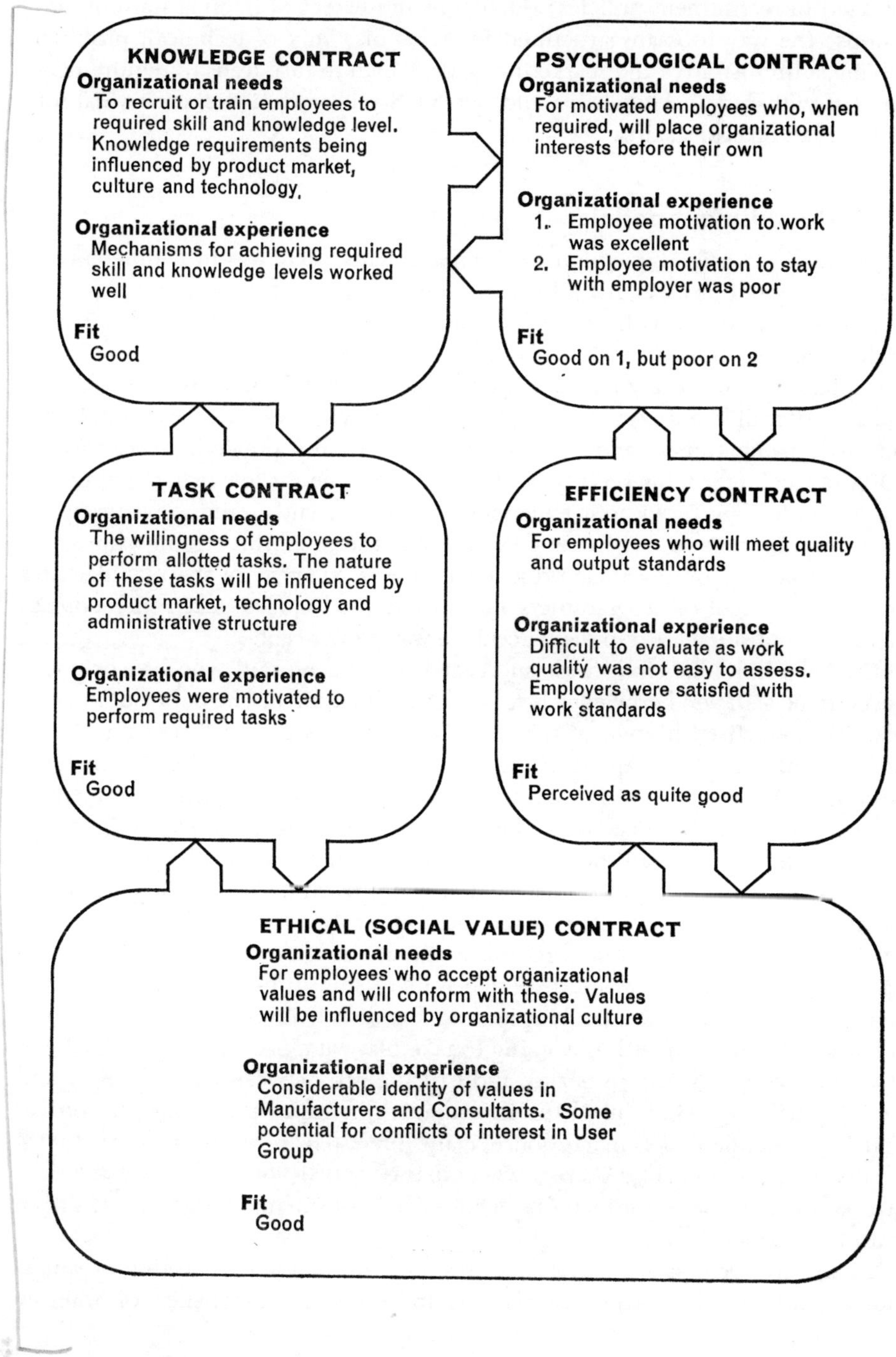

of programmers and systems analysts – usually the head of the EDP department and the personnel manager.

The skills required and the organisation's success in obtaining these skills are reflected in recruitment policies; the nature and extent of internal training provisions; the way jobs are structured in terms of a mix of technical, problem-solving, administrative and marketing skills, which in turn leads to requirements for staff with certain knowledge and personality characteristics, creative ability and human relations skills.

Recruitment policies

If we start by considering educational requirements, there was little difference in the tendency of our users, manufacturers and consultants to recruit programmers and systems analysts with degrees. In each group the proportion of staff with higher qualifications varied from one third to one half with the exception of consultant systems analysts, 68 per cent of whom had university degrees. A much greater difference was found in regard to previous experience and training. Few user programmers and systems analysts had any previous experience in EDP work before joining their present employers, whereas few manufacturer and consultant staff were without experience. Similarly, with training, virtually no user programmers and systems analysts had taken data processing courses of any kind before joining their present employers, whereas in the manufacturer group 35 per cent of programmers and systems analysts had taken such courses and in the consultant group the percentage was 76 per cent.

On the whole our eight firms succeeded in securing staff who had or could develop the skill and knowledge level which they required. The policy of internal recruiting practised by two of the users meant that they had little difficulty in finding staff with the potential to make good programmers and systems analysts, although there was of necessity a time lag between recruitment and attainment of the necessary level of expertise. The mail order company, which preferred to recruit from outside, had the most problems and therefore paid great attention to measures for keeping those staff which it did recruit. The manufacturers and consultants did not have serious recruitment problems when our survey was carried out although labour forecasts made at the time suggested that manufacturers, in particular, would experience increasing difficulty as the computer industry expanded in size. Looking at these forecasts from the viewpoint of 1972 it is clear that this expansion is going to take place at a pace that is much slower than was envisaged two years ago, and that the gap between labour supply and demand will not widen until the investment climate in the country improves and large numbers of firms are once again interested in pressing forward with computer developments. Today, we find the British computer industry in a state of uncertainty about its future while many consultants are having to search hard for business in order to avoid reducing staff numbers.

In all three groups the buffer that prevented difficulties in meeting organisational skill and knowledge needs was training. The excellence of training provisions allowed two of our three users to recruit internally without problems and enabled the mail order company to bring inexperienced university graduates into the company and train them successfully to the necessary level of expertise.

If these training facilities had not existed then our firms would have had to seek more experienced staff in an extremely tight labour market, with no guarantee that once recruited they would stay with the firm for any length of time. In the user and consultant groups two-thirds of staff had taken internal training courses in data processing subjects. We found that the need to enable their staff to keep up with a rapidly developing technology made the manufacturers prolific organisers of courses, 82 per cent of their staff had taken internal EDP courses and some had taken as many as ten of these. The consultants provided rather less training particularly at systems analyst level, but made sure that their recruits were very well qualified before accepting them as members of staff.

Training differences were related to the skill mixes required by the three groups. Users required staff who would be competent to design and program systems to meet organisational needs, using the firm's own hardware. Manufacturing staff, in contrast, had to be familiar with their firm's complete range of computer applications and able to relate these to the needs of a wide variety of clients. When assisting clients, consultants were presented with different makes of computer, different kinds of software and a wide variety of EDP problems. These factors influenced the technical and problem-solving skills required by firms in the three groups – with manufacturers and consultants, as a rule, requiring more technical and problem-solving versatility. Administrative skill was necessary in all three groups, but again it was especially important in the manufacturer and consultant groups which were totally dependent on outside clients for the survival of their businesses. Marketing skill, defined as selling to other organisations within the company's product market, was also essential in the manufacturer and consultant groups. Although many staff would not be in direct contact with customers, nevertheless the shadow of the customer and his requirements affected the attitudes and behaviour of everyone. Selling anything inevitably places the salesman in a potential conflict situation between the needs of his own organisation and the needs of the customer and we found that nearly 50 per cent of staff working for manufacturers and consultants experienced this kind of conflict. But they had all developed methods for coping with this and thus avoiding personal stress.

The differences in the required technical, problem-solving, administrative and marketing skill mix also led to differences in the personal attributes required of programmers and systems analysts. User EDP staff had to be able to accept and work within the cultural constraints of their own companies if they were to be successful innovators. They therefore had to show tact, understanding and patience. Manufacturer and consultant staff also required these attributes but success in the manufacturing group was defined by the employers as assisting the firm to sell computer hardware and more forceful personality characteristics were required by those in direct contact with the customer. Success in the consultants was seen as assisting the client to solve his problems, this requiring personality characteristics closer to the user than the manufacturer.

For all these reasons 'having the right temperament' was seen as crucial to job success and there was a sharp division in the way in which programmers and systems analysts defined temperamental requirements. Programmers saw the right temperament in terms of acquiring the patience and perseverance to write successful programs. Systems analysts saw required temperament in terms of personality attributes which enabled them to establish good relationships with user and client groups.

Users and consultants required staff who could develop satisfactory long-term relationships with user and client departments. Staff of this kind would also be beneficial to manufacturers. However, their staff were likely to encounter a conflict of interest between their desire to help the customer and their wish to achieve a large number of sales.

Our firms were reasonably happy with the skill and knowledge mixes of their employees and there were no regrets that they did not have staff with a different set of talents. But we found that the necessary skills had not always been easy to acquire. Programmers told us that they had experienced difficulty in developing the temperamental qualities of patience and thoroughness while systems analysts said that they had been slow to acquire the skills associated with human relations and management.

We found that all three groups had carefully worked out mechanisms for securing staff with the skill and knowledge level or potential they required, despite the tightness of the labour market. Users secured this knowledge level through internal training and on the job experience; manufacturers and consultants through the recruitment of trained staff and the further development of skills and knowledge by means of internal training.

Requirements for motivated employees

Two aspects of motivation are important to an employing organisation. One is the motivation of staff to work in the company's interests, the other is their motivation to remain with the company. The best workers are of limited value if they are only intending to stay one or two years and this applies particularly to data processing departments where there can be a period of several years between the formulation and implementation of a new computer system.

Our evidence shows that firms had few problems over the motivation of EDP staff to do the work required of them. Programmers and systems analysts were enthusiasts with strong desires to perform effectively and to design good systems. The problem lay in the second area, that of motivation to remain with the company. It will be remembered that 45 per cent of the people interviewed told us that they were thinking of leaving their present employer and that this percentage was even higher in those firms where the fit between what employees were seeking from work and what the employer was providing had unsatisfactory elements. We do not know how many of these individuals actually did leave but it is likely that the sudden depression in the computer market that occurred in 1971 caused many to change their plans.

Reasons for leaving were similar in all three groups. Programmers spoke of a wish to gain wider experience in data processing and a number referred to a particular type of computer application which attracted them. Systems analysts, in contrast, nearly all said that they were seeking an opportunity to develop managerial skills and that this could not be done within their present firms. Their principal reason for moving was therefore the promotion blockage within the data processing hierarchy. This was a difficult problem for our user organisations to solve. Senior systems analysts saw management as data processing management and perceived our three firms as offering very limited promotion opportunities. User firms could provide management jobs outside the data processing department but except in the government department this was not the kind of managerial appointment that systems analysts were seeking. Computer manufacturers might be expected to have more data processing management jobs than users or consultants, yet in both manufacturers we found that more than 50 per cent of systems analysts were either thinking of leaving, looking around for another job, had applied for or been offered another job. The situation in the consultants was similar for although many staff had expressed a long-term interest in moving into general management, the vast majority were seeking their immediate promotion within the data processing area and believed that these management jobs did not exist within their own companies. The fit between organisational requirements and organisational experience on this variable was therefore good for motivation to work but poor on motivation to stay.

Efficiency needs

We have seen that there was a good fit on this variable from the employee's point of view in that he felt the effort-reward bargain to be a fair one and he had few objections to the work and supervisory controls that were used. But there were more problems from the organisation's point of view. Firms tended to view the effort-reward bargain as too biased in the employee's favour. Very high salaries had to be paid to attract and keep good data processing personnel and in the user firms this distorted company salary differentials and caused personnel managers some problems. Although practice varied on the extent that work controls were routinised into standard procedures management problems arose from the fact that it was difficult to evaluate the speed and competence of individual programmers and systems analysts and to arrive at realistic time estimates for programming and systems projects. This caused difficulties when time estimates had to be given to customers for these could later turn out to be inaccurate. In the user group, Industrial Products had introduced its work measurement scheme in an attempt to improve the accuracy of its time forecasts. These forecasting difficulties caused problems for organisations and staff alike. The credibility of the data processing specialists was reduced in the eyes of the users if forecasts were wrong, while programmers and systems analysts could find that they came under considerable pressure towards the ends of jobs, when there were desperate attempts to meet target dates. For many this was the most stressful aspect of their work. From the organisation's point of view the fit between needs and experience on this variable was less good than on other variables.

Social values

An organisation's values are reflected in the expectations of the leaders on how other members should behave if organisational goals are to be achieved and the organisation is to remain a viable enterprise. Values influence the selection of goals and cover beliefs on personal conduct and ideas on the nature of duty and responsibility (2). Leaders seek, not always successfully, to get their values accepted throughout the organisation. If this can be done it assists an identity between organisational objectives and the objectives of subgroups. It also ensures that management behaviour is viewed as legitimate by people at lower levels in the authority hierarchy.

In the manufacturer and consultant groups, there was little conflict between organisational and subgroup goals and we found a general acceptance of the innovative values of employers. There seemed a greater potential for conflict in the user group where the innovative goals of data processing departments might on occasion get out of line with the interests of user departments. Our research into the introduction of computer systems in these firms showed that this could happen and we found line managers troubled that their lack of experience with computers and computer systems made it difficult for them to challenge decisions that were being taken by the data processing department. These value differences were eased in Industrial Products and the government department by the practice of internal recruiting. This meant that although there could be conflict between EDP and line departments, most EDP staff had had a long indoctrination into the overall value system of the company.

As the needs of an organisation change so the balance of power shifts and the group which can best help the organisation to achieve its goals at a particular moment in time will secure power because its functions are seen as highly relevant by top management. But the fact that a group has top management support does not automatically secure the approval and cooperation of other groups, although this support gives legitimacy to its activities. Local interests which see themselves as threatened by the power group may make a pretence at cooperation but in reality attempt to frustrate its objectives. Successful innovation can then be seriously threatened unless mechanisms are developed for bringing this conflict into the open and resolving it. The process of doing this can of itself bring the value position of the two groups closer together and so make the proposed system easier to introduce and more acceptable to the users. A divergence of values between innovative and user groups working together within the same organisation can only be solved by each group recognising the validity of the value position of the other. If a client firm dislikes the values of the computer manufacturer or consultant it is doing business with then it can always sever relationships. In contrast, innovators and users associating within the same company have usually no alternative but to work together.

The fit on this variable between organisational needs and requirements was therefore good in the manufacturer and consultant groups. But there was a potential for conflict in the user group where the technical/rational values of the computer staff might not fit the value position of user departments.

Task requirements

An organisation's task requirements are a consequence of the demands of the product market it serves, the technology it uses to make the product, and the administrative network of roles and relations it creates to progress the product through the organisation to the customer. They are also influenced by the state of the labour market, for if labour is of poor quality, hard to get and difficult to train then tasks will have to be simplified so that the labour available can cope with them. This last point was not a problem with data processing staff, for although there was a tight labour market for experienced personnel, there were many people available with the interest and potential to make good programmers and systems analysts.

Data processing activities are still relatively free of technological constraints of a kind that limit discretion on how work shall be carried out. Although data processing people often use their technology to tighten controls on others, they do not suffer from many externally imposed restrictions themselves. They have a great deal of personal control over what they do and how they do it. This is in contrast to the job of the clerk or the shop floor worker who frequently has a very limited amount of job discretion.

In the manufacturer and consultant groups there were few problems on task structure and the way work was organised appeared related to both the needs of the firm and the needs of its staff. In the users the structure of EDP tasks was usually a product of the way the data processing manager chose to organise the work of his department and how he allocated work responsibilities. Here again task structure arrangements appeared to be successful and the only complaints we received were of occasional coordination problems due to an overlap between the work of programmers and systems analysts. It seemed that organisational needs were well catered for by the structure of EDP tasks that had evolved in our firms and the fit between organisational needs and experience on this variable was a good one.

Conclusions

The fit between organisational needs and organisational experience on our five variables was therefore generally good. The weakest area was the efficiency variable, not because we had any evidence that programmers and systems analysts were not meeting work standards but because it was not easy for firms to evaluate programmer and systems analyst performance. A potential problem area in the user group was the ethical fit where there could be a conflict between the innovative values of the EDP group and the more conservative value systems of user departments. This is a large problem and has been discussed in previous publications by the author (6, 7, 8).

Figure 7.5 sets out in simplified form the fit between organisational needs and experience on the five variables.

The fit between organisational and employee needs

In looking at the fit between organisational and employee needs in the data processing area we have in fact been examining the extent to which there was identity or conflict of interest between computer personnel and their employers. Sociologists pay a great deal of attention to conflicts of interest because the manner in which these manifest themselves can throw a great deal of light on the workings of an enterprise. Alan Fox suggests that organisations can be viewed as 'disputed ground' which individuals and groups seek to capture for their own interests (2). Order is preserved by the development of shared values which assist cooperation between different interest groups, or which enable conflict to be contained and resolved with the least amount of disruption to the organisation. Conflicts of interest are not necessarily dysfunctional. They can assist organisational health by challenging the assumptions behind current norms and practice and thus acting as a stimulus for change. An absence of conflict can lead to a stagnant organisation which finds it difficult to recognise the need for change. Nevertheless too much, or the wrong kind of conflict, can prevent an organisation realising its objectives and thus put its ability to survive in jeopardy.

Harmony or conflict with organisational interests will differ in form and extent from one occupational group to another. For example, as a general rule there will be more conflict related to economic issues at the bottom than at the top of an organisation. Too much conflict within the ranks of management or between key specialist groups and senior management hinders the ability of the organisation to perform efficiently and respond to changes in its environment. However the fact that a management or specialist group has power usually indicates that its objectives are broadly in line with the objectives of the organisation's leaders, for power at this level is more likely to be allocated than taken and cannot easily endure without top management sanction.

In the present study we have been considering the ability of eight organisations to secure and use effectively a particular group of specialist staff, together with the success of these specialists in meeting their needs in work and in achieving job satisfaction. We have found that on our five analytical variables – knowledge, psychological, efficiency, ethical and task structure needs – the fit has been a good one and has led to effective and harmonious relationships. Our employing organisations have not been frustrated in meeting their objectives through the deficiencies of their staff and our programmers and systems analysts have believed that their personal needs were being successfully catered for. In the manufacturer and consultant groups this fit was assisted by the fact that organisational values were generally accepted and supported; management and employees each perceiving the needs and behaviour of the other as legitimate.

Alan Fox suggests that where the fit between organisational and employee needs is good and the individual has high expectations of his work, then a category of occupational privilege emerges (2). Fox believes that some forms of work enable men to grow towards what their societies define as full human stature and the work of our data processing specialists would certainly come into this category. Unfortunately this is true of a minority rather than a majority of jobs for the demands of a consumer-orientated society led managements to break a great deal of work down into small, routinised segments in the interests of cost savings and productivity.

To summarise our findings on the fit between organisational and employee needs. In the manufacturer and consultant groups, we found that our firms were able to meet the needs of their staff on all five variables while at the same time being satisfied that these staff were assisting the attainment of organisational objectives. This is not to suggest that there were no conflicts of interest between different functions within these firms. But our survey was not designed to study these and they did not appear to be sources of job dissatisfaction to the staff we interviewed.

In the user group the fit between organisational and EDP staff needs was good at the time of our survey but these staff were working in a more differentiated internal environment than the staff of the manufacturers and consultants and they had the difficult challenge of convincing their own management of the validity of their technological and innovative values and objectives. Our survey was carried out in 1969 when top management was greatly influenced by the promises and hopes held out by its computer men and believed that the business goals of top management were congruent with the innovative goals of computer personnel. The economic recession of the early 1970s caused many managements to think hard about the return they had received on their computer investment and society itself started to question the rightness of the technical ethic more forcibly than it had done in the past. All of these things could affect the fit between organisation and employee needs and if our survey was carried out in the user firms today we might find less top management satisfaction with the performance of computer personnel and less job satisfaction within the data processing group.

Fig. 7.6 Interaction of organisational and individual needs

	Both sets of needs met	Organizational needs met but not individual	Individual needs met but not organizational
Knowledge contract	**Effective utilization of skills and knowledge**	* Individual frustration, due to recruiting too well qualified staff	* Organizational dissatisfaction with competence, due to recruiting staff who are not well qualified enough
Psychological contract	**Psychological health**	* Conformity to organizational goals, together with low morale	* Individuals identifying with sub-group goals not organizational goals
Efficiency contract	**Good work performance**	* Productivity and quality, together with low morale	* High morale and deteriorating product
Ethical contract	**Organizational and individual values seen as legitimate**	* Conformity to organizational values, but little identity with these	* Identification with peer group values. Little support for organizational values
Task structure contract	**Task structure fits technological constraints and individual needs**	* Technological determinism, boredom or stress	* Job interest and high production costs

If this proved to be the case it would be closer to the situation in most occupational groups where a perfect fit between organisational and employee needs is difficult if not impossible to establish and maintain and a compromise has to be achieved between the needs which the organisation most wishes to meet and those needs which its employees most wish to meet. Talcott Parsons suggests that the optimum of job satisfaction is the best that can be obtained from existing conditions, given the individual's existing set of needs and the availability of resources to meet these needs.[1] Figure 7.6 sets out the consequences of a good and bad fit on each of our five variables.

It must be stressed that the fit between organisational and employee needs is not necessarily a stable one but will alter as employee job needs and job expectations change and as conditions change in the environment of the firm, particularly in the product and labour markets and in the technological environment.[2]

The diagram below sets out those environmental factors that impinge on the work of an EDP department in a user firm and affect its needs and functions.

In conclusion it is important to stress again the point made at the beginning of this chapter; that a good fit between employee and organisational needs on our five variables will contribute to organisational health by creating job satisfaction and effective relationships. But these alone will not ensure the viability and survival of the enterprise. In addition there must be *organisational* flexibility which enables an organisation to respond to pressures and change in its environment. There must also be *organisational development* so that as these external demands increase and become more complex the organisation can build up the necessary intellectual and technical growth to enable it to respond successfully. An absence of job satisfaction and of effective relationships will make this flexibility and development difficult to secure.

Methodological conclusion

This book presents a new approach to the study of job satisfaction in that it attempts to integrate existing theory and to provide a method of analysis that covers factors both extrinsic to work. Louis Davis in a challenging article entitled 'Job satisfaction research: the post-industrial view' (1) points out that most studies of job satisfaction examine all aspects of the work situation except the work itself. The concept of job satisfaction, as conventionally drawn, is therefore almost exclusively concerned with adaptation to jobs which we are increasingly coming to believe are more suited to machines than men. Davis claims that in most psychological and sociological studies of job satisfaction, only the

[1] Talcott Parsons' actual words are 'the optimum of gratification is the best that can be obtained from existing conditions, given the existing set of need dispositions and the availability of objects' (8).

[2] Figures 2, 3 and 4 in Appendix B show how alterations in the product and labour markets and in the technological environment can alter the nature of the fit between organisational and employee needs.

Fig. 7.7 Environmental factors and the EDP department

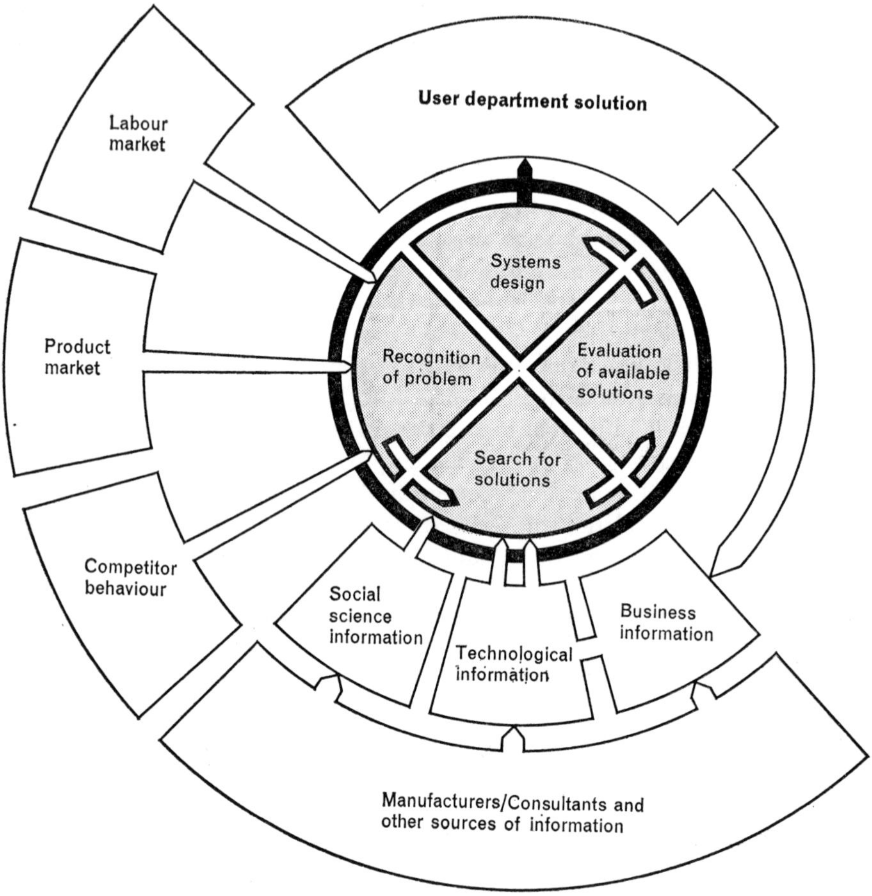

variables not influenced by technology are typically examined and the most striking feature of past and present research is the failure to study the job itself. Davis is, of course, referring to job satisfaction studies of blue-collar rather than white-collar jobs, but his general criticism is valid.

We hope, by our approach, to have avoided this criticism and in looking at job satisfaction from a broader perspective than is usual we have established that with computer specialists it is the task itself and not extrinsic factors such as pay or promotion which contributes most to job satisfaction.

The Computer Research Unit at Manchester Business School is now embarking on a series of studies on job design. It is hoped that by using our job satisfaction model as an analytical tool, information can be obtained which assists systems designers to create jobs which meet human needs for interesting and challenging jobs; set within a work situation which also provides satisfaction on our knowledge, psychological, efficiency and ethical variables. By doing this an accommodation may be found between the demands of the organisation on the one hand and the needs of the employee on the other.

Our method can be useful in obtaining other personnel information that is of value to a company. First of all, asking a firm what its needs are and thus making it set out its role requirements of staff assists job definition. Firms do not always think as clearly as they might about what they require of staff and why they want some things and not others. The exercise of defining jobs in terms of our five variables can assist a firm in working out its present needs. The assessment of likely changes in product and labour markets and in technological environment can assist it to establish how needs are likely to change in the future. Second, the examination of individual needs can provide useful information on those areas where job satisfaction is not as good as it might be and help identify factors that could be changed to secure improvement. Regular attitude surveys using our method can show how the morale of a group is changing over time and provide useful feedback information which may help management ensure that a serious deterioration in morale does not take place.

It must of course be recognised that the possession of such information does not always make a remedy possible. What is good for the organisation is not necessarily good for the employees and management may have to make difficult decisions on which set of interests are to be given priority. However a knowledge of organisational and employee needs will enable this choice to be made in an informed manner and if organisational interests are given priority then management will be aware that they may have to face a deterioration in job satisfaction and perhaps work performance.

We suggest that our method can be of value in four ways which are of interest to management.

1. It can be used, as we have done here, as an indicator of job satisfaction.
2. It can be used as a selection tool to identify what kind of staff the organisation is seeking and how these role requirements fit with the personal needs of particular job candidates.
3. When new systems are being introduced and new jobs created it can be used as a diagnostic tool to ascertain what employees are seeking from work in terms of both extrinsic and intrinsic job factors, and so assist job design.
4. It can be used as a monitoring tool when introducing change. Job satisfaction on our five variables can be ascertained before the change takes place and the fact that change is taking place can be made a vehicle for improving areas where the fit between organisational and individual needs is known to be poor. Once the change is implemented then it is possible, using the method, to establish whether job satisfaction has improved or deteriorated.

Job satisfaction is not something that remains constant; it alters during an individual's lifetime as his needs, expectations and aspirations alter. It can be argued that with groups as important and expensive as computer specialists management cannot afford to allow job satisfaction to deteriorate. Nor can it afford to have high job satisfaction if employee attitudes and performance are out of line with organisational needs. Our method is a small contribution to the personnel information process.

It is appropriate to end this book with the words of Adlai Stevenson: 'The image of the automation engineer may not excite the imagination as does the image of the astronaut, but the fate of mankind in the foreseeable future will depend more on what we do manipulating machines on earth than on how we do hurtling them through the heavens.'

Appendix A: Factors influencing the approach of a company to EDP

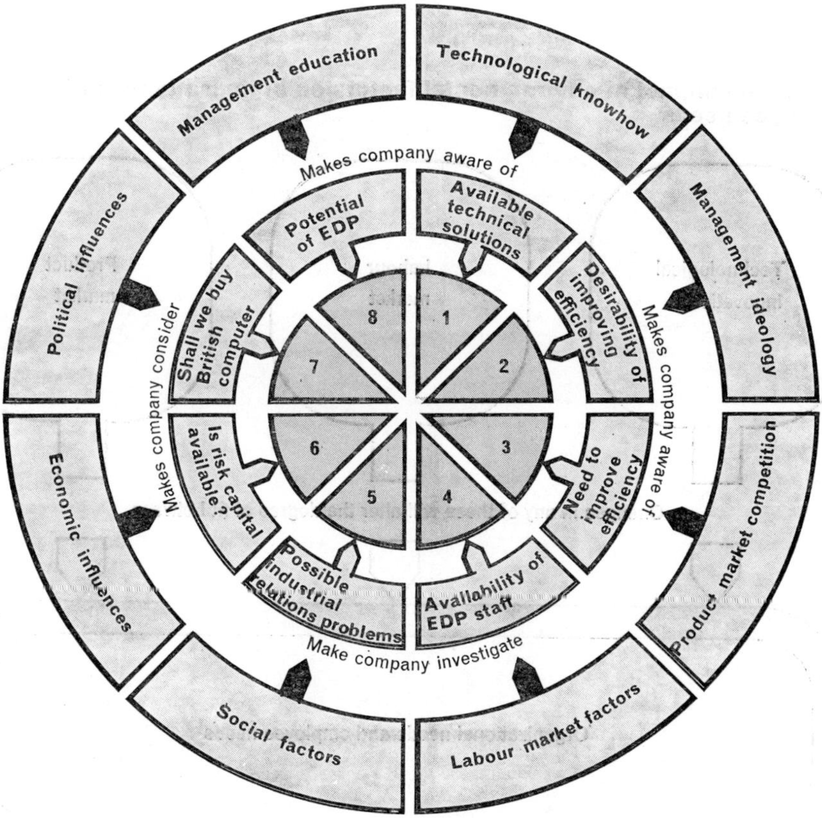

8 Decision to use EDP

7 Decision to buy British computer

6 Decision to use EDP

5 Industrial relations policies for EDP

1 Choice of EDP technical solution

2 Decision to use EDP

3 Choice of EDP area

4 Recruitment and training policies for EDP

Appendix B: Organizational needs / employee needs

Fig. 1. The impact of environmental factors on organisational and employee needs

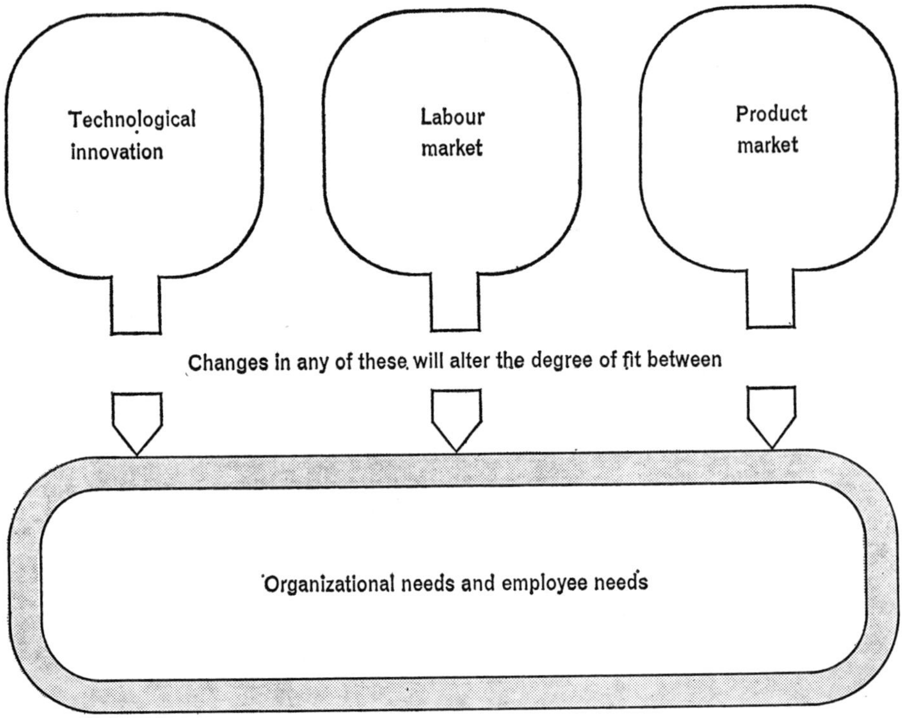

Fig. 2. Likely consequences of a tightening of the labour market

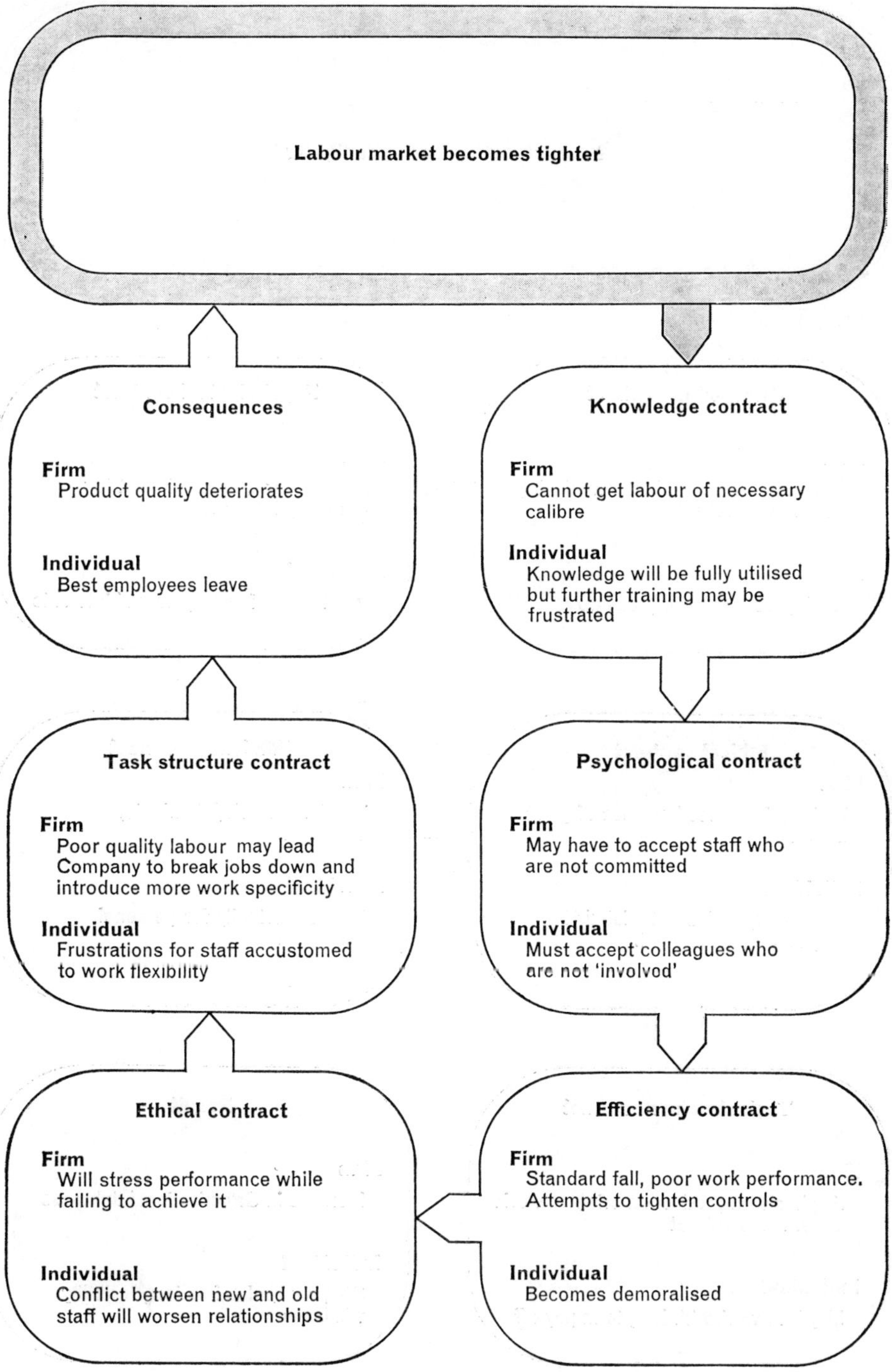

Fig. 3. Likely consequences of a tightening of the product market

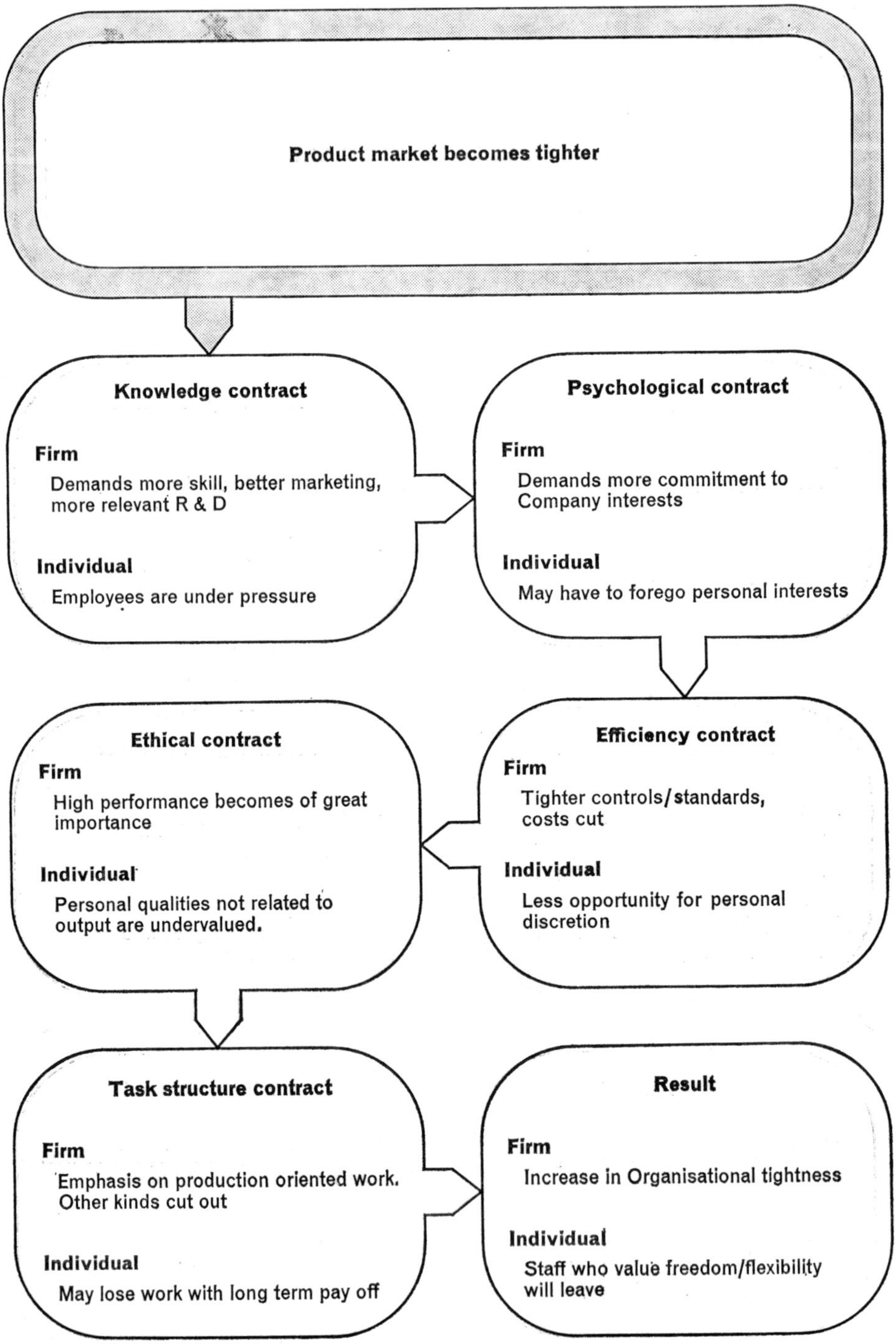

Fig. 4. Likely consequences of technological innovation

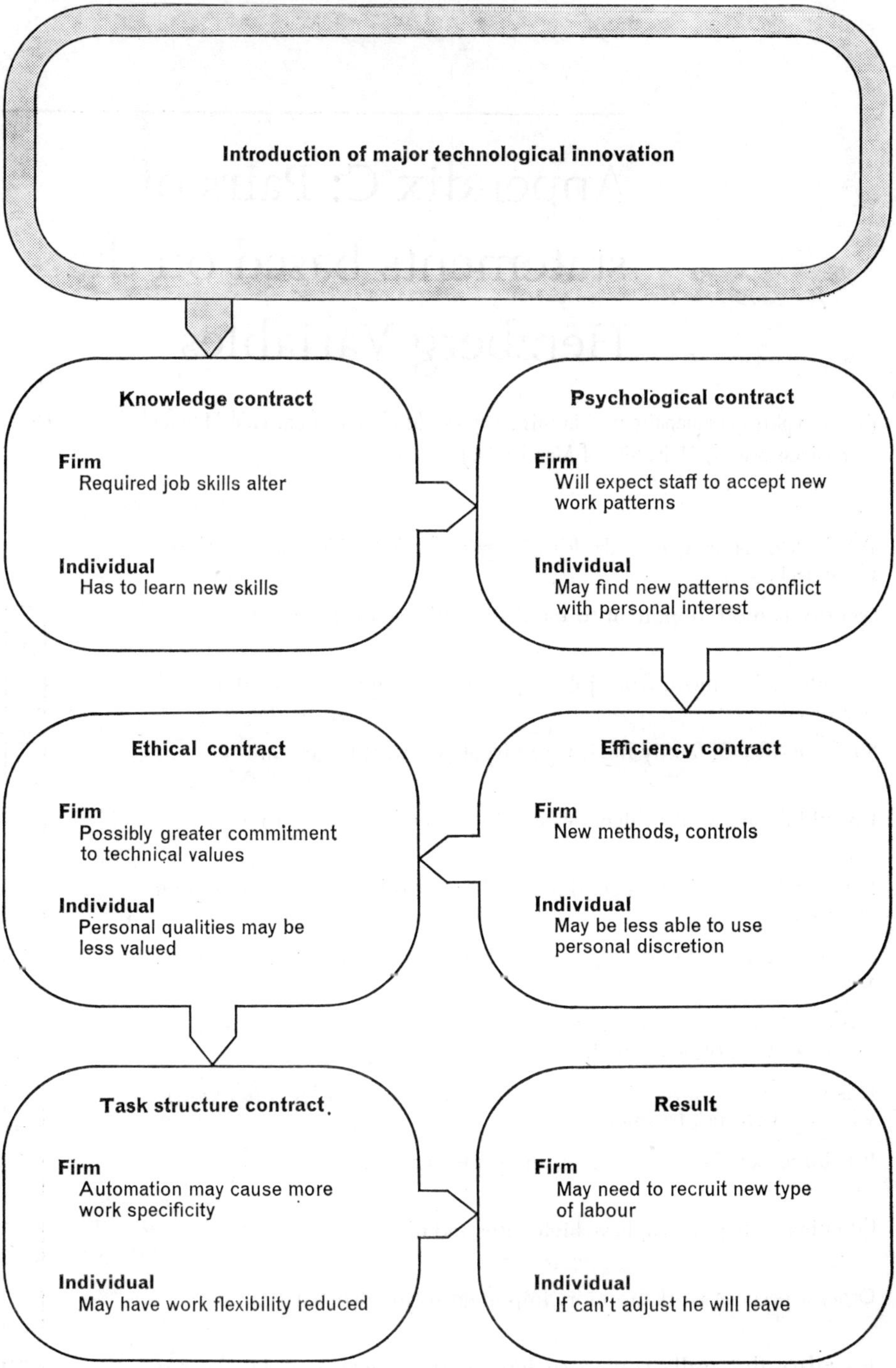

Appendix C: Pairs of statements based on the Herzberg Variables

(The complete questionnaire used in this study can be obtained from Enid Mumford, Manchester Business School, University of Manchester.)

Which statement in each of the following pairs fits best with your own views? Please tick.

Security is more important to me than challenge or excitement. ☐

I would rather move from job to job than put up with boredom and routine. ☐

Some sacrifice of family life is necessary if you want to get on. ☐

I wouldn't take a job which meant being away from home a lot. ☐

I know when I'm doing a good job, and I want other people to recognise this too. ☐

So long as I know I'm doing good work, it doesn't matter to me if others aren't aware of this. ☐

Self-development is never possible, one has to accept that one's potential will not be realised. ☐

It is essential to have a job which allows for personal 'growth'. Otherwise one becomes frustrated. ☐

It is important for me to get on, and get to the top. ☐

I'd rather be happy than have high status and ulcers. ☐

Other aspects of work are more important to me than salary. ☐

It's salary that really counts, so long as the money is right, the rest doesn't matter. ☐

It's the people you work with that make a job good or bad. Working with a pleasant crowd is essential. ☐

I don't bother too much about the others at work, it's the job that is important. ☐

I'd rather get on quietly with my own work, than have responsibility for the work of others. ☐

Responsibility is a challenge. I enjoy it. ☐

I wouldn't work for a firm I didn't believe in and think efficient. ☐

So long as the firm pays well and provides me with interesting work, I'm not too worried about its image. ☐

Status is important to me. I like to be respected. ☐

I don't care about rank and job titles, it's what you're doing that is important. ☐

I must have interesting work all the time, if not I get fed up. ☐

I enjoy spells of routine and find them relaxing. ☐

Appendix D: Questions about managerial philosophy

The following statements indicate some common management viewpoints. Please indicate the extent to which (*a*) you agree in principle with them, and (*b*) you have found them of practical help (there should be 2 ticks on each line).

	AGREE	DON'T KNOW	DISAGREE	OF PRACTICAL HELP	OF NO PRACTICAL HELP
1. Give a man a secure job and he will give you loyalty and hard work in return.					
2. Delegation ought to be designed into the organisation, and not left to individual whim.					
3. Keep people informed about everything. They like it and it pays off.					
4. The man at the top must carry the ultimate 'can', else why give him authority and a big salary?					
5. No man should have more than one boss.					
6. Always define lines of promotion clearly, and base promotion on objective criteria (e.g. written qualifications, measured performance).					

	AGREE	DON'T KNOW	DISAGREE	OF PRACTICAL HELP	OF NO PRACTICAL HELP
7. People value the esteem of their fellows more than anything else, and you can't bestow it with cash.					
8. There's never time to find the perfect solution. But you can always find one that will get you 'over the hump'.					
9. Everyone's job should be clearly defined. People like it that way, and it's more efficient.					
10. Authority to get things done and responsibility for the consequences ought to rest with the men in the position, and with the knowledge to get them done, regardless of formal title and status.					
11. Whatever else moves people, it's safe to assume that if you offer them enough cash they will give you the performance you want.					
12. It's better to take on 'self-starters' of whatever shape and let them define their own jobs, than fit square pegs into square boxes in organisation charts.					
13. There's always a best way to do any job, and it ought to be done that way.					
14. Treat people *as* people and you won't have to supervise them closely; they'll do the job for you.					
15. A little unemployment and a little tougher management would do wonders for industrial efficiency.					

	AGREE	DON'T KNOW	DISAGREE	OF PRACTICAL HELP	OF NO PRACTICAL HELP
16. If a man sets his own targets he is likely to reach them quicker than if they were set for him, and he is a happier man for it.					
17. An efficient information system is one which lets people have only the information which is necessary for them to do their job efficiently.					
18. Personal style in management is much more important than technical qualifications.					
19. A man ought to earn the deference of his colleagues by the example of his technical competence and personal behaviour, and not expect it because of the authority that goes with formal title.					
20. Meticulous planning, close control and well-designed systems of reward and discipline – these are the key to efficiency.					
21. Good communication = satisfied people = efficiency.					
22. It's management's job and nobody else's to decide what's to be done and how it's to be done.					
23. Conflict is inevitable and usually has a positive function.					
24. Identity with common purpose is the ideal to be aimed at.					

References

CHAPTER 1 Job satisfaction and computer specialists

1. BEER, STAFFORD. *Decision and Control*, London: Wiley, 1966.
2. BJERRUM, C. A. 'Forecasts of computer developments and applications 1968–2000', *Futures*, June 1969.
3. BLAKE, R. N. and MOUTON, J. S. *The Managerial Grid*, Houston: Gulf, 1964.
4. BLAXTER, E. and MORRIS, W. E. M., eds. *Economic Evaluation of Computer Based Systems*, vol. 2, National Computing Centre, 1971.
5. BRANDON, D. H. 'The dark side of data processing', *Data Systems*, July 1967.
6. BROWN, W. D. E. *Exploration in Management*, London: Heinemann, 1960.
7. BURNS, T. and STALKER, G. M. *The Management of Innovation*, London: Tavistock, 1961.
8. COOPER, R. 'Memorandum on Motivation' unpublished paper, University of Liverpool School of Business Studies, 1970.
9. CROZIER, M. *The Bureaucratic Phenomenon*, London: Tavistock, 1964.
10. FIEDLER, F. E. *A Theory of Leadership Effectiveness*, McGraw-Hill, 1967.
11. GULOWSEN, J., HAUG, O. and TYSLAND, T. 'Norwegian firm taps total human resources', *Industrial Engineering*, August 1969.
12. GOULDNER, A. *Patterns of Industrial Bureaucracy* London: Routledge & Kegan Paul, 1955.
13. GOWLER, D. and LEGGE, KAREN. 'The wage payment system: a primary infrastructure', in *Local Labour Markets and Wage Structures*, London; Gower Press, 1970.
14. HELMAN, T. 'Systems of the analyst', *Management Today*, Annual Review, 1969.
15. HERZBERG, F. *Work and the Nature of Man*, London: Staples Press, 1966.
16. HICKSON, D. J., HININGS, C. R., LEE, C. A., SCHNECK, R. E., and FENNINGS, J. M. 'A strategic contingencies theory of intra-organisational power', *Administrative Science Quarterly*, 16, No 2, 1971, 216–229.
17. HERBST, P. G. *Socio-technical Design*, London: Tavistock, 1972.
18. HUNTER, MAXWELL. 'Are technical upheavals inevitable', *Harvard Business Review*, Sept.–Oct. 1969.
19. JAQUES, E. *Equitable Payment*, London: Heinemann, 1961.
20. LAWRENCE, P. R. and LORSCH, J. W. *Organisation and Environment*, Boston, Graduate School of Business Administration, Harvard University, 1967.
21. LIKERT, R. *The Human Organisation*, New York: McGraw-Hill, 1967.
22. LUPTON, T. and GOWLER, D. *Selecting a Wage Payment System*, London: Engineering Employers' Federation, Research Paper 3, 1969.

23. MCGREGOR, D. *The Human Side of Enterprise*. New York: McGraw-Hill, 1960.
24. MCKINSEY ASSOCIATES. 'Unlocking the computer's profit potential,' *The McKinsey Quarterly*, 5, no. 2, 1968.
25. MASLOW, A. H. *Motivation and Personality*, New York: Harper, 1954.
26. MEYER, M. W. 'Automation and bureaucratic structure', *American Journal of Sociology*, 74, no. 3, 1968.
27. MUMFORD, ENID. 'A new approach using an old theory', *Sociological Review*, 18, no. 1, 1970.
28. MUMFORD, LEWIS. *The Pentagon of Power*, New York: Harcourt Brace, Jovanovich, 1970.
29. PAPETTI, S. *Personnel Problems in Data Processing*, Anbar Publications, Monograph no. 10, 1967.
30. PARSON, T. and SHILS, E., eds. *Towards a General Theory of Action*, Harvard University Press, 1951.
31. ROSE, J. *Automation, its Uses and Consequences*, London: Oliver & Boyd, 1967, p. 51.
32. ROSE, M. *Computers, Managers and Society*, Penguin (Pelican Library of Business and Management), 1969, p. 17.
33. SAYLES, L. *Behaviour of Industrial Work Groups*, New York: Wiley, 1958.
34. SCHON, D. A. *Technology and Change*, Oxford: Pergamon, 1967.
35. SIMON, H. *The Shape of Automation*, New York: Harper & Row, 1965.
36. STEINER, G. *The Creative Organisation*, University of Chicago Press, 1965.
37. THORSRUD, E. 'Socio-technical Approach to Job Design and Organisational Development', unpublished paper, Work Research Institutes, Oslo, 1967.
38. VROOM, V. H. *Work and Motivation*, New York: Wiley, 1964.
39. WALKER, C. R. and GUEST, R. H. *The Man on the Assembly Line*, Harvard University Press, 1952.
40. WIENER, NORBERT. *The Human Use of Human Beings*, New York: Houghton Mifflin, 1950.
41. WOODWARD, JOAN. *Industrial Organisation: Theory and Practice*, Oxford University Press, 1965.

CHAPTER 2 The knowledge contract

1. ASHILL, MAURICE. 'Professional status helps BCS in its role for the future', *Computer Weekly*, 8 October 1970.
2. BRITISH COMPUTER SOCIETY, Working Party 10. 'Education and training of systems analysts', *The Computer Bulletin*, June 1967, pp. 11–17.
3. BRUNER, JEROME S. 'Some observations on effective cognitive processes', in *The Creative Organisation*, ed. Gary A. Steiner, University of Chicago Press, 1965.
4. BUREAU OF EMPLOYMENT SERVICE. *Occupations in electronic computer Systems*, US Department of Labour, July 1965.
5. CLARK, WILLIAM. 'Confused ideas', *Computer Weekly*, 25 July 1968.
6. DEPARTMENT OF EDUCATION AND SCIENCE, Scottish Education Department, Ministry of Education for Northern Ireland. *Computer Education*, HMSO, 1967.
7. ENGINEERING INDUSTRY TRAINING BOARD. *The Training of Systems Analysts*, London, 1967.
8. GILLIS, WARREN K. 'Personnel Requirements in Data Processing'. *Computers and Autotion*, September 1968. 24–6.
9. HENNEY, ALEX. 'The education and training of systems analysts and programmers', *Data Systems*, November 1968, pp. 30–2.
10. JOHNSON, TIMOTHY. 'Computers: the cuckoo in the economic nest', *The Sunday Times*, 4 October 1970.

11. KNIGHT, KENNETH. 'A descriptive model of the intra-firm innovation process' *The Journal of Business*, 40. No 4, 1967, 478–496.
12. LANYON, N. L. H. 'Training for systems analysts', *Computer Weekly*, 6 June 1968.
13. LEE, SANG M. 'Organisational identification of scientists', *Academy of Management Journal* 12, no. 5, 1969, 327–37.
14. MAUNDER, M. and STYLES, A. 'A formal training scheme for systems analysts', *Computer Weekly*, 24 April 1969.
15. PAPETTI, S. *Personnel Problems in Data Processing*, Anbar Publication, Monograph no. 10, 1967.
16. *Retail Business*, October 1966.
17. 'Review of recent developments in computer education', *The Computer Bulletin*, June 1967, pp. 6–10.
18. TORRANCE, E. PAUL. 'Scientific views of creativity and factors affecting its growth', *Daedalus*, Journal of the American Academy of Arts and Sciences, Summer 1965.
19. VROOM, V. H. *Work and Motivation*, New York: Wiley, 1964.
20. YEATES, DONALD, 'Training for the future', *Computer Weekly*, 25 July 1968.

CHAPTER 3 The psychological contract

1. BEHLING, O.; LABOVITZ, G. and KOSMO, R. 'The Herzberg Controversy: a critical reappraisal,' *Academy of Management Journal*, 11, no. 1. 1968, 99–108.
2. CHUNG KAE, K. 'Toward a general theory of motivation and performance', *California Management Review*, 11, no. 3. 1969, 81–7.
3. CHUNG KAE, H. 'A Markov chain model of human needs: an extension of Maslow's need theory', *Academy of Management Journal*, 12. no. 2, 1969, 223–34.
4. GLASER, B. *Organisational Scientists*, New York: Bobbs-Merrill, 1964.
5. HAIRE, M. *Psychology in Management*, New York: McGraw-Hill, 1965.
6. HALL, D. T.; SCHNEIDER, B. and NYGREN, H. T. 'Personal factors of organisational identification', *Administrative Science Quarterly*, 15, no. 2, 1970, 176–90.
7. HERZBERG, F.; MAUSNER, B and SNYDERMAN, B. *The motivation to work*. New York: Wiley, 1967.
8. HERZBERG, F. *Work and the Nature of Man*, London: Staples Press, 1968.
9. IRI STUDY GROUP. 'Motivation incentives, and rewards for R & D personnel', *Research Management*, 12, no. 3, 1969.
10. KAHN, R. L.; WOLFE, D.; QUINN, R. P.; SNOEK, J. D. and ROSENTHAL, R. A. *Organisational Stress*, New York: Wiley, 1964.
11. KAST, F. E. and ROSENZWEIG, J. E. *Organisation and Management: a systems approach*, New York: McGraw-Hill, 1970.
12. LEGGATT, T. W. N.E.D.O. *Management Project, Institute of Manpower Studies Aims, Organisation and Research Project Programme* 1969–1970, Institute of Manpower Studies, 1970.
13. LIKERT, R. *The Human Organisation*, New York: McGraw-Hill, 1967.
14. MASLOW, A. *Motivation and Personality*, New York: Harper, 1964.
15. MCCLELLAND, D. 'Business drive and national achievement', *Harvard Business Review*, July–August 1962. 99–112.
16. MCGREGOR, D. *The Human Side of Enterprise*, New York: McGraw-Hill, 1960.
17. PARSONS, T. and SHILS, E. eds *Towards a General Theory of Action*, Harvard University Press, 1951.
18. PORTER, J. 'The future of upward mobility', *American Sociological Review*, 33, no. 1, 1968, 5–19.

19. PORTER, L. W. 'Job attitudes in management: 1. Perceived deficiencies in need fulfilment as a function of job level', *Journal of Applied Psychology*, 46, 1962, 375–84.
20. PORTER, L. W. 'Job attitudes in management: 11. Perceived importance of needs as a function of job level', *Journal of Applied Psychology*, 47, 1963, 141–8.
21. SCHEIN, E. H. *Organisational Psychology*, Englewood Cliffs, New Jersey: Prentice-Hall, 1965.
22. TASKMASTER, 'Changing jobs can be a hobby', *Computer Weekly*, 18 May 1967.
23. VROOM, V. H. *Work and Motivation*, New York: Wiley, 1964.
24. WILLIAMS, R. and GUEST, D. 'Are the middle classes becoming work shy?', *New Society*, no. 457, 1 July 1971.
25. YEARSLEY, R. 'Some thoughts on the computer personnel and its solution', *Data Systems*, January 1969, pp. 30–1.

CHAPTER 4 The efficiency contract

1. BRADLEY, W. R. 'The job of the modern research manager', *Research Management*, 11, no. 3, 1968, 167–75.
2. *Cornmarket Salary Survey*, 1970, Careers Register Ltd, Cornmarket Press Ltd.
3. FIEDLER, F. E.; O'BRIEN, G. E.; and ILGEN, D. R. 'The effect of leadership style upon the performance and adjustment of volunteer teams operating in a stressful foreign environment', *Human Relations*, 22, no. 6, 1969, 503–14.
4. FIEDLER, F. E. 'Leadership experience and leader performance – another hypothesis shot to hell', *Organisational Behaviour and Human Performance*, 5, 1970, 1–14.
5. FRANK, E. R. 'Motivation by objectives – a case study', *Research Management*, 12, no. 6, 1969, 391–400.
6. GREENWOOD, F. *Managing the Systems Analysis Function*, AMA 1968.
7. HELMAN, T. 'Systems of the analyst', *Management Today Annual Review*, 1969, 24–6.
8. HERSEY, P. and BLANCHARD, K. H. 'Managing research and development personnel: an application of leadership theory', *Research Management*, 12, no. 5, 1969, 331–8.
9. LIKERT, R. *New Patterns of Management*, New York: McGraw-Hill, 1961.
10. LOCKE, E. A. 'Toward a theory of task motivation and incentives', *Organisation Behaviour and Human Performance*, 3, 1968, 157–89.
11. MAIER, N. R. F. *Psychology in Industry*, Boston: Houghton-Mifflin, 1955.
12. MANN, F. In *Leadership and Productivity*, San Francisco: Chandler, 1965.
13. NOWLAN, F. 'What does a DP manager do?', *Data Systems*, October 1967, pp. 36–40.
14. STUART, W. J. 'An experiment in data processing management', *Datamation*, June 1968, pp. 64–5.
15. TOMLIN, R. 'A PERT plan for computer installation', *European Business*, April 1970, pp. 24–35.
16. VITELES, M. S. *Motivation and Morale in Industry*, New York: Norton, 1953.
17. VROOM, V. H. *Work and Motivation*, New York: Wiley, 1964.
18. WESTMACOTT, H. P. and SPENCE, W. 'Does your programming department earn its keep?', *Computer Weekly*, 15 October 1970.

CHAPTER 5 The ethical contract

1. ALLPORT, G. W.; VERNON, P. E. and LINDZEY, G. *Study of Values*, Boston: Houghton Mifflin, 1951.

2. ARGYRIS, C. *Interpersonal competence and organisational effectiveness*, Homewood, Ill:, Dorsey, 1962.
3. BANKS, J. A. 'The structure of industrial enterprise in industrial society', *The Sociological Review* Monograph No. 8. University of Keele, October 1964.
4. BENNIS, W. 'Theory and method in applying behavioural science to planned organisational change', *Journal of Applied Behavioural Science*, 1, no. 4, 1965, 338–60.
5. BERELSON, B. and STEINER, G. A. *Human Behaviour*, New York: Harcourt, Brace & World, 1964.
6. CAIN, M. E. 'Some suggested developments for role and reference group analysis', *British Journal of Sociology*, 18, no. 2, June 1968.
7. CORWIN, R. G. 'Patterns or organisational conflict', *Administrative Science Quarterly*, 14, no. 4, December 1969, 507–20.
8. ELLUL, J. *The Technological Society*, Cape, 1965.
9. FERGUSON, C. K. 'Concerning the nature of human systems and the consultant's role', *Journal of Applied Behavioural Science* 4, no. 2, April–June 1968, 179–93.
10. HEDLEY, A. R. 'Organisational objectives and managerial controls – a study of computerisation', in *Industrial Organisation: Behaviour and Control*, ed. J. Woodward, Oxford University Press, 1970.
11. HUTTON, G. 'Work groups and job design', *Work Study and Management Services*, March 1970, pp. 211–16.
12. JAHODA, M. and WARREN, N., eds. *Attitudes*, Penguin Books, 1966.
13. KAHN, R. L., WOLFE, D. M., QUINN, R. P., SNOEK, J. D. and ROSENTHAL, R. A. *Organisational Stress*, New York: Wiley, 1964.
14. KLEIN, J. *The Study of Groups*, New York: Humanities Press, 1956.
15. LYNTON, R. P. 'Linking an innovative subsystem into the system', *Administrative Science Quarterly*, 14, no. 3, 1969, 398–417.
16. MARTIN, J. and NORMAN, A. R. D. *The Computerised Society*, Englewood Cliffs, N.J.: Prentice-Hall, 1970.
17. MERTON, R. K. *Social Theory and Social Structure*, New York: Free Press of Glencoe, 1949.
18. MITCHELL, G. D. *A Dictionary of Sociology*, London: Routledge & Kegan Paul, 1968.
19. MUMFORD, E. *Systems Design for People*, National Computing Centre, 1971.
20. NEAL, M. A. *Values and Interests in Social Change*, Englewood Cliffs, N.J. Prentice-Hall, 1965.
21. PARSONS T. and SHILS, E. *Toward a General Theory of Action*, Harvard University Press, 1951.
22. PONDY, L. R. 'Varieties of Organisational Conflict', *Administrative Science Quarterly*, 14, no. 4, 1969, 499–505.
23. REID, J. G. 'Management services – innovators or helpers?', *Work Study and Management Services*, December 1968, pp. 732–8.
24. ROSS, J. E., 'Data processing training for managers: objectives and curriculum content', *Computers and Automation*, September 1968, pp. 16–20.
25. SACKMAN, H. *Computers, System Science, and Evolving Society*, New York: Wiley, 1967.
26. SHERIF, M. *The Psychology of Social Norms*, New York: Harper & Row, 1963.
27. SIEGAL, A. E. and SIEGAL, S. 'Reference groups, membership groups and attitude change', *Journal of Abnormal and Social Psychology*, 55, 1957, 360–4.
28. SILBERMAN, C. E. *The Myths of Automation*, New York: Harper and Row, 1966.
29. SMELSER, N. 'Memorandum to Stouffer', quoted in Neal, M.A., *Values and Interests in Social Change*, Englewood Cliffs, N.J., Prentice-Hall, 1965.
30. STEIN, M. D. 'Social change skills and creativity' in *Comparative Theories of Social Change*, Foundation for Research on Human Behaviour, Ann Arbor, 1966.

31. STEWART, R. 'The Computer Disillusion', *Management Today*, September 1967, pp. 96–9.
32. WALTON, R. E., DUTTON, J. M. and CAFFERTY, T. P. 'Organisational context and inter-departmental conflict', *Administrative Science Quarterly*, 14, no. 4, 1969, 522–42.
33. WOODWARD, J. *Industrial Organisation: behaviour and control*, Oxford University Press, 1970.

Chapter 6 The task contract

1. COOPER, R. 'Memorandum on motivation', unpublished paper, School of Business Studies, University of Liverpool, August 1970.
2. EMERY, F. E. *Systems Thinking*, Penguin, Modern Management Readings, 1969.
3. HALL, D. T. and LAWLER, E. E. 'Job characteristics and pressures and the organisational integration of professionals', *Administrative Science Quarterly*, 15, no. 3, 1970, 271–81.
4. HERBST, P. G. *Socio-technical Design*, London: Tavistock Publications, 1972.
5. HERBST, P. G. *Autonomous Group Functioning: an exploration in behaviour theory and measurement*, London: Tavistock Publications, 1962.
6. HERZBERG, F. *Work and the Nature of Man*, Cleveland: World Publishing Co., 1966.
7. HERZBERG, F., MAUSNER, B. and SYNDERMAN, B. *The Motivation to Work*, New York: Wiley, 1959.
8. JAQUES, E. *Equitable Payment*, London: Heinemann, 1961.
9. JAQUES, E. *Time Span Handbook*, London: Heinemann, 1964.
10. LEAVITT, H. J. 'Unhuman organisations', *Harvard Business Review*, July–August 1962, pp. 90–98.
11. LIKERT, R. *The Human Organisation*, New York: McGraw-Hill, 1967.
12. LOCKE, E. A. 'Job satisfaction and job performance', *Organisational Behaviour and Human Performance*, 5, 1970, 484–500.
13. MILLER, E. J. and RICE, A. K. *Systems of Organisation*, London: Tavistock Publications, 1967.
14. MUMFORD, ENID. 'Computer people and their impact', *New Society*, 26 September 1968.
15. MUMFORD, ENID. *Systems Design for People*, National Computing Centre, 1971.
16. PAPETTI, S. *Personnel Problems in Data Processing*, Anbar Monograph, no. 10.
17. PAUL, W. J. and ROBERTSON, K. B. *Job Enrichment and Employee Motivation*, London: Gower Press, 1970.
18. RYAN, T. A. *Work and Effort: the psychology of production*, New York: Ronald Press, 1947.
19. SHEPARD, J. M. 'Functional specialisation, alienation and job satisfaction', *Industrial and Labour Relations Review*, Jan. 1970, pp. 207–19.
20. TAYLOR, F. W. *Scientific Management*, New York: Harper, 1947.
21. TURNER, A. N. and LAWRENCE, P. R. *Industrial Jobs and the Worker*, Boston: Harvard University School of Business Administration, 1965.
22. VROOM, V. H. *Work and Motivation*, New York: Wiley, 1964.

Chapter 7 Job satisfaction and organisational health

1. DAVIS, L. E. 'Job satisfaction research: the post-industrial view', *Industrial Relations*, May 1971, pp. 176–93.
2. FOX, A. *A Sociology of Work in Industry*, London: Macmillan, 1971.
3. GOLDTHORPE, J., LOCKWOOD, D., BECHOFER, F. and PLATT, J. *The Affluent Worker*, Cambridge University Press, 1968.

4. HERZBERG, F., MAUSNER, B. and SYNDERMAN, B. *The Motivation to Work*, New York: Wiley, 1967.
5. HERZBERG, F. *Work and the Nature of Man*, London: Staples Press, 1968.
6. MUMFORD, E. and BANKS, O. *The Computer and the Clerk*, London: Routledge & Kegan Paul, 1967.
7. MUMFORD, E. and WARD, T. B. *Computers: planning for people*. London: Batsford, 1968.
8. MUMFORD, E. *Computers, Planning and Personnel Management*, London: Institute of Personnel Management, 1969.
9. PARSONS, T. and SHILS, E., eds. *Towards a General Theory of Action*, Harvard University Press, 1951.
10. SCOTT, W., MUMFORD, E., MCGIVERING, I. and KIRKBY, J. *Coal and Conflict*, Liverpool University Press, 1963.
11. TAYLOR, J. C. 'Some effects of technology in organizational change', *Human Relations*, 24, no. 2, 1971, 105–23.
12. WHYTE, W. F. *Money and Motivation*, New York: Harper & Row, 1955.

Index of names

Index of subjects

R

S

T

U

V

W